Remainders

Eric Korn
Remainders

from the *Times Literary Supplement* 1980–1989

CARCANET

First published in 1989 by
Carcanet Press Limited
208-212 Corn Exchange Buildings
Manchester M4 3BQ   U.K.

Copyright © Eric Korn 1989

All Rights Reserved

British Library Cataloguing in Publication Data

Korn, Eric
  Remainders.
  I. Title
  828'.91407

ISBN 0-85635-847-9

The Publisher acknowledges financial assistance from the
Arts Council of Great Britain

Typeset by Paragon Photoset, Aylesbury
Printed in England by SRP Ltd., Exeter

For David and Andrew

*What thou lovest
well remains, the rest is dross.*
        EZRA POUND

'When the Reader sees some *Errors* in the Orthogravy, some *Passages* omitted without design, and some *transpos'd*; he is desir'd to think the *Translator* living at a Distance from the Press, an Excuse.'

Bouhours, *Pensées Ingenieuses or a collection of the Bright Sayings, Sublime Thoughts and Witty Sentences of the Most Celebrated Fathers of the Church* (1710)

· —— ·

'In treating of the most trivial matters I have been careful to be accurate; and to avoid, even in my gossip, anything resembling the *blague* of the *boulevardier*, concerning which by the way, Renan once asked me, with a quizzical smile, whether perhaps it might not be the debilitated offspring of Cartesian scepticism.'

Anon, *Things I shouldn't tell* (1924)

· —— ·

I acknowledge with gratitude the limitless patience of editors (John Gross, Jeremy Treglown) and editorial staff at *The Times Literary Supplement*, Lindsay Duguid, Alan Hollinghurst and Holly Eley, who have allowed me freedom to pursue any eccentricity that took my fancy. I am equally grateful to those readers who have taken the time to offer material, to correct, to chide and sometimes even to encourage.

Natural indolence has enabled me to resist the temptation to update, edit, or improve, though I have added the occasional footnote. *HRIW* stands for 'How Right I Was'.

Eric Korn *1989*

PLAN OF THE BOOK

There is no plan.

Table of contents

A is for Albania
logical approach to, 70–73
Omar Khayyam, work of, in, 107
Useful phrases for tourist, 125
Zenobia, travels with, to, 125

B is for Biblio
-fantasy, displayed by Ulster bookseller, 173
-machy, or the battle of the Bookers, 169–72
-mimesis, or book-forgery, 148
-poly, a short guide to bookselling, 140
-poloclasty, or destroying booksellers, methods of, 152
-phagy, practised by Borzoi, 65
-phobia, shown by New York fairgoers, 163–4
-praxis, 142–7
-theoria or book-fair-haunting, 141
and also for Borges, J. L., 174–6
and Buckingham, unsuitability of for romantic encounters 145

C is for Computer
admirable application of by French postal authorities, 28
avoidance of, by booksellers, advocated, 63
brutal behaviour of, 137
future development of novel, implications for, 120–21
improbable prediction concerning, 138
production of gibberish by, accidental, 206
  ”   ”   , deliberate, 190
regrettable tendency to lose text by, 94
to run Marathon, 85
and Coffee, British recipe for, 176

D is for Disbelief concerning
complete veracity of author unfairly displayed by readers, 198
current decade as period of scepticism, 51
Merryweather's Tempest Prognosticator, 60
  ”   ”   ”   , shown to be unjustified, 62
miraculous intelligence of Rhodian dogs, 116
rattlesnake theory of Mayan art and architecture, 79

readiness of God to practise dentistry, 81
sinfulness of locution 'hopefully', 96
and also dyslexia 100, 147
and also Darwin, Charles R. 157–63

E is for Eccentricity, displayed by
Braun, A., A., discoverer of new thought process, 68
Johnson, 'Reversible', of Abeokuta, 45
Ker, John Bellenden, expounder of nursery-rhymes, 40–41
Swift, Theophilus, the Reverend, litigious wooer, 38
and also   eternity, 212
             end, the, 213

F is for Frauds, Fakers, Forgers, Flim-Flammers, and Failures, Heroic
Exposed by *Truth* magazine, various, 23
Fox, a wily, preying on bookcollectors' natural urge for self-improvement, 148–50
Groom, Charles Otley, 7–12, 14
Groom-Napier *see* Groom
Macintosh, Burr, heroic failure, his *The Little I saw of Cuba*, 48
Napier,   *see* Groom-Napier
Madagascar, King of, 11
             Queen of, 23
Merchiston *see* Napier
Montferrat, Prince of, *see* Merchiston
Sahara, Empress of, 23

G is for God
Botham, suitability for role of, 19
reluctance of, to fill teeth, 81
see also   Satanism, Versifiers

H is for Head
of famed psychic, exploding, 16

I is for Intemperate criticism of
Auctioneers, 154
Chesteron, G. K.,   *see* Levin, B.
Levin, B., 189, 191–2
London Underground, 103
Post Office, British, 76, 81
      "   "   in matter of Special Delivery, 83

REMAINDERS

J is for Joyceans,
dozing, aroused, (wrongly as it transpires), 57
Dublin given over to rejoicings by, 182–7, 188

K is for Kulib'yaka
epiphany concerning, 59
and also for Koestler, Arthur 166–8

L is for Languages
Albanian, *q.v., passim*
Batak 95
English as a Foreign Language (for Norse fisherfolk), 151–2
German textbook comfortingly found to contain anti-Hitlerite satire, 63
Ido, 131–3
Kwéyòl, 96
Malagasy, 98
Malayalam, 103, 104–5,
Maltese, 89–93
NeoMelanesian, 102
Polyglot, 77
Spanish, ambiguity of,
Tibetan, 102

M is for Monomania
concerning bustickets, 153
    "   Cherished Numbers, 153
    "   cigarette lighters, 64
    "   withdrawal slips, 65
of Marathon organizers, 85
  "   "   runners, 86
  "   "   spectators, 87
on subject of palindromes, 109 et seq

N is for Newspapers
Narrative economy of Mexican local, admired, 123
Veracity, lack of, proudly displayed absence of, deplored, 12
What, Say, The, 123

O is for Obscenity, Indecency, Blasphemy and Other Offensiveness
Browning, unwitting o. of, 8
Buckingham, unsuitability for, 145
'Joseph' preaches against, 155
non-Maltese dress, of, 92

Obscene Publications, good fortune of author in obtaining, 179–81
　　　"　　　"　　Act, Obscenity of, 193–6
of performance, claimed by lawyer, 199
pusillanimity of Press in suppression of, 201

P is for Poetasters, (vile versifiers and writers of rhyming rot)
Griffin, R., 'the Bughouse poet', 3–6
Hoobler, Idella Clarence, of Worcester, Mass, 181
Numerous to list, too, of Korea, 54
Sault, Joseph W., of Welwyn Garden City, 66
Unconscious, of Tombstone, Ariz., 168
and also for　pamplemousse, 106
　　　　　　　paper-bag-cookery, 169
　　　　　　　palindromes, world's longest, 103
　　　　　　　　　　more about, 107
　　　　　　　　　　still more about, 109
　　　　　　　　　　yet more about, 112, 113
　　　　　　　　　　even more about, 114–15
　　　　　　　　　　see also monomania

Q is for Quips (and cranks and wanton wiles)
Scholarly investigation of, at International Humour Conferences, 128
Unavailability of Tirana as venue for, 128

R is for Racine, Jean, shameless distortion of, 207–12
and also for Rushdie, Salman, 203–6

S is for Sundry Subjects
Sex Manuals, 37
Sexism of Limericks, 92
Sexual frustration in dogs, and its consequences, 196–8
Sexually Transmitted Diseases, 207
Snake at watertrough, in Kentish Town, 173
Soap operas, deconstruction of, 133–4
Spoonerism, rare example recorded, 207

T is for Tee-shirts (and related literary forms)
Botham, Ian, appearance on, 19
Brilliant examples of, 135
Bumper and other stickers, 76, 139
Curious encounter as consequence of heedless wearing of, 29
Literature, the T-shirtification of, 127–8
'Love', logograph, semasiological investigation of, 131

U is for Unrecorded
Constable, Peter, Elizabethan poet, u. heretofore, 36
Marvell, Andrew, u. poem hesitantly attributed to, 15, 19

V is for Voyages
to Belize 135–7, 138
to California, 81, 116
to Dublin, 182–7
to Mexico, 79
and also Verses: Diabolical *see* Poetasters
             Satanic *see* Rushdie, S.

W is for Woks
Wok-Jokes 1
Woks of reference: B.U.C.O.P., 6–7
                    B.I.L., 30–3
                    Best 'n Most in DFS, 41–3
                    Canadian Pacific Railway List, 165
                    Magazines for Libraries, 24–7
                    N.U.C., 24, 27, 35
and also for Welshness, not made mock of, 177–9

X is for X-words,
in *Bloodless Phlebotomist, The*, 78
in *North Frontenac News*, 89
in *William in Trouble*, 89

Y is for Yugoslavia
unexpected absence of references to, but indexed nonetheless, 000

Z is for Zoology
adopt-a-carnivore scheme, 100
Cannery Row, zoological pleasures of, 119
lobsters, 3
monkeys, inability to compose works of Shakespeare rigorously
   proven, 139
pandas, lust in, 36

REMAINDERS

☆   21.3.86

I write, when I do, groaning and sweating with infacility, like a bantam trying to lay an ostrich egg, or more forcefully, a kiwi trying to lay an Aepyornis egg, clucking and cursing while the unhatched, uncounted chick is already fossilized in my (strictly literary) oviducts; sometimes it takes a morning of labour and travail and digression and *Angst*, a tide of crumpled paper ascending from feet to knees, before I light on *mots justes* like 'cheque herewith' or 'sorry for delay'. Am I really sorry? If not really sorry, do I want it thought that I am sorry? If I don't want it thought that I am sorry, do I want it thought that I want it thought that ... whining with doubt I touch firm ground and it shimmies away like jelly on a plate; I palpate the rocks of certitude and they turn to mud or melted chocolate. How many Hs in 'with'? Is the word 'delay' English or what: run it round the mouth a few times and it turns Venusian. Isn't 'herewith' an Anglo-Saxon legal term for the right to shear moles on your cater-cousin's socage? Wasn't Herewith the Czech a Viking who daringly led his fleet of dragon-beaked foam-riders up the Vltva, *stupor slovachorum*, who ruled Bohemia until defenestrated by his own thegns at the Castle of Stary Gezy? The painfully constructed confection of phrase and sense turns to a pease pudding of delirium, a verbal junket, what Eliot called the Word in the Dessert.

So I'm envious of the fluent, and above all envious of such supersalespersons of the Logos who can conjure a whole book, or better still a publishing concept, out of not-a-lot. There's a man here with an anthology of short stories set in railway stations, it's to be called *Intercity*: there's a video, a sit-com, a washing-powder and a set of give-away tumblers, and BR have made him a huge advance; then again there's a man who has published a dictionary containing a few hundred words, albeit long ones, along with the letters he wrote to authors to ask them why they used words he didn't know like pinguid; and their (often) patient replies.

I recall vividly the exact traffic island in Chinatown where I conceived, planned, plotted, copy-edited and all but completed (traffic was heavy) *My Hundred Best Wok Jokes*. And I've been cuddling it to myself all these years.

We got all kinds of wok: punk wok, Brighton wok, wok of ages with the cleft handles, woks populi, our cheapest line. We got wokoko or bawoque wok, Ayers wok for Australian epistemologists, woks in beauty like the night, all night wok shops (that's wok around the clock), and just a closer wok with thee. We got gay jokes (a wok on the Wilde side), lonely cannibal jokes (wokking my baby back home), Tantalus jokes (my daddy woks me) and even Irish literary jokes: what do you get if you stir-fry a mess of linguistic roots? Finnegans wok, be the powers.

The trouble with this kind of associative lava-flow (out of the cradle endlessly wokking), is that ten seconds of creative magma provides enough restaurant names (the wokkery, where e'er you wok, wok a little faster) to last an entrepreneurial (the woxworks) lifetime, without counting the abstruse ones like Peters (on this wok I shall build) or the banal (don't knock the wok, Lambeth wok, Madame will you wok).

Well, there you are. It's off my chest, the torch is passed, and now I shall never get out a little book with illustrations by one of those monosyllabic cartoonists, ('brilliantly caught by GLUP's inimitable pen'), just in time for the moon-cake-and-year-of-the-antlion market.

It could have been called *Woks in the Head* or *Woks et praeterea Nihil*, or *Getting your Woks off*, depending on the market segment we are targeting.

Just the soy-sauce tie-ins alone would have made me rich.

☆ 10.3.89

BUSH COMMITTED TO TOWER* said the headline (Ceefax, February 22) and my heart thrilled in unison with the hearts of every loyal subject of Ermajesty. I could see it all. Prince Philip must have master-minded it, with trusty loyal Howe and some trusty loyal Guardsmen in mufti, after the funeral of his late Imperial Zoological Highness-whom-alas-too-often-heavy-affairs-of-state-drew-away-from-first-love-Nudibranchiata-of-Greater-Pacific-Co-Prosperity-Sphere.

'Hallo, Mr President, lovely funeral, few of the boys are having a night-cap and a chat about trade imbalances, fancy joining us, splendid; quick, Howe, run and ask Mitterand if we can borrow his Concorde and if he argues remind him who invented it, no nothing Mr President, just having a word with my Minister chappie here about getting some munchies...'

Bush, already jet-lagged, *distrait* and Orientally disoriented, succumbs promptly to the Royal Mickey Finn. Once aboard the lugger and the man is ours, swiftly disemplaned at (rich irony!) a disused USAF base in the Essex marshes, by helicopter of the

---

* John Tower: a now-long-forgotten politician, to whose support Bush vainly pledged himself.

Queen's Flight to a hastily commandeered City Airport, then bundled, like Lenin through Finland, into a sealed coach of the Docklands Light Railway, through the Traitors' Gate and to the dankest, dampest, dimmest, darkest, dirtiest, deadliest dungeon of the lot.

No 'Mr President' palaver now. 'Treasonably and feloniously against the peace of his most gracious and puissant Sovereign George Ye Third...'

☆ *16.5.86*

I have a rectangle of paper here that figures a drowsy crustacean and is headed, touchingly, HOW TO CARE FOR YOUR LOBSTER. A salutary lesson, this seems, for those who thought caring for lobsters came naturally, like mother love. 'Do refrigerate me when I arrive' it suggests. Do save the seaweed, I like to sleep on top of it. Don't put me in the bathtub, I drown in fresh water. Then, unexpectedly: Do eat me as soon as possible.

'Any questions? Call the lobster hotline.' 'Hallo, is that 0-800 LOBSTER? I have a few questions. Moral questions. Theological questions about the nature of care. Questions about the lobster with the altruistic gene, whimpering to be eaten. Questions...'

Lobsterline (cheliped over mouthpiece): 'Got another one here, third today. I'll take it, angel. Yes, Sir, that's the absolute paternal care that we may die of if we do well, as your non-Crustacean poet Eliot has it. You need to listen to station K-LAW, the Voice of the Lobster, where even Homard sometimes nods, and talk to our in-house decapod preacher, Richard Griffin...'

Which is how I came to hear of Richard Griffin, lobster Laureate and a lunatic of major importance, author of at least three books of verse, *The Delaware Bride*, *A Tale of Fraunces' Tavern (AD 1765)* and, most relevant to our concerns, *The Lobster's Gizzard*, 1916, the author, no place, but surely New York). The first lines of the title poem reveal the master

> Put on your thinking cap
> Scorn your notched ear-lobe
> Go run another lap
> What a botched queer globe.

It's a ballad, of sorts, about Mike O'Hara on the Hill of Tara, determined to get the gizzard in a frightful blizzard, urged on, ambiguously by the equivocal figure of the Wizard. ('Up in the apple tree/There waits your lobster./Farewell and think of me/

Don't fail your Slobster'). Michael pursues his quarry, but it turns out to be a phantom lobster and he is drowned in a bog like the last of the Baskervilles 'The king of the blizzard/Triumphant the Wizard/Now laughs at the lizard./The fake lobster's gizzard/Comes in for its joke/O Why did Mike croak?/Unfortunate bloke/O Why did he croak?/Poor bloke O Poor Bloke'.

And there is a photograph of the poet, staring eyes and little hatchet, with a lobster on a fork.

Other topics dealt with by Griffin are Pendennis McGuire, who fatally swallows a centipede in his coffee, legal flogging in Delaware, the Woman Without any Ears, death in prison ('They buried him in the jailyard,/Along with a bunch of yeggs/Departed chums of the lockstep, society's lowest dregs/In a pit of lime, one puddle of grime, like ill-conditioned eggs'), the Dodo ('Thy graceful beak is seen no more, thy voice no longer holds the floor') and memorably, a fire in an asylum, a Blakean vision entitled 'Water on the Brain':

> See the carcases all charred
> Filling up the Bug House Yard,
> Twisted into many shapes
> Like huge worms, those made like tapes
> Of all sizes, big and little,
> Crisp and brown, both soft and brittle,
> But quite free from Earthly pain.
> No more water on the brain.

☆   *13.6.86*

> Oh! There was a man with a celluloid throat
> Who once sailed along in a little green boat;
> His wife she was troubled with ossified liver;
> Her thumb, it was pierced with a sharp oaken sliver.
> Now this sliver, this liver, this boat and this throat,
> Were at last swallowed up by a petrified goat.

(*From* 'Oh! There')

Requests, demands, for more of the works and life of Richard Griffin, sweet singer of the scampi, reach me by every post. (They don't.) There is little I can feed to his hungry public. Biographies are dumb. National Union Catalog knows that he was born in 1857, but not whether he has died. His books, all self-published, are scantily held by undiscerning libraries: *The Camel's Last Gasp, The Melancholy Yak, The Dead Rabbit Riot* AD *1857, Bughouse*

REMAINDERS

Poetry (1917), *Bughouse Poetry* (1919) and *Bughouse Poetry: The Collected Works of Richard Griffin* (1922). The more Griffin I read (and I scarcely do anything else now) the less can I decide whether we are dealing with self-conscious Manhattan Dada, or barking crustacicidal lunacy. (That he spent a little time inside or, as the Romanians so delicately put it, *up river*, is certain: textual references abound.)

The rare portrait, reproduced here, does not clinch matters. Another frontispiece shows the poet in the role of Guy Barnabas Bone, who lives in the alkali desert and deals in whip-scorpions or *vinegarones* (the word, unexpectedly, is in the *OED*, though one of the citations, from the *Glasgow Herald* of 1920, reads suspiciously like a review of Griffin, if such a thing is imaginable).

I wish I could quote in full the hospital ballad with the refrain 'The uric acid gathers in the corner of my thumb' – 'That woman with the cancer in the gullet, hear her stammer./The gentle nurse, ungentle now, raises the staff to slam her./Why don't they end the case at once and hit her with a hammer?'; I would like you to taste the sinister *enjambements* of 'Pink Tea' ('They held a 'pink tea' at the Rink/The Gink had a kink in his blink./He took a pink drink – hear the clink/of his glass. As he gulps see him wink./Hank pays for the drink. Hear the chink/Of the tin in his purse. See the link'). But perhaps the metrical innovations of 'The Elm of Nax' are his most deserving and enduring memorial.

> The bright Angel feels
>   A sort of a flickety
> Shock through the heels.
>   Wheels scrape a clickety
> Knock. See the keels
>   Decidedly rickety.

> The bright Angel cracks
>   To slivers the branch
> Of th'Elm called Nacks,
>   'Tis on my own ranch.
> My classic lip smacks
>   Saying, 'Dick, be Stanch.'

☆   29.2.80

I've been glancing idly through BUCOP, the British Union Catalogue of Periodicals, to see if they are keeping up with the rush of new literary periodicals. By no means: though it comes hot from the microchip four times a year, it still takes a couple of years before the two thousand-odd new magazines, journals, periodicals and supplements that come into British libraries annually are properly accessed and kitted out with an international standard serial number and an approved abbreviation. Some skill and subtlety are exercised here. *Products Of India* becomes *Prud India* instead of *Prod India*, which might be taken for an offensive slogan, like Wake Up, England, only ruder. Nor, alas, is *Mind Your Own Business* abbreviated to MYOB.

    They come from far and near: the *Rev. Invest. Cent. Invest. Pesq. (Cuba)* and *London Transport Scrapbook; Veg. Hot Humid Trop.* (from Mayaguez, from what is now called Institut. de Trop.) and *Urbandoc News* of Edinburgh – a pair perhaps of Celtic heroes, Bandoc and Urbandoc, coming with pipes and terrier from misty Skye; *Computerweek* of Braamfontein, the coy *Perinatal News* and the severe *World Stainl. Steel Stat.*, the euphonious *Omaly Si Anio* (= *Hier et Aujourd'hui*) and the intriguing *New Directions in Attribution Research*. Gastronomy is well provided for, with *Pasticceria Internazionale* and something called *Top Curr. Phys. Anthrop.*, presumably *Topping Curried Physical*

Anthropologist, the gourmet guide to dining out in Melanesia. Among magazines of less general appeal there is *Offshore Scout* (for oil riggers), *Planetarian* (for the owners of planetaria), *Soc. Netw.* from the International Network for Social Network Analysis and *Shorthorn J.* (didn't he play for Essex?).

Abrupt and enigmatic titles are favoured by switched-on scientists as well as dropped-out poets: thus *Open Earth* which sounds as though it is published by the Rivendell Commune, Frodo Farm, Glastonbury, actually comes from the Geology Department at Milton Keynes. *Angina Pectoris* seems clear enough (a more forward-looking editorial board would have chosen *Heartache* or *Pang*), but what is *Winged Bean Flyer*? Does *Matrix* carry concrete poetry or obstetrical reports? *WAME* clearly should be *Rev. Obstet. Soc. Scotland*, but actually is something disappointing like *West African Mining Engineer*, or *World Association for Monitoring Entropy. Soc. Serv. Deliv. System* must be about designing self-propelled trays for Meals on Wheels, but what are *PIMA* magazine, *Other Clare, Somatostatin* and *Zed's Magazine* (of Sherborne)? One could find out from *Rev. Soc. Stud. Surreal. Period. Nomencl.*, but it hasn't been published yet.

☆   *8.8.86*

I really shouldn't be allowed to go to auctions. I bought a copy of John Evelyn's book on salad-making, *Acetaria*, simply because of the aptness of the catalogue description: 'a few leaves browned or spotted'.

Then I paid too much for the fairly insignificant anonymous epistolary novelette *Letters of a Betrothed* (Longman Brown, 1858) because the association piqued me so much. It is by a certain Marguerite Power, niece to the Countess of Blessington, of whom *DNB* relates that she wrote *Virginia's Hand*, 'a story in poor blank verse, evidently under the influence of Mrs Browning's *Aurora Leigh*', and this copy is given to Robert Browning 'by desire of the author' by Anna Jameson, a close friend of both Brownings and, presumably, of Marguerite Power. It's signed by Robert Browning and according to the catalogue of the 1913 Browning Sale, once had a further note in R. B.'s hand, though this has been lost, filched or eroded. But the association is not just that of literary ladies or Victorian enthusiasts for marriage. On the title page Ms Power has chosen to have printed as epigraph, in, I am morally certain, all sweet innocence, one of the more scabrous *double ententes* from

Twelfth Night: 'By my life, this is my lady's hand! These be her very C's, her U's, and her T's, and thus makes she her great Ps'. A most suitable token for Robert who, as every schoolboy knows, wrote *Pippa Passes* under the impression that 'twat' was an item of ecclesiastical headgear. What misconstruction led him to this we cannot now ever be sure: '*11 across*. Every nun has one (*4 letters*)': something like that I suppose.

☆   19.4.85

Did you notice, when you were last reading your copy of *The Book of Nature and the Book of Man* . . .

You what?

But Good Heavens, don't you know that Victor Hugo said it was 'miraculous', that Carlyle called it his 'daily solace', that Garibaldi described it as 'a star of the first magnitude' and that Emerson remarked to Longfellow 'of all the meteors which fly through the atmosphere of philosophy, none shine with more brilliancy'?

Moreover, Dickens spoke of 'the essential oil of wit with which its pages are flavoured', Darwin liked it, quite ('no grander book exists'), while Charles Reade, often inclined to ascend a short distance further over the top than his fellows, declared it 'the concentration of his author's powers to a focus of light so radiant that the very eye recoils from its dazzling effulgence'.

I recently found *The Book of Nature and the Book of Man*, with these impressive testimonials, in a plump octavo volume, the Gonzaga coat of arms on the cover, described on the general title-page as *Works of H. R. and M. S. H. The Prince of Mantua and Montferrat, Prince of Ferrara, Nevers, Rethel, and Alençon* (Dulau & Co, 1886, New Edition for Private Circulation). Curious, I realized I already had a copy of the *Book of Nature etc*, published by John Camden Hotten in 1870, with an admiring preface by the late Lord Brougham. The author of that edition, however, was Charles O. Groom Napier of Merchiston, naturalist, author of *The Food, Use, and Beauty of Birds* (1865); but in 1865 his name was Charles Ottley Groom.

The 1870 edition is not rare, although most copies are 'author's presentation' or 'author's lending' copies; there is a special issue, which I have seen, with thirty-two rather ill-assorted photographic plates, Several Birds' Nests and Tintern Abbey Facing West; many relics of the Dodo, some from the Author's own Collection;

Stonehenge, Lower Forms of Life, and 'a portrait of an American lady, who attended a recent meeting of the British Association for the Advancement of Science, and is considered by Redfield greatly to resemble the elephant'.

Dulau's edition (not in the British Library) consists of the sheets of Hotten's printing, with the new preliminaries containing the striking opinions of numerous celebrities. Bound with it are two volumes of *The Burlington House Magazine* (antiquities, anthropology, round the galleries, anti-vivisection, most of the articles signed 'C.O.G.' or 'C.O.G.N.' or 'Turkish Pasha', 'Hungarian', 'Vital Reformer'); also a novel, *The True Story of Emily Ulster*, 'edited and abridged by her distant kinsman the Prince of Mantua (Hugh Graham)'.

I hadn't been too excited by Groom-Napier's work, a not-more-than-usually-dotty piece of anti-evolutionary twaddle: there had to be a Recreation of species after the Flood, because plants can't stand salt-water: the ark's passengers were preserved only as a precious memento of the prediluvian world. How could I have been so indifferent to a work that had such an effect on Sir Charles Lyell as he recounts in the 1886 introduction?

> One night this almost forgotten text ['thus far and no farther'] came to me, I rose from my bed, I lighted my candle; I got down some books; among others the presentation copy of 'The Book of Nature and the Book of Man'. *I sat up all night reading its pages. From that night I was an altered man.* I began, like Job, to abhor myself in dust and ashes . . . There is not a shadow of true philosophy in the progressive development theory. Poor Darwin! I went to see him, but I cannot undo the mischief which my support has done him; may God forgive me. I cannot do more with my feeble health than thank you from the bottom of my heart for your work.

Somewhere about here, or perhaps a little earlier, I began to realize that I was being had. If the Pope had sent for him, if the Sultan of Turkey had sent two black horses, if Disraeli had wanted him as Secretary of State for Science, if Doré, Cruikshank and Landseer had all been eager to illustrate his works, why hadn't I come across him? Why did the sixteen-volume French edition never turn up at auction – no, we know the answer to that, 'all but a few proof copies (two on vellum) were destroyed after the death of the Comte de Chambord'.

Everyone wants to write their own blurbs, and not a few do. Few do it as spectacularly as the Prince: did I tell you that the introduction – which runs to sixty-odd pages – purports to be edited by Charles Reade, who provides footnotes about each of the great celebrities? Thus when Owen Jones writes to thank the Prince for giving him 'many fine original ideas which will be useful in his profession', Reade quotes the Prince's high opinion of Jones and vice versa. Various factitious intermediaries, the Baron von Müller, J. Montgomery, Mr Mocatta, receive and comment on these letters; Carlyle writes to Montgomery, attacking Darwin and praising the Prince: 'no better specimens of Carlyle's style exist than these letters' comments 'Charles Reade', which is perhaps the Everest of chutzpah.

The correspondents of the pseudo-Prince (perhaps I should not call him that, for there is an affidavit from twelve representatives of the Twelve Tribes of Israel acknowledging his descent through the Houses of Palaeologus and Gonzaga from Zerrubbabel, according to a manuscript Genealogical Table in the hand of Moses Maimonides) were mostly dead when their letters were published, which may have simplified matters. General Gordon writes that he is off to Khartoum, and will collect some birds there if he is spared; the Prince Imperial is also off to Africa, with a limp leather copy of the Prince's ornithology work 'to serve as a pocket book'; it didn't save him. ('A Zulu brought to the coast, a year after the death of this dear young Prince, a copy of *The Food of Birds* much stained with blood; it had evidently been stabbed with a sharp instrument.')

Was he a jester, a fraud or a madman? I cannot decide. His pamphlets on the vegetarian cure for intemperance suggest dementia, though even there he methodically covers his traces.

> The author instructed Dr Meckelwörth, a German physician, in his system, and he has sent him forty cases of successful treatment in Mosco. Dr Meckelwörth's Swedish brother-in-law, Dr Herman Swegelhörst, has an even greater number of successes ... a pupil of Dr Swegelhörst has applied the system in America.

On the other hand, the pamphlets describing the great banquet (Vegetarian and Temperance) given in a gigantic tent in Greenwich, hung with the Prince's pedigrees embroidered on vellum, do read more like an elaborate jest. There's a recipe for bird's nest soup (75 oz of birds' nests at 30/- per ounce in the Canton market, 5 oz truffles, 24 oz carrageen moss jelly, 14 oz shallots, butter, button mushrooms, pepper, salt and raspberry vinegar, simmer for two hours in a steam-tight container, serves 1,200), a detailed description of vegetarian sucking pig, and curry champagne, and a remarkable account of the million-pound museum presented to him by a grateful German Baron. (People were always giving him things: 355 grateful Welsh miners, whose distress had aroused the Prince's practical pity, so that he had taught them how to extract gold ore from slag, by which means they made a million pounds profit in a couple of months, presented him with nuggets containing some four hundred pounds of gold 'worked into a carriage, a sword of state, a chair of state and various gold articles'.) There's a little crop of pamphlets, all apparently printed in Dunfermline, giving variant accounts of these events, in a style that looks like surreal waggery: on the other hand there is an obsessional reiteration of certain themes and characters: the Jew Vegetarian, Sophy of Bayswater, The Dodo and the Solitaire, bird nesting, metallurgy.

The only biographical account I have found is unhelpful. This is an article 'A London Munchausen', in *Cornhill* in 1912, by one C. C. Osborne, a man both smug, credulous and incurious. 'With the private life and character of the Prince of Mantua and Montferrat we are not concerned,' he starts, unpromisingly, but quotes an unnamed source (all his sources are unnamed) to the effect that the Prince's appearance and manner contained not the slightest hint of eccentricity. He believes that the Prince (unlike other pseudo-princes such as Orelie Antoine, Roi d'Araucanie et Patagonie, George, King of Mosquitia, Francisco Birget y Vidal of Madagascar and Theodore of Corsica – there's a jolly research programme) was entirely benign, not merely making no profit but actually sending expensive gifts to those he sought to honour. Certainly there was a report of the Mantua and Montserrat Medal Fund, but can Osborne be sure that the grateful letters from those honoured actually existed? He has fun at the expense of Ruskin and Owen, who apparently accepted their honours with glee, and congratulates Froude, who sent a non-committal response, for being less of a dupe; but Osborne hadn't seen the testimonials to the author of the *Book of Nature*, and may have underestimated Graham Groom-Napier-Murchiston-Montferrat's subtlety. Conversely, he is deeply shocked that Groom's Mum (that's the dowager Duchess of Mantua) shared his deception. 'One can scarcely imagine the condition of mind of these persons.' He may have profited from his quackery: equally, some of the letters might even be genuine.

The Great University Caper seems to have been his best wheeze, if wheeze it were. He announced that there was a tidy sum of money available to found a university, and he was prepared to receive submissions about the most suitable site.

There was agitation for a Welsh University about then, and the Prince let it be known that he was favourably disposed to the idea: mayors, aldermen and dignitaries from all over came rushing to praise the air of Aber or the beef and morals of Brecon. A public meeting was held in Essex Hall, at which the Prince read copies of letters to his ancestors, including an affecting one from Shakespeare ('I wish it was in my power to come to Italy . . . If I could do so I'm sure my next plays would be better written') and temporized with the Welsh. The meeting did take place: *The Times* reports it, deadpan. Didn't the Welsh get suspicious? They should have done so, for one Jim Storrie of Cardiff Museum had written to the press, to recount his experiences with the Prince, who had hired him as curator of *his* museum: 'During the time I was in his employ I was wholly engaged in trying to incorporate a lot of second-hand rubbish picked up at auctions into a decent-looking collection. When I found that Groom had no museum and was unable to pay my wages I left him . . .'. He also revealed, to those who needed telling, that the Great Vegetarian and Temperance banquet had not taken place.

The letter had little effect. The Brecon alderman said it was 'the most scandalous communication ever to appear in any paper', and Swansea was convinced it was a wicked Cardiff plot to snatch the University grant while Swansea was looking the other way . . .

☆ *15.6.84*

What England wants . . .
What England needs . . .
What England doesn't have is a newspaper that tells lies.*

Yes, of course, but I mean really prime fibs like the whoppers in the *Weekly World News*, printed in Lantana, Florida and permeating the continent like rancid orange juice, with stories like DUMBO DOCTORS GOOF AND MOM GIVES BIRTH TO TEST TUBE MONSTER (being kept alive for dark purposes in a secret Russian mutation factory, the tale goes on): COPS DISCOVER SAVAGE KILLER OF 37 IS A WEREWOLF and – the headline I'd most like to be marooned on a desert island with – FAMED PSYCHIC'S HEAD EXPLODES. Seems that the Russians (them again) were measuring one Red spoonbender's power to deflect incoming missiles to less vulnerable targets, for example the launch pads they had come from, and thought it would be educational to match him against another psychokinetic whiz who could bend the trajectories straight again. So there they were in their respective silos, engaged in fierce mental duel, eyes slitted to show intense concentration, magnetic power waves radiating from

---

* This was written some years ago.

bulging orbits, throbbing, thrilling chords on soundtrack and then suddenly boom!! plop! squelch . . .

The advertisements are helpful too: hypnotic eyes in five minutes, the new 19X water machine gun, and the Sacred Seal of Solomon ('Incredible! Get everything you Want!'). You can 'Develop a Rock-Hard Lean Stomach with 'Speed-Shaper' (No Doorknobs Needed)', or you can 'Cast your spell with Your New Irresistible Man-Catching Enchanting Bust', though what happens when an irresistible bust meets a rock-hard stomach is unpleasant to contemplate. A man called Bob, whose address, for some reason, is Dulles International Airport, suggests that if we want the Lost Secret 'Wealth Formula' ('a brand-new $200,000 dollar home completely paid for, and MOST IMPORTANT OF ALL, $1000 a day coming in every day for the next seventy years') we should write to him within seven days; but no one can outbid the Lourdes Cross, perhaps the most blasphemous thing in print. 'When you own this REAL diamond Cross of Lourdes with its *Genuine* eternal light and *Genuine* Lourdes water wrapped in *Genuine* Gold, watch how fast you 'Luck into' THOUSANDS OF DOLLARS,' And all the kindly and pious manufacturers want from me is sixteen bucks and my promise that *once I experience my miracle* I will let them know so they can register it in the Book of Miracles (now preparing), which will be sent on completion to the Vatican . . . to Jerusalem . . . to Mecca . . . to New Delhi and other great religious centres. There is a reverent description of the process of manufacture ('very carefully water drawn from the miraculous spring of Our Lady of Lourdes, France, is entered into the magnificent Chamber of the diamond cross . . . with slow painstaking effort, a gold replica of Our Saviour is united with the body of the Cross') and a tabulation of the kind of miracles you can expect, lest you have some lingering fear that you are only being offered spiritual gifts:

– Miracles that can make you rich (with wads of bills to spend as you please)
– Miracles that deliver you expensive new cars
– Miracles that let you win at Bingo, the lottery, the track, the casinos (wherever you go you hit the jackpot.)

Sounds like the meek are going to inherit the earth sooner than you might expect.

Weekly World News also features, in a nifty little story entitled 'Shopping Mall Monster', what may be the World's Worst Misaligned Participle: 'Then he drove them to his home where, still blindfolded and tied, he raped them'.

☆   *31.5.85*

A little more light has been shed on the unconvincing career of Charles Otley Groom Napier of Merchiston, Prince Bourbon d'Este Paleologue Gonzaga, Prince of Mantua and Montferrat, eminent Victorian fraudster or trickster and general adder-to-the-gaiety-of-nations, of whom I wrote last month. The torch is being pointed by a diligent and amiable North Californian painter, who just happened to be reading the memoirs of the astronomer Sir Robert Ball, an improbable enough exercise in itself. *The Reminiscences of R. B.* (I have complained – see p. 19 below – about the worrying excess of writers with those initials, but nothing seems to have been done about it) was published by Cassell in 1915, edited by his son W. Valentine Ball (a most inconsiderate choice of forename).

I was wrong about the Mantua-Montferrat Gold Medal for persons of Supreme Excellence – previous recipients Julius Caesar, Shakespeare and Dante, to name but a few. I took it for a simple fantasy, but it seems he did mail the medals out. Deciding it was time to honour the Irish contribution to civilization, he consulted Trinity College and the Irish Academy, who nominated respectively Dr Samuel Haughton, geologist, physician and zoophile (when a man was bitten by a monkey in Dublin Zoo he called round to ask after the monkey), and Sir Samuel Ferguson, Oghamist and miscellaneous littérateur. Ferguson was shyly delighted, Haughton took his medal to the lab and assayed it. The glistering prize was not gold. (As might have been deduced, syllogistically: All that glisters is not-gold.) Though urged by friends not to spoil Ferguson's innocent pleasure, Haughton felt his colleague should not be imposed on, and revealed the metallurgical imposition. Ferguson accordingly wrote the Prince a letter of masterly sensitivity. He was deeply grateful for the honour and the medal, but felt obliged to tell him that his servants or the Irish postal service had substituted base metal for the gold: if he could have the Prince's assurance that a gold medal had been sent, he would treasure the base metal as though it were gold: but if not, he would send it back. And back it eventually went.

☆   *16.10.87*

Gentleman in Rome quotes a handbook of Islamic Dietary Law: 'Pastries prepared with lard (pork-fat) or geltain deserts like jells and marshmellows are also *haram*': he is very moved, and so am I, by the geltain desert, which sounds a worse place to be adrift than the Rub' 'al Kali' (apostrophes inserted at random and without legal force) or Empty Quarter. It would sound equally well in romaunt or allegory or paramyth: Sir Maldefoy on the Jell Perilleuse: How Pilgrim encountered a most dire marshmellow, which betokeneth Carnal Distraction, and Overcame; Lord Necrobot the Neutrinobrained, voivode of the Geltain Desert.

But you don't have to be a risible foreign person to misspell. *The Times*, no less, recently advertised a rural property in a sort-after-district with fishing rites.

☆   26.2.82

> *Good* Ramus *pardon me, for I*
> *Have always lov'd* Trichotomy
> *But now I doe affect it more*
> *By far, than ever I did before.*
> *How many doe I daily see*
> *Given up to Muliebritie!*
> *A female head to a male face*
> *Is marryed now in every place.*
> *And some doe make, so vain they are,*
> *A Galaxias in their haire.*
> *Now sure Trichotomy it is*
> *Can banish these sad vanities*
>
>   A.M.

A bookseller's lot (Lot 727 in this case) is not always an unhappy one. I have been getting a heap of quiet pleasure from *Comarum ἀκοσμια: the Loathsomnesse of LONG HAIRE or, a treatise Wherein you have the Question stated, many Arguments against it produc'd, and the most materiall Arguments for it refell'd and answered with the concurrent judgement of divines both old and new.*

Published in 1654, it is by Thomas Hall (1610-1665), presbyterian and pamphleteer, curate of King's Norton, Worcestershire, and Master of the school there, ejected 1662, scholar, busybody. It is a vigorous piece, written in a tone of genial exasperation ('the Lord he knows that I doe it not out of any Pharasaicall selfconceited humour'), though it gets a lot less genial in the second part, *An Appendix . . . Against Painting, Spots, nak'd Backs, Breasts, Arms &c together with a discovery of the Nakedness Madness, and Folly of the Adamits of our times, a Refutation of all their Cavills, and removing of all the Fig-leaves, under which they would hide themselves.* He gets hot below the bands about those 'impudent flyblown kind of anabaptists' and is altogether down on 'that which is the Bedlams madness, and the Beggars misery, *viz* Nakednesse, that is the Whores pride, and the Strumpets glory . . . .

It's all much as you would expect, but then my eye was caught by those commendatory verses signed A. M. Every bookseller wants his oil-polluted geese to be black swans, many an arithmetic book with 'best wishes from Uncle Al' gets 'possible Einstein presentation' pencilled onto the flyleaf, and I would dearly like these verses to be by Andrew Marvell ('Previously unattributed. Not in Margoliouth or Grosart. Of the highest rarity and importance in casting light on a previously obscure period of Marvell's life and on the development of his verse. £5,000,000 o.n.o.'). Well, they aren't in Margoliouth or Grosart, or in Crum, or in *Hobbled Pegasus*, and they have the right sort of sound to my uninformed ear. In 1654 Marvell was alive and well and writing in Eton, at the house of John Oxenridge, having just left off tutoring Lord Fairfax's daughter in Yorkshire and failed to get a job with Milton. He became familiar here with John Hales 'the ever-memorable'. Could there be a connection through the schoolmasterly world with the Master of King's Norton Grammar School?

I have done a certain amount of research, laborious, delightful and much of it no doubt misdirected, like looking through a century of indexes to *Notes and Queries* to see if anyone there has preceded me. Apparently not, though J. E. Vaughan was working on a life of Hall in 1960, from the MS biography, but all that seems to have appeared in his *Guide Book to the Church and School of King's Norton*; no clue there to A.M. or the latinists D.U., R.D. or G.A. who also contributed verses to this volume. (I've since consulted the MS in the Dr Williams Library. It doesn't help.) But Hall was learned, bookish (his library went to Birmingham), and received pupils from far and wide.

I also looked through Lowndes for other possible A.M.'s. They are a sorry lot. Andrew Melville the presbyterian died in 1622; Andrew Moore, *History of the Turks* 1660, four volumes, he wouldn't have had the time; Alexander More, who quarrelled with Milton, author of *Fides Publica Contra Calumnias J. Miltoni* and supposed author of *Regii Sanguinis Clamor ad Coelum*, actually by Peter du Moulin who let More take the blame and claimed the credit later; Alexander Mudie, author of *Scotiae Indiculum*; A. Murmurer (London), that's a pseudonym; Ann Moore, the pretended fasting woman of Tetbury, 1813, irrelevant but I must find out more about her; Andrew Mure, *The discovery of St Peter's Well*. From Wing's *STC* I add Adam Miles, *The Countryman's Friend*; Alexander Mingzeis, *Mirth for Citizens*; and Adam Moore, *Bread for the Poore*. This last is probably irrelevant but I must add him to my collection of rhyming authors and titles, which I may have mentioned: *Omphalos* by P. H. Gosse, *Appointment in Samarra* by John O'Hara, *The Ill-Made Knight* by T. H. White. I have about a score from Johannes Freke, *De Linguae Graecae*, to René Levesque, *L'avenir de Québec*, and will give a bottle of fairly good claret, from Freddie Barrett, for the longest list to reach me by 22 March [see p. 21].

From *DNB* I get, as well as a fractured eye-muscle and a parcel of rowdy Highlanders, more about More, a churlish character, though he did publish poems, albeit in Latin and in Paris. 'Unless grossly calumniated throughout his public career, his morals must have been far less strict than his theology.' Also, much more disturbingly, Adam Martindale, a presbyterian divine from Cheshire, who wrote on everything: on natural salt from Cheshire, *Divinity Knots Unbound, Improvement of Mossie Land by Burning, Twelve Problems in Compound Interest, An antidote to the Poison of the Times, A Token for Ship-boys*. When a maypole was put up in the village his wife 'whipt it downe in the night with a framing-saw'. They don't make killjoys like that these days.

I examined Guffy's *Concordance to Marvell* and derived little comfort from that. Marvell uses none of the obscure words in this piece, though he does use 'affect', 'pardon me', 'daily', and of course 'I', 'they', and 'is'. He uses 'vain' forty times, but only once or twice in the sense of 'conceited' rather than 'fruitless'. He does use 'in every place', in the sense of 'everywhere' ('whilst fame in every place her trumpet blows'). But I do not expect much from computers; my own computer assures me that the lines can't be by Marvell since they do not contain the word which heads his relative frequency table, 'the'. By the same token, they cannot be by any other English poet either.

The volume also contains a longer and more entertaining set of verses 'To the Long-hair'd Gallants of these Times', which is signed R. B., and has a striking passage on *Plica Polonica* or *Polish plait*:

> Have you not been inform' o'th' hand
> Of God on *Poland* lately laid:
> Enough to make all Lands afraid,
> And your long dangles stand on end?
> Feare him that did that *Plica* send.

> And those sad Crawlers: and have more
> Unheard of Judgements still in store . . .

There is a long side-note about *Plica polonica*: 'A most loathsome and horrible disease in the haire, unheard of in former times; bred by moderne luxury and excess. It seizeth specially upon women; and by reason of a viscous venemous humour, glues together (as it were) the haire of the head with a prodigious ugly implication and intanglement, sometimes taking the forme of a great snake, sometimes of many little serpents: full of nastiness, vermin, and noysome smell . . .'.

There are all too many R. B.'s. Richard Broughton, author of *Monastichon Britannicum*; Richard Baxter (*The Saint's Everlasting Rest* and three score more besides); Richard Brome, the playwright; Robert Brathwaite, author of *The English Gentleman* (but he is a Royalist and surely out of consideration); Robert Democritus Burton – no, he died in 1640. I, of course, would like it to be Brome, editor (according to some authorities) of *Lachrymae Musarum . . . Elegies written by Divers Persons of Nobility and Worth upon the Death of Henry, Lord Hastings*, 1650, to which Marvell contributed one of the very few poems that was published in his lifetime. Brome died in 1652 or 1653, which doesn't exclude him entirely. It could just as well be Richard Baxter, who wrote approvingly of Thomas Hall (in *Reliquiae Baxterianae*), but Baxter lists all the books for which he wrote poetical epistles – or at least all he can remember: there is a mention of 'one or two others' – and doesn't refer to it there or in his commendation of Hall.

If Brome, then Marvell; if Baxter, then Martindale; or two other people entirely. But before leaving it to the experts, I looked up some of the odd words in the poems in *OED*, and this has confounded me entirely. 'Muliebrity' is recorded from Kyd (1592) and Urquhart's Rabelais (1693). The uncommon form 'galaxias' is reported only from Ussher (1625). So far so good. 'Plica' is not recorded from before 1684 – must remember to send them a postcard – when it is used by **Robert Boyle**. Boyle was around in 1650, (and not too far from Worcestershire;) but surely he is a red herring. 'RB', in the note on plica, cites his authority as Dr Bolton, who turns out to be a **Robert Bolton**. He died in 1631; his patron was one **Richard Brett**. I don't think I can stand it.

'Trichotomy' as a logical term is commonly used, but 'trichotomy' as a joke for hair-cutting is recorded by *OED* only from 1875, when it was used (hair is now beginning to crawl on the back of my neck in plica fashion) by **Richard Burton**, Richard Francis Burton that was.

Did you know that Robert Boyle and Richard Baxter had the same executor? Did you know that Peter du Moulin, or Petrus Molinaeus, son of Pierre du Moulin, or Petrus Molinaeus, (a pair of conspirators if I ever heard of any), wrote eulogies of both Robert Boyle and Roger Boyle? Have I stumbled on a secret society of R. B.'s extending Pynchon-like through the centuries? An arboretum of unacknowledged arbitrators (R. B. traitors). pointed arbalest-like at the heart of civilization, involving Robert Bridges and Rupert Brooke (alive in Grantchester under an alias) and Rhoda Broughton and Richard Boston and Rabbie Burns and Rabbi Bar-Jeshuah, first King of Merovingia? Is Elizabeth Taylor aware of the fact that her ex-husband is the noted Victorian traveller and pornographer, and also the 300-year-old encyclopediast (what's he got to be melancholy about)? And Rhett Butler and Ret B. Traven-Marut and if I'm found suddenly dead (poisoned by Rubidium in my rum-baba), tell England . . .

☆ 5.9.86

GOD (SOMERSET CC AND ENGLAND) IS NOT DEAD!
If the T-shirts are not yet proclaiming the Assumption of the Holy Batman, they soon will. I hadn't realized how far Ian Botham had become saviour-of-the-month in home theogonics circles until I heard a sports commentator say 'Well, that's it then; not even Botham can stop the rain', and realized that *he didn't believe it.* It was in fact one of those without-prejudice prayers offered by folk paddling in the shallows of belief: 'Oh-oh, no one can help me now, I bet', we exclaim, raising our voices and coughing slightly in the hope that Someone will overhear us.

We could do a lot worse than Botham. We need a few uncomplicated minor worshippees, not your omnipotent and eternal Creator of the Universe, King of Kings and all that; lord of Lords maybe, an unassuming, rustic and temporary Kingship only: 'that's a majestic stroke', declared my commentator; 'a bucolic stroke maybe, but a majestic one'. This combination is just what we look for in the modern god-concept. As the consumer magazine *What Deity?* observed in a recent editorial:

> In an energy-poor society, the old style all-purpose divinity, the labour-intensive, prayer-guzzling juggernaut is increasingly being replaced by the more modest single-function, dedicated demiurge. Today's worshipper is not prepared to pay the going rate for transcendence, and immanence is seen as something of an embarrass-

ment. Prudent votaries are trading in Eternal Judges for a matched set of culture heroes, nature deities and totemic figures.

The glossy adverts tell the same story. Sinlessness is seen as priggish, slowness to anger as irrelevant to the challenges of today. The major dealers (Many Mansions of Manchester, House of Gods, Stockport) have a full inventory of micro and mini gods, lares, idols, fetishes and nats. And the Blessed Botham makes a useful addition to the range, along with Dagon and Dagan, Gilgamesh and Gilgalad, Cu Chulain and Kukulkan (another day we'll go into that one, how the Irish discovered Central America, the Mayo-Maya connection). These are persons with superhuman strength and human failings, bags of charisma but a touch unreliable, given to errors and rages, madness, heroic laments for the loss of comrades, travellers, exiles (omnipresence, once fashionable in deities, is specifically forbidden by the laws of cricket), teachers of useful arts, herb lore and new songs, strikers of great strokes and victims of inexplicable bans.

The name is a hint. As Any Good Dictionary relates, *botham* is an obsolete form of *bottom*: 'tha he on botme (thaereon helle) stod' says Caedmon's *Satan*, playing the usual apostate's trick of turning the elder gods into demons; reminding us of that other botham, the zoocephalic Bottom, weaver of the web and the weft of the world, Guardian of the boundaries, from whence he will return to judge the living and the dead: and then I wouldn't be in a Test Selector's boots for all the chai in China.

☆   *30.4.82*

You've probably had enough of what Holinshed calls 'images of sore and terrible countenances, all armed in curious worke of argentine',[*] so you won't mind if I go on about Thomas Hall's treatise against long hair, and the commendatory verse signed 'A.M.'

My little Marvell turned out to be something less than a nine days' wonder, exciting a whirlwind of indifference. I am still waiting for the definitive dismissive missive, doubtless this very moment being penned in some distant academic litcritorium: 'I have thought that the Hall canard was so long ago exposed. Is Mr Korn really unfamiliar with the most convincing refutation of his

---

[*] See date. There was a war on at the time. The Shetlands was it? Or the Faeroes?

attribution in *Skrifter fràn den Kongligas Haarkundshistorisk Institut in Søensø?*

John Lehmann wrote civilly; but I'm not convinced that a posthumous portrait of Marvell, published in 1681, showing him with long hair, proves that he might not have written an epigram (epigrammatists are not on oath) in a different sense, at another place, at another age, under another régime. The Restoration was also a hair-restorer. Or as a recent correspondent suggests, Marvell's hair in 1681 may have been wiggish.

Or Whiggish. On the precise meaning of which at the turn of the eighteenth century depends another hotly debated issue, the precise date of the first recorded of the drinking songs with which the men of Brasenose College, Oxford (and doubtless the women too) launch their annual mardigratifications, before settling down to the rigorous business of supping themselves into a stupor. See *Brasenose Ale. A Collection of Verses annually presented on Shrove Tuesday by the Butler of Brasenose College.* (Privately Printed, Boston, Lincolnshire, 1878):

> Then in true English Liquor, my masters, begin
> Six go-downs upon rep. to our true English King,
> In this orthodox health let each man keep his station
> For a Whig will conform upon such an occasion.

The editor, while sticking to the date of 1705 or thereabouts does point out that there wasn't anyone around at the time you could call both English and a king, and puts the whole thing down to Jacobitism. But the exclusionists of the 1680s, who opposed the Duke of York, were also Whigs ... The other words present no difficulty. 'Rep' is a kind of corded fabric, or else a worthless fiddle, while a 'go-down' is of course 'a (sometimes subterranean) storehouse in India and other parts of Eastern Asia'. More interesting is the second recorded ale-chanty:

> O may my verse be strong and clear
> To spread its glory wider
> Not windy like to bottled beer
> Or gripe-compelling cyder

lines you would hardly recognize as coming from the sobersided pen of Reginald Heber, he of the spicy breezes and the icy mountains. ('The only brews that Heber cares for', they used to jest, 'are he-brews'.)

I would have offered a bottle of audit ale for anyone knowing that, but my last challenge gleaned but a single response. I asked for rhyming titles and authors, along the lines of *The Ill-Made Knight*, by T. H. White, *The Wandering Jew*, by Eugene Sue, *The Sorrows of Werther* (Goethe) and, obscurer, *Maria Again* by Mrs John Lane, *There's Rosemary, There's Rue*, by Lady Fortescue, *The Flame and the Rose*, by Helena Grose, and – my favourite of all for its air of deadpan inevitability – *How to Examine the Chest* by Samuel West (Late Physician to the City of London Hospital for Diseases of the Chest, Victoria Park). My sole respondent offered, quite to prey on the helpless, like the children's homes that maltreated defiance of propriety, *King Lear* by William Shakespeare, Aphra Behn's *Poetical Remains, Collected Poems* by Oliver Wendell Holmes and, outrageously, *Wars I have Seen* by Gertrude Stein, which is almost as bad as my own *The Silver Tassie*, by Sean O'Casey. Nonetheless, the due meed of success (from Dew Mead Bottling Co of Honiton) will soon be on its way to Anthony Thwaite, who is of course known as the author of *Poems on the Victorian Great*, the travel books *Pomegranate and Date* and *The Sukiyaki Came Late*, and a study of the role of the Arts Council *Hand it out on a plate or make 'em wait: Can poets create with the aid of the State? Notes on the Great Debate.*

☆   2.9.83

You and I, of course, being persons of the world, would be unlikely to advance any money to one Colonel Graves, sometime Commander-in-Chief to the armies of the Queen of Madagascar, later Commander-in-Chief of the forces of Jacques Lebaudy, Emperor of the Sahara. Nor to the Comte de Toulouse-Lautréc (sic) nor to Deacon Hann Yusp of the tribe of Jilu. We would not be likely to rush our subs to the Anti-Expectoration League, The National Thrift Society, The Children's Non-Socialist League; nor buy space in the Colonial Advertising Catalogue of the Britannia and International Language Co – not even if, especially not if, solicited by an agent called Charles Septimus Malpass, clearly the kind of villain who is hissed on every entrance, and snickers up his sleeve.

Nowadays we have television and radio to expose frauds, sharps, swindlers, bunco-steerers and flat-traps. But in 1913 they only had the admirable *Cautionary List* of *Truth* magazine to prevent people giving all their money to Mr H. Haverley, the Branded Man of Haverstock Hill, founder of the Aggressive Christian Union ('tells a cock-and-bull story about being kidnapped by papists and branded with an H on his forehead. The H may be taken as standing for "humbug" '), to the London Institute for Lost and

Starving Cats ('money collected is mainly expended on killing cats') or to the 'gang of bogus bishops' who ran The Shaftesbury Memorial Shoeblack Outdoor Brigade for Homeless Destitute Deaf Dumb and Crippled Boys ('appeals among the most blasphemous and canting issued by any charity-monger').

Truth Cautionary List (it ran for many years) describes hundreds of bogus organizations, not often as candid as the man collecting for the Samuel Smiles Centenary (self-help begins at home), and individual hypocrites like George Brooks: 'originally a Nonconformist Minister and a violent Radical. Became a still more violent Tory, self-constituted champion of property and vested interests generally. Addresses pathetic appeals to wealthy representatives of these classes, describing his personal and domestic distresses. When not relieved, becomes abusive.' Some preyed on deserving victims – like John T. Higgins ('improvident young heirs falling into the toils of this vampire have been bled in the most unscrupulous manner'), like P. Saunders of Savile Row, who claimed 418 per cent interest on a loan to a 'wealthy inebriate'; or like the Societé Academique d'Histoire International, which would send you a gold medal and a diploma for twenty guineas. But many preferred to prey on the helpless, like the children's homes that maltreated their inmates, or Gibbs & Co who passed off over-priced sewing-machines to servant-girls and enforced payment with the 'penny frightener' an imposing blue paper headed 'Notice before proceding to Law'.

There were bogus share promoters and promoters of bogus shares, bogus biographers (Joshua Hatton, writing as Guy Roslyn, now reduced to poverty and begging from those he had biographed in the past), bogus printers and bogus editors of bogus papers, like *The Gentlewomen's Court Journal* and *The New Church Quarterly*, which existed only to collect review copies.

Medical frauds were numerous, even though The Aural Remedies Co had lost its chief consultant, Dr Crippen, since the 1910 edition; there was still Amritam and Antineurasthenin, Brainine for the brain and Crystolis for the hair, Antidipso or Eucrasy or Alcola for drunkenness, Madame Temple's Cure for Blushing, the Magic Foot Draft, and bust enhancement by Diano, the Institute Venus-Carnis and the Académie Neuzonic. The Brothers Grant advertised themselves as 'human X-rays', while the Health and Vim Supply Co 'undertakes to cure obnoxious diseases.'

Truth was hard on Bernard and Jennie Barton of Bugsworth ('a married couple who carried on a disgusting business') and on the Reverend Basil Collet, 'an inhibited clergyman, the whining note of whose appeals betrays the practised mendicant'. I cannot withhold admiration from the Kew Seed Co, which promised for many years that 'every day 40 readers who reply to this advert will receive £1' and was as good as its word: every day forty readers who replied and sent for 4s 9d worth of goods received £1. Which made sixpence each. But my favourite style of crook – and I suspect *Truth*'s – is the Seaside Lapidary: 'a class of persons who carry on a curious business by substituting real gems for worthless pebbles. The pebbles are picked up on the beach by people and sent to the lapidary, who returns to them inexpensive gems, such as topazes and aquamarines, the price charged for cutting showing a profit to the lapidary'. Surely this is not fraud but the acceptable face of something or other?

☆   11.4.80

1980 should see the completion of one undertaking on which publisher and computer can congratulate one another. The *National Union Catalogue of pre-1956 Imprints* records what some seven hundred North American Libraries hold by way of books printed in the first four centuries after Gutenberg – which makes it the largest and for many purposes the most useful bibliographic tool ever fashioned. Unlike the stalagmitic growth of Channel Tunnel or French Academy Dictionary, NUC has kept astoundingly close to schedule, smiling in the face of biblioflation.

The introduction to Volume 1 (August 1968) spoke of 610 volumes published at the rate of sixty a year. They started late in the year: Volume 5 was the first to bear the date 1969; and 1979 accordingly began with Volume 605. At last count, the British Library's shelves had Volume 659, accessed back in December. The alphabet as you see, has proved slightly longer than anticipated, or contributors more co-operative; 659 reaches only WRIGHT, FRANCES TERESA: or rather it doesn't because she is '*See Annabel Lee*', hundreds of volumes in the past. The latest actual entry is Frances Laing Wright, who edited *The White Heron* (1937), an Anthology of Louisiana Poets of Today (held, I regret to say, nowhere in their home state, but only at Texas U and by those Damyankees at DLC, an insult to Southron Womanhood indeed).

The White Heron also perches about midway through Volume 162 of the 167-volume Library of Congress Catalogue of 1946, which suggests that the NUC will reach its omega or zzz at Volume

167-divided-by-161.5-times-659, or a rather slim volume 682 (then, of course, the supplementaries will begin). That's 11 per cent over the original estimate for size, and rate of completion maintained to a whisker, which makes most civil engineers look very sick.

☆   13.3.81

While one may argue whether ambergris or Lomotil (TM) is the most beautiful word in the language, can there be any doubt that Euro-MP is the ugliest?

☆   5.12.86

As I may have remarked, I have enough trouble deciding whether *Time Out* or *City Limits* is the magazine for me, and I'm not helped in the least by having the data for an informed choice among 6,500 of the beastly, seductive, time-voracious things. Such, however, is what I am offered by Katz's and Katz's *Magazines for Libraries*, now in its fifth remorseless edition.

Katz and Katz (that's Bill and Linda Sternberg Katz, published by Bowker, pp xviii + 1094, £95 and was ever money better spent?) haven't, obviously, read through sixty-five hundred periodicals from *Cinemacabre* to *Muscle Development*. Of course not: they have read through sixty-five thousand, from *Thrust* to *Vibrant Life*; from *Sinerjy* to *Sipapu*; from *Tel Quel* to *Teenage Mutant Ninja Turtles* (I'll come back to that in a minute); from *Motheroot* to *National Hog Farmer*; from *Old West* to *New Albania*; from *CelebrAsian* to *EGgink*; from (I'm enjoying this) *A + to ETC*; from (I can stop whenever I want) *The Journal of Presbyterian History* to *Petersen's Pickups and Minitrucks*; from *The Police Chief* to *Hustler*; from (just a little one) *Yelmo* to *Yup*; from *Hanging Loose* to *Addictive Behavior*; from (I can't fight it any longer) *Alive! for young teens, Archie's Pals and Gals, El Heraldo de Brownsville, High Technology, High Fidelity, High Times, Highlights for Children, Highway and Heavy Construction, Interface* (source of timely information on specialist libraries), *Interface Journal of New Music research, Interface Age, Interfaces, Inter*...

Sorry about that.

They've read all those magazines and then they have (pedantically speaking) decimated them. They have called on experts savvy enough to tell you which skydiving mag should be in every library and which is only for specialist parachuting collections; the twelve most significant Urban Studies periodicals; what to go for if your budget only runs to seventeen journals on management science; and the best source of information on cata-, tri-, and poly-marans. The last one isn't too difficult really: there is just *Multihulls* ('the only periodical that offers diverse and thorough coverage of this boating niche'), and their conclusions have a pleasantly pleonastic ring or rather ring-ring: 'if there is a perceived demand for publications about multihulled boats, *Multihulls* should be given primary consideration'.

They have a humbling bank of expertise. I have been rather preening myself for knowing about comics ('Sequential art' is the preferred term), despite not being a sequential artlover; I will for example pontificate about *Teenage Mutant Ninja Turtles*, a joke that accidentally got taken seriously and now serves as a sort of Caliban's mirror of the first edition market: as each new number hits the stands the previous issue quadruples in price and is declared rare. K. and K.'s Man on the Strip knows all about this, knew back last spring that Superman was going contemporary, knows all about the markets for *Heavy Metal, Love and Rockets, Care Bears* ('message of spreading happiness ... aimed at children just beginning social contact') and *Katy Keene* ('for fashion-conscious children'). Their resident expert (we are told who he is and he lives in Culver City, Calif) is not so hot on British Comics, or maybe *Mandy, Dandy, Blandy* and the rest don't come up to snuff: though there is no excuse for omitting the hugely influential *2000 AD*.

The signed reviews are enjoyably judgmental: the hefty philosophy section enthuses over *Praxis* ('as those who read the Serbo-Croatian will understand'), commends fifty others, faint-praises *Sophia* ('artisan-like, printed no doubt from a justified word-processing program') and damns *Mind* ('lost its grip'), *Topoi* ('not enough for a steady diet, only a vitamin supplement') and *Philosophy and Phenomenological Research* ('sad ending for a pioneer'). But there's no *Radical Philosophy* in this section, in fact no radical anything in the index except *Radical America*. There are no British computing magazines, except the academic *Computer Journal*; I started to wonder if Britain was underrepresented. But there stand *The British Journal of Aesthetics* and the *British Journal of Criminology, Punch* and *Country Life* and the *TLS* ('often witty and provocative letters to the editor').

Wading through the wetlands of single-author journals becomes an easy outing with an assertive local guide. Some writers are for all libraries: *The Blake Quarterly*, *The Keats-Shelley Journal*, *The James Joyce Review* ('the twentieth century's most important – if tedious – novelist'); Saul Bellow, Conrad, Dickens and Donne are suitable for medium-to-large institutions, while only the biggest and most specialized need to bother about Claudel or Hawthorne, *The Flannery O'Connor Bulletin*, or poor Emily Dickinson ('Somewhat insignificant despite its high cost').

Gender politics crowds the magazine racks. The section called 'Men' contains nothing more than five Wild West/Survivalist journals, a high-class rag-trade rag, *Playboy* ('gauge community needs and select accordingly'), *Hustler* ('healthy sexual attitudes'), and *Screw*. Women by contrast get pages and pages of stuff, all the way from *Barbie* and *Playgirl* and *Big Beautiful Women* to *Hecate*, *Sinister Wisdom* and *Off Our Backs*. Not to be confused with *On our Backs* in the 'Lesbian and Gay' (didn't that use to be 'Gay and Lesbian'? Or is it always ladies first?) category, which gets very positive treatment: 'prove your commitment to intellectual freedom by subscribing to this daring magazine.' The man who graded the Singles magazines had a lot less fun. 'Best of its type in south central Texas' is but grudging praise of *Touch of Class* (San Antonio), especially when he adds 'primarily of interest to middle-class yuppies'. *Cupid's Destiny* gets a dart square between the shoulder-blades: 'from the looks of some of the photos, a person would have to be desperately unwed to resort to the Destiny League'. Only *Living Single* in Columbus, Ohio, seems to turn him on; 'definitely one of the best . . . emphasis is on the glamour and excitement of single living. Articles on skiing, night life and exciting personalities exemplify the happiness that single life can hold . . .'. If solitary night skiing with a bunch of exciting Ohioans isn't your bag, there's nothing left for you but *Laugh*, *Poolife*, *Muzzle Blasts* and *Suicide and Life-Threatening Behavior*.

☆ 26.9.80

When I wrote the other month about that benign biliomastodon, the National Union Catalogue, and how it progressed with such admirable steadiness, without pause or gap, of course I knew that it had omitted five volumes' worth of *BIBLE*, but didn't want to draw attention to what seemed like a moment of absentmindedness. But now we are at volume 692 and there's still no sign of holy writ, and I feel obliged to warn the editors about the dangers of postponing a disagreeable chore. One knows too well the self-deceptions and excuses, palm striking forehead, oh dear me those *BIBLE* entries, yes, I really must get down to them after the weekend, when I get my desk cleared, when we get that awkward *TOBOLSK* to *TOLSTOY* out of the way ... and soon comes the seductive whisper suggesting we leave the whole thing over till the second edition or perhaps if we just jump straight from Biberian J. *Springtime in Yerevan* to Bibuji Ram Dass *Analysis of N-space tensors*, no one will ever notice the difference.

Meanwhile, the wave-front has reached *YMCA (NEW HAMP-SHIRE)*, an unpublished hymnsheet called *Songs for Young Soldiers*, which is preserved in the Presbyterian Historical Society of Pennsylvania. Anyone take any bets that the next volume will start with a duplicated collection of limericks from the YMCA of New Mexico?

☆   29.2.80

Apropos des Bottins: the most portentous news item for publishers, and indeed for all word-heavers, comes, unexpectedly, from the French Post Office. Some forward-looking pragmatist has looked at the costs of continuously updating, printing, binding and distributing many kilotons of directories each year, and has concluded that it would be cheaper to kit out the entire Francophone population with a small computer terminal and a visual display unit on which the required number will magically appear.

This is not speculation, projection, nor pious intent. Manufacture and distribution of the data terminals will, we are told, begin at once. This may make life difficult for Luddites and for bumbling indecisives who can't remember if they want Phillips with one or two, and are sure that it's either Coronation Road or Jubilee Grove or Abdication Avenue; but then life has always been difficult for people like us: directories give us short shrift, and inquiries operators no shrift at all.

So there will be some ten million French homes with the capacity for receiving unlimited quantities of verbal information on a VDU. How long before another forward-looking pragmatist does his sums and offers storage capacity for hire – if not on this year's model, then maybe on the next generation of PTT-computers (or compététuteurs)? And how long before publishers are discussing the viewdata rights? And how long after that before books are printed only in limited editions for antiquarians? It could be the end of French letters as we know them.*

☆   *18.10.85*

I was walking along Manette Street, between the shop that sells puffed stuffer fish, stuffed puffer fish, and the corner where the find-the-lady gang have their pitch, when a semi-English-speaking man accosted me. 'Where, please, can I find the enemy?' he articulated. 'No, no, we are all friends here', I simpered, 'whatever our nations may have done in the past we . . .' 'I am looking for the enemy', he enunciated carefully, 'the journal, the enemy.' I was flattered that he had recognized my professional status. 'You mean *The Enemy: A Review of Art and Literature*, ed. Wyndham Lewis, nos 1-3 (all published) 1927-1929, wrappers, v.g?' 'Nein. Enemy. En.Em.EE. Oder die Melody Maker?' he elucidated, pointing firmly at my midriff.

I tumbled to it at last. 'Ah, of course you mean *NME*, the *New Musical Express*, that sapient and savvy observer of all that is fresh and innovative upon the socio-musical and politico-punk stage, that shrewd and literate dissector of dreams, that rapier of hype, that deflator of bombast . . . yes: I don't know, actually, I suppose newsagents sell it.'

My habit of wearing T-shirts without reading them had got me into another fine *malentendu*. This time it had been a heavy metal group called Twisted Sister, a gift from a witty and non-twisted sister-in-law. At other times people have come up to me and offered to help me save whales, or Wales, to stamp out godlessness or God, to run for mental health or for dear life. We are giving out signals without being aware of it, like a female dragonfly that has been sprayed with female dragonfly pheromone by some insect endocrinologist when she isn't in the mood, and can't understand why she is suddenly the cynosure of all those multifaceted eyes. The cause of so many of our troubles is all these androids about the place, chaps who have been seized by Martian snatch-squads, taken aboard the mother ship and duplicated down to the nearest molecule just as they were at the moment, so that the simulacra go around the world permanently switched on to emitting rage or

---

* HRIW. I didn't foresee that they would also use it for Bourse updates, buying from the local supermarché by Direct debit, and porno telephone calls. In backward England, porno telephone calls have to be made manually.

bewilderment or sexual arousal or rejection. There are various politicians who . . . But you knew that already.

☆   25.12.81

Speaking of which, have you come across any Faroese daily papers recently? *Føroyska Politiken*, as it might be, or *Thorhamni Tidningar*? They are pretty thin on the ground, if George Kurian's *Book of International Lists* (444pp. Macmillan. £5.95. 0 333 32386 6) is anything to go by, and the point I'm making is that *The Book of International Lists* isn't anything to go by, except as providing more support for my belief that anything that can be expressed numerically is not worth saying. The book (which I shall henceforth refer to as BIL, so that I can later make some joke about suffering, like Pierre Louÿs, from BIL-itis) is the soft-bound edition of *The Book of International Rankings*, this title being thought more appropriate for the hardback. BIR was published in 1979 and some of the data (the cost of a taxi in Frankfurt, Olympic medals in 1976 per capita of population – well done Bermuda!) have not grown more pertinent with the passage of time.

I was struck by the fact that the Faroese, though highly literate – 99%, on a par with Britain, Gibraltar and Greenland and just below educational Utopias like Bermuda, Nauru and Macao – are shamefully near the bottom of the list for newspaper circulation; just between Rwanda and Mauritania, with a figure of 0.1 per thousand. Given the population of 42,000, this makes a print-run of 4.2 newspapers, the odd one no doubt being torn up for stuffing cod.

There are a lot of oddities about island life. The Faroese, together with the Falkland Islanders and the inhabitants of St Pierre and Miquelon, come top of the league for number of rooms per house, which I thought might have something to do with boat building and extended families, but Table 286 shows that the little French dependency has 7,000 scientists engaged in basic research, and since there are only some 5,000 St Pierroises and Miquelonnaises if that is the right adjective, you can see why they need the extra rooms. Unaccountably, St Pierre and Miquelon is absent from the population table (it should be at number 186, between Nauru and Tuvalu) but you can work it out from the number of cinema seats per thousand, and the total seating capacity (Table 306). They do have a lot of cinema seats (fourth in the world per capita, or rather per fundamenta, behind Falklanders, Cook Islanders, and Cypríots) but they don't use them much, averaging only three times a year (Table 304). I suppose they have to entertain their guests, making endless cups of black coffee for those research scientists, sitting on seine nets making basic discoveries.

The Falklanders are not eager cinema patrons either (well, they have 322 sheep per head, for one thing) but the Macao-folk go eighty times a year each, undeterred by the fact that they only have ten thousand cinema seats. This works out as each seat being filled seven times a day, which must mean very short movies, unless they sit on one another's laps a lot; or perhaps they all go to drive-ins which, oddly, don't count.

The Cayman Islanders, we learn, have 0.1 cinema seats per thousand, and one thousand seats in all, which makes the population ten million, which is a lot of tax exiles. Again, this territory doesn't figure in the population lists, so I can't tell if it should be ten seats per thousand and ten thousand Caymanners in all, or 0.1 per thousand as it says and only one seat (reserved for the Grand Cayman, no doubt), or whatever other possibilities suggest themselves.

George Kurian does explain that the figures have to be treated with caution, drawing attention to certain anomalies like the finding (Table 280) that in the Vatican City there are 1,192,000 university professors for every million people; he even goes as far as to say that the figures for proportion of Christians (Brazil 100%, Rumania 100%) 'do not correspond to reality in a mathematical sense'. But other anomalies you have to find for yourself, like the fact that 75.9% of the population of Gabon lives in towns of over 50,000 people, (Table 17), although only 32% live in towns of any size (Table 16); or that 31% of all married Panamanians are divorced, even though the divorce rate there is only 0.5 per thousand. 'Maybe they go to Honduras for their divorces', suggested my actuarial consultant, a notably fair-minded man, who also argued that the bizarrely low annual death rate for Pitcairn Island – less than two per thousand – doesn't necessarily mean that all Pitcairners live to be 500; they may be a very young population (boatloads of mutinous babes coming in on every tide); or maybe they all go to nearby Christmas Island to die, which would account for that misnamed spot having the highest death rate in the world.

Now I'm not really complaining about anomalous, inadequate or improbable figures from a bunch of Pacific atolls with populations too small to maintain an adequate Civil Service, and better things to do with their time, like lying in the surf eating copra and smoking rongo-rongo. ('Ya Sinalau, the damned *orang blanda* has just brought another three questionnaires from the United World Statistical Service.' 'Bring me my fishing-spear, and tell them the answers are 3.8, 42, and 11 kilograms per hectare.') This is just the top of the atoll. If this patent piffle is being peddled as sober fact, what confidence can I have in the respectable-seeming middle of every table? Does the Netherlands really produce twice as much cement as Malaysia, for example, or has one figure or another slipped its decimal moorings, like the Faroese and the Caymen? And I am not talking about simple misprints, like the endearing transposition of columns that tells us there are 83, 673, 128 libraries in Denmark (can't you see them, packed solid and piled ten deep from Flensburg to Elsinore? They'd have to keep the pigs in the stacks. No bed for Bacon, indeed) or the blunder that gives Macao two separate entries in Table 386 (vocational training), once at a respectable 40th and again at a shameful 139th. What does worry me is that this elaborately fatuous stuff can go from computer to book and thence back to computer, without ever – even after two years in print, where any layman can fall over absurdities – without seeming to have been proof-read, edited or passed through a vertebrate brain.

Consider the rather important Table 61: Percentage of National Income received by the poorest 20% of population. You may be surprised that Liberia tops the chart as the most egalitarian state, with 13% of National Income going to the poorest fifth. Kurian advises us that this chart should be read in conjunction with the preceding chart, showing Percentage of National Income received by the richest 5%. It should indeed . Turn to the preceding chart, and lo! Liberia's name leads all the rest, with a cool 60% of National Income going to the fat cats. But this only leaves 27% to be distributed among the middle 75% which makes them poorer than the poorest people in the country, which makes nonsense of everything.

Worse than the mistakes are the stupidities; minor sillinesses like listing carefully, by continent, the *lowest* cities over 3,000 feet in altitude, or the least populous cities with more than half a million inhabitants; major follies like the quasi-numerical enumeration of what can not be enumerated: the Press Freedom Index, the Political Opposition Index, the List of Most Powerful Nations. Such indexes display what the indexer knows or believes to be the case; they cannot tell us anything we don't know already. To the extent that they give mathematical precision, they are wrong or wrongheaded. The Press Freedom Index, designed by the Freedom of Information Center, School of Journalism, University of Missouri, tells us that the Press in Upper Volta is freer than the press in

Ethiopia but less free than the press in the Soviet Union. Thank you. The Most Powerful Nation Table, (size, economics, national will), with USA at the top, natch, shows Burma as more powerful than Vietnam, Mongolia more powerful than East Germany, Guinea as more powerful than Switzerland. Thank you. The Political Opposition Index shows Guatemala and Lesotho near the top, necessitating a comment: 'the most stable democracies are generally found in the middle of the ranks. The US, for example, with an index of 1.49 seems to have the optimum conditions for a workable democracy'. (Three inches is a very good height indeed.)

Most obviously crazy is the Civil Disorder Index, which is introduced by some pseudoscientific rumbling: 'the study of disorder in international and national affairs, just as the study of entropy in physics, is becoming quite a discipline in itself'. In a disciplined fashion we are told that in the years 1975-78, Spain had the most instances of civil disorder, far outranking Chad or Lebanon, despite their civil wars, while among the least disorderly were the Central African Empire, under the homicidal lunatic Bokassa, and Equatorial Guinea, under the lunatic homicide Macias Nguema.

George Kurian's religious prejudices are worth examining. He describes Hinduism as 'not essentially different from the animist religions of Africa', and provides the following gratuitous account of Islam:

> an expansionary (sic) religion and backed by petrodollars, it has been making gains in Africa, a continent that had been ravaged by Arab slave traders until the twentieth century. (Islam is one of the few religions that expressly sanctions slavery.) Islam's appeal is enhanced by a number of factors, particularly its approval of polygamy, its easy divorce laws, and its simple theology, almost entirely borrowed from Judaism.

Which is not to say that simple pleasure cannot be extracted from this riot of dubious data. Here is a list of countries that — as far as my unrigorous examination goes — top the charts once and once only each. Can you guess what peculiar excellence distinguishes: Mali, French Polynesia, Djibuti, Yemen Arab Republic, Luxembourg, Turks and Caicos Islands, England and Wales? Answers at the foot of this column.

Answers: Mali: fertility rate; French Polynesia: fatal industrial accidents; Djibuti: divorce; Y.A.R: expenditure on Civil Service as proportion of total budget; Luxembourg; beer-making; Turks and Caicos; receiving letters; England and Wales: counterfeiting.

☆   *21.2.86*

Reading a recent number of the *Mechanics' Magazine* (relatively recent, about 1834 in point of fact) I came across a suggestion that seemed to have a lot of merit. Man called Snowden looking at railway carriages, had a brainwave, took out a patent. Take a few seats out of each carriage, replace by cogged wheel, connected by cunning gearing to wheels underneath. Find two brace of brawny working-class chaps to turn the wheel: they could have a sort of treadmill arrangement, splendid exercise for the calf musculature, or a kind of rowing-machine apparatus, equally good for the biceps. Dispense with locomotive entirely, save 100 per cent on coal: 'expense of fuel and inconvenience of smoke altogether done away with, accidents and explosions rendered impossible'. Save on engineering costs, don't need to level off the ground; effort efficiently adjusted to load, fellows just coast downhill, work a little harder on the upgrade. I won't give his figures, based on undercutting the Liverpool and Manchester Ry Co's 2d per passenger-mile, twopence three farthings per ton; but the principle is plainly as valid as ever. United strength of four men in the shafts would produce 144lbs of force, sufficient to propel 'for what might be termed a working day of eight hours', three tons at twenty miles per; not quite your Intercity 125, but no problem of burning brake linings either. But the great advantages are not environmental or financial but social: 'the grand object is obtained, that of securing employment for the many individuals now seeking work but looking for it in vain'; no longer pretext for gloomy Malthusians to speak of redundant population, 'neither will any willing labourer afterwards be driven to participate the paupers' mess for want of remunerative employ, but on the contrary the whole body of society will receive a new and vigorous impulse that cannot fail to diffuse health and happiness to all'.

I see no possible objections. The Greens will be enthusiastic, the market-forces will be mobilized, unemployment will vanish at a series of strokes, employers no less public-spirited than in 1837 will put men before technology, inflation will be frustrated and Victorian values will triumph again.*

* HRIW.

REMAINDERS

☆   31.7.81

I've a great admiration for the editorial efficiency displayed by Mansell, the publishers of the 700-odd volume *National Union Catalogue of pre-1956 Imprints* but among a billion catalogue card entries from all over North America, a few black sheep are bound to gatecrash. I recently bought an obscure English obstetrics book, and on looking it up in *NUC* was taken aback to find printed beneath the bibliographic details, the following words: 'Whoever shells out good bucks for the crap in this catalogue is being royally screwed by us'.

Footnote: John Commander, c-in-c of the project, refused to believe that I had stumbled by chance on what (he piously hoped) was the only printer's graffito in the entire work. (He offered me a bottle – or possibly a case – of champagne if I found another.) He was convinced someone had broken a vow of confidentiality and blabbed. But it was the purest coincidence. I just happened to buy the book and happened to look it up. If you want to check up, it was . . .
O God, I've forgotten.
It began with W.

☆   25.7.80

I foresee hot competition over the film and paperback rights of *Zoological Society of London: Scientific Report 1977-79*, which has lust, mayhem and violent death on every page, to say nothing of an astoundingly beautiful X-ray photograph of a stork's skull. Aesthetics is not, though, the main concern of the dedicated workers at Regent's Park: artificial insemination is more what they are keen on. It's full steam ahead for the Puma, the Yak, and the Sooty Mangabey, but 'the program aimed at the artificial insemination of the female elephant "Toto" was abandoned in 1978 owing to increasing practical difficulties', they laconically tell us. (Baron Corvo would have understood.) They are more explicit about the business of pandering to pandas, unrewarding work: 'no sign of oestrus, but subsexual play, bleating and interest were shown in May 1979'. Since May 1979 interest rates and bleating levels have both risen sharply, at least in my neck of the woods, but I can't tell about the other.

Meanwhile the pathologists tell sad stories of the death of birds, slender meerkats (it has been an especially rough year for slender meerkats) and gentoo penguins (broom bristles, alas). Lethargy in a Californian sealion is probably unavoidable, but hepatitis B in wildcaught chimpanzees had a more shocking origin: local animal dealers apparently inject them with human serum, with the intention of providing protection against human diseases, thereby making them carriers for a disease harmless to primates but potentially deadly to Man. But there are successes:

> a particularly nervous Black rhinoceros was transferred to Regent's Park from another collection but even after two weeks had refused to walk from the house into the paddock. Tranquillisation with 500 grams of Diazepam ('Valium'), given orally every 24-36 hours for three to five days at a time, persuaded the animal to accept its new environment.

Now 500 grams of Valium would persuade your average literary journalist to accept his environment for about ninety-two years, or to put it another way, would soothe some 50,000 particularly nervous booksellers. But when the black rhino gets nervous, boy, he get nervous, and the keeper who wandered up to him with a large pail full of pills is an unsung hero – though still greater feats of heroism are implied by the sentence: 'a substantial number of faecal samples from animals with diarrhoea have now been examined.' I learn also that ruffed lemurs have been suffering from BIDS syndrome, which sounds like the occupational disease of auctioneers, but actually stands for Brittle Hair, Impaired Intellect, Diminished Fertility and Short Stature, a totally different kettle of fish.

The tone in which these Gothic horrors are described is generally genial, but the writers become quite severe on the subject of budgie care: 'Despite considerable publicity over the past two decades concerning the sensitivity of parakeets to iodine deficiency, thyroid pathology associated with a low iodine intake is still seen frequently, especially in pet Budgerigars submitted for autopsy.' Even the report's list of acknowledgments is fascinating: 'thanks are due to Dr Such for the supply of ram semen and computer facilities'. Now that's what I call a well-rounded man.

☆   *18.2.83*

The man who can best help me with my enquiries is a Constable. He is Peter Constable, an Elizabethan Recusant poet who appears, under the name of Pietro Contestabile, as the contributor of a twenty-line English poem beginning with the words 'If to the church, rightly we may Compar/the Mone . . ' to a polyglot collection of elegies on the death of Ludovicus (Luigi, Louis) Cardinal D'Este, the man who completed the building of the Villa D'Este and patronized Tasso.

The collection, *Varii Lamenti d'Europa Nella Morte dell'Illustriss.e Reverendiss. Monsignor* etc, edited by one Sebastiano Forno Ardesi (Padua Franc. Capponi, 1587), seems to be rare, a word I use sparingly: it is not in the British Library, nor in various other UK Libraries, nor in any of the United States Libraries contributing to NUC – at least not under Forno or Ardesi or Este or Deste or Varii or even Europe (miscellaneous). The printer is not listed by Cosenza, the lister of Italian printers, though the *Clavis Typographorum* records that Capponi was active in the one year 1587, so the book must be known in Italy.

There are various Catholic Constables, most notably the poet Henry Constable, author of *Diana*. Peter Constable is not mentioned in accounts of Henry, nor in Gillow's *English Catholics*; nor is he an alumnus of Oxford or Cambridge. The poem is conceitful, the kind of thing that was easier to write in the sixteenth century with lots of East/Este quibbles:

> Sith East doth want what hop doth then remayn
> That in the world the sun shall rise agayn

The text is corrupted, but not half as badly as the unfortunate anonymous 'Todeschi' in which 'Kirchen' becomes 'Kinchen' in the next line and 'Rinchen' two lines further on.

How can I make my new poetaster sound more thrilling? There are numerous references to Constables in Shakespeare, of which the most gnomic is 'Dun's the Mouse, the Constable's own word'. Mouse had better be a corruption of 'Muse' and we know who Duns is . . .

☆   6.5.83

WE ARE GIVING YOU A $7.50 BOOK *FOR FREE* BECAUSE WE THINK YOU WILL WANT TO CARRY IT.

Well, yes if I can have something opaque to carry it in, the book being Margo Woods's *Masturbation Tantra and Self-Love* (Omphaloskepsis Press, San Diego). 'One of those extraordinary happy books that comes along just when you're beginning to feel that sex is a dark closed room with a door that has no handle', as Michael Perkins of *Screw* magazine felicitously puts it, though presumably staffers on *Screw* are inside the dark closed room trying to get out.

You don't need to know anything about the book (reciting the Shiva/Shaki mantram to call the archetypal energies up, and apricot kernel oil from your local health store, that class of chat), but on page 21 there is a striking phrase: 'I had just read Dr R——'s book, and thanks to his graphic description of an orgasm, I realized I had never had one'. Rarely has the function of the literary enterprise been so clearly illuminated. For orgasm, substitute if you will True Love/an Oedipus Complex/Utopia/an unhappy childhood/a dacha in the pine woods/a boat trip down the Thames/a room of one's own/a fall in front of a train. Candidates are advised to choose no more than three.

☆   5.8.83

Spare an uncharitable thought, if you will, for Theophilus Swift, possibly the least amiable character (I shall get letters vindicating him) in Regency Dublin. He came my way through a copy of *The Touchstone of Truth*, third edition, or more fully, *The Touchstone of Truth; uniting Mr Swift's Late Correspondence with the Reverend Doctor Dobbin and His Family; and the detailed account of their subsequent challenge and imposture. Third Edition; enlarged with several new remarks and observations by* Theophilus Swift, Esquire. *Jubent renovare dolorem* (Virg.) Dublin 1811. (The two previous editions have different though equally cumbrous titles.) The Correspondence, which is presented with three prefaces, two introductions, a Stricture, an Advertisement, a Challenge, five Appendices and a Postscript, demonstrates a most sustained persecution of the unfortunate Dobbins whose offence was not to marry or, respectively, wish their daughter/sister/kinswoman to marry this ancient and quarrelsome buffoon.

    Theophilus had had some practice: the son of Deane (*sic*) Swift, who was the cousin of Dean Swift (so was Deane's wife, as it happens), he was born in England in 1746 and moved to Dublin on receipt of a legacy, where, says *DNB*, 'his eccentric opinions and habits attracted attention'. He had previously written a pamphlet on Colonel Lennox's duel with the Duke of York, that had led him into a duel with Colonel Lennox, in which Swift was injured. He abused the faculty of Trinity College for failing to honour his son, 'the cleverest lad in all Ireland'. The Faculty replied in kind and there was a trial after which both Swift and one of his victims were jailed for libel on each other. In 1805 he conceived himself to be enamoured of, and then engaged to, the unfortunate Emma Dobbin:

> Hear, Emma, Hear!
> The Vow comes watered with a gushing tear!
> Delightful drop, if thou accept the strain!
> A drop of Pleasure in a Fount of Pain!
> ***************************

His asterisks, not mine; they are justified in a characteristic footnote: 'having lost the paper-slip on which I had set down these Lines when I returned home, I have depended for their correctness on a memory that was never a good one. At the end of five years, every hour of which has been edged by some keen reflexion, or barbed with some bitter thorn, I may be allowed to forget some Evanescent Verses . . .'. Somewhere between 1805 and 1807 Miss Dobbin, if she had ever considered herself engaged, came to consider herself disengaged, and became affianced to a Reverend Lefanu, one of the literary Lefanus. Swift, reasonably, felt himself slighted; and eccentrically, conceived that his honour was impugned, since unless Miss Dobbin avowed that she had abandoned him, he would be thought to have abandoned her. She chose silence, an error with Swift, who had a marvellous skill at creating no-win entanglements and finding secondary grievances.

He wrote her what he describes as a 'hasty but affectionate' letter (there is an appendix explaining the reasons for his haste and the conclusions which may and may not be drawn from it) saying that if the report was true he wanted his previous letters back. 'That I may not be misunderstood I would say explicitly that having besought her to return my letter should it be true that she was preferring another to me, her Reservation of them implied and gave me reason to conclude that she was *not* preferring another.'

Dobbin senior writes back to say explicitly that Swift is not going to have his daughter. Swift replies that this is not explicit enough. Emma Dobbin writes to say that she is not going to marry him, and returning his letters. Swift publishes the letters with sardonic commentary ('My friends are now in possession of Miss Dobbin's talent as a letter writer. They will not wonder that I was delighted at her correspondence . . .') and issues a series of involved challenges: 'ninthly, What was the reason that when she positively declined the Proposal she did not positively decline the Contract?' A member of the family sends him a challenge, to which he replies in suitable terms. Then realizing it is a hoax, he sends a letter asking for his reply back. The family returns the second letter, not the first, which dishonourable conduct is denounced at length. He deals with another abusive letter in a magisterial way: ' "You are in your second childhood?" So I was when I proved for seven years my fidelity to an undeserving woman. "You are deranged?" So, I could have told her, are well known to be certain "individuals of a family" whom She would be very sorry I should name.' He resigns her to Lefanu in a letter full of malice; Lefanu gets the girl, and Swift is sent a piece of wedding cake. Swift, unconscious of pathos, reprints the letter that accompanied the cake, with a final footnote: 'The Bride-Cake was surmounted with a Trophy of White Ribband'. So next time chaps bemoan the passing of Swiftian pamphleteering, let them think whether they'd like this kind of treatment, which word processors could no doubt issue at a fearful rate. Though without the White Ribband.

Loonier than Theophilus was John Bellenden Ker, who wrote *An Essay on the Archaiology of English Popular Phrases and Nursery Rhymes*. (Southampton and London 1834.) The good news is that it is the first scholarly study of the Nursery Rhyme. The bad news is that it is demented. Rather in the manner of *Mots d'heure, Gueuzes, Rames* – but he means it – or the contemporary scholar who appears to maintain, if I've been following him, that the Hebrew Bible is actually in Greek, Ker believes that nursery rhymes and many popular expressions are ignorant peasant corruptions of Low Dutch originals, meaning something quite different, mostly sly attacks on the rapacity of the pre-Reformation clergy. He uses Dutch, which he knows, more or less, as an approach to Anglo-Saxon, which he doesn't. (A bit like searching for a lost ear-ring under the light because you'll never find it over there in the dark.) What he says is clear enough.

> It will not be denied, I suppose, that English and Anglo-Saxon, are, at least, sister-languages, and if so, as the offspring of a same parent, at one stage of existence an identical language. And if we believe (which I do) the Anglo-Saxon and the Low Saxon (still surviving, in the main, in what we now call the Dutch) were the same language, our own must at one period have been as these once were, also the same language.

Do not delay over-long near that strangely migrainous sentence, but drill yourselves on these simple examples of the Ker technique. 'BLUE DEVILS = *bloed-evels q.e.* bad blood; DEAD AS A DOORNAIL = *dood als er doornagled q.e.* dead as if pierced through and through; HEAD OVER HEELS = *heet over ijls q.e.* hotly over-hasty; HE LAUGHS IN HIS SLEEVE = *hij laffe's in hys liefde q.e.* he is basely deficient on the score of affection; IT IS ALL MY ARSE IN A BAND-BOX = *het is al mêe aes in eeno beender-bos q.e.* it is altogether no more than carrion in a shrine, however showy this state-coffin may be, it contains but mere carrion after all; and thus notwithstanding your display of words, or promises, I put no value upon them, knowing them to come from a worthless person; one undeserving of my confidence.'

I think we are now ready to undertake one of the nursery-rhymes. All are quotable; but fond as I am of *'Ryd er Ghack-horsé! Toe ban by't wrêe kruys:* Ride your Cock-horse (your people; parishioners). Bestow upon them the curse of cruel vexation!'; and *'Bat er keck, Bat er keck, Bekers-man:* Put a bold face on it, be assuming in your claims, my man of the cup', I think the palm must go to number XXVII:

> There was an old woman who lived under the hill
> And if she is not gone she lives there still.
> *Daer Wasse een ouwel-wije hummend luid aen der Heer hilde:*
> *End of sij is nauwt gae an, sij lief's daer still.*

'There you hear rise a holy-wafer-humming noise in honour of the Lord Pantry. And if it is not paid for, the holy-wafer-chaunters would rather be quiet (not give themselves the trouble of mumbling over their church-office for nothing).'

☆ 30.7.82

Speaking of sinecures, how about the job of passport examiner at Jakarta airport? I don't mean big bustling Jakarta/Halim Perdanak, of course, but its tranquil sister Jakarta/Kemayoran. Last year just six passengers took wing thence to foreign parts, and a smaller number (my authority rather cavalierly describes them as 'NM', for 'not meaningful', which would be a hell of a thing to have stamped on one's passport) arrived, perhaps by mistake, to help it earn its place near the bottom of the list of busy cosmopolitan skyports. It is actually a place or two above San Carlos (I mean of course San Carlos de Bariloche, in the Andes; oh, *that* San Carlos) or for the matter of that La Guardia, which is shown by some quirk as having no foreign traffic at all (not true, I arrived there myself). But some of these heaven-havens have busy domestic traffic, so you might be happier, or at any rate idler, as a ticket clerk and airport announcer (you probably have to lend a hand in the aerobistro at quiet moments) in Morlaix/Plojean which had only five thousand passengers last year, about twelve a day, fifteen when it gets hectic. Or at Bobo-Dioulasso, the airport for Bobo-Dioulasso (1,000 out, 700 in) or Kandahar (3,500 each way; no one stays in Kandahar), or Tozeur, Tunisia, where 3,924 people flew in and

3,868 flew out, the odd fifty-six no doubt resting in the tinkling streams of that divine oasis, or bitten by sand flies and bleaching in the shimmering salt-flats? Or would you rather be an air-hostperson with Airworks India (seventy-six passengers carried in fiscal 1980), the airline that treats you as someone special. I'm not knocking Airworks, clearly a comer (it carried only thirty-nine passengers in 1979, and any fool with a slide rule can still tell you that means it will carry 24 million bodies in AD 2000): but you might be happier with one of the bigger, more impersonal lines like Pushpaka Airlines, with 2,300 fare-paying passengers, that's more than six passengers every day, or the sombrely named Flugstodin of Iceland (1,085) or our own dear Burnthills Aviation, which carried 794 folk between, I should like to think, High Wycombe and Ventnor, Isle of Wight.

All of these job opportunities, and more, much more, come from *The Best'n'Most Guides in DFS 1982*, a title that bewilders and irritates in about equal amounts. *The B'n'M in DFS* (Volume SV, whatever that means, a stout paperback of 560 pages, some of them attractively tinted like the eighteenth-century *Livre de Quatre Couleurs*, and published by Genepub of Ornskoldsvik, Sweden, apparently at $65) turns out to be another demonstration of the awe-inspiring ability of a computer to produce rubbish. No; to be fair to computers (and being fair to computers is going to be the major critical task of the coming century) it demonstrates the computer's ability to multiply rubbish, to sort, classify, arrange, collate and print-out it by the ton. Measure, rather carelessly, the height of sixty-five not-very-randomly selected policemen, and it will give you alphabetical, chronological and geographical rankings, with probits and regression coefficients and standard deviations (if policemen may be said to show standard deviations), all ready for some human intelligence to discuss the effect of social status on height in Derbyshire, or the prospect of no person under the rank of sergeant exceeding fourteen inches in stature by the middle of the next century.

The book comes with a snappy epigraph from the chairman of the British Airports Authority, a copyright notice rather sweetly laid out in the shape of an airliner, and an apology for its otherwise unrelieved ugliness: 'the nearly 100 per cent use of computer technology may result in the book's printed pages having a slightly less aesthetically pleasing appearance than previously'. The data concern the booze, carcinogens and stinks (drinks, smokes and fragrances, as editor Yngve Bia prefers to call them) available from duty-free shops (DFS) in airports, planes and ferries around the world. Bia is valiant, although perturbed by the possibility that the

EEC will ban the whole business, a threat to which he in rather Strindbergian fashion attributes 'the all pervading gloom overshadowing everything, particularly with regard to the subject matter and content of this book'. He explains expansively if not always explicitly. 'The title *The Best 'n' the Most* consists of two superlatives "the Best" and "the Most".' It seems that 'Best' means 'most popular', and most popular means – I had to trek through column-miles of typographically and intellectually unjustified prose to be sure of this, encountering *en route* oases like 'the attribute Sex refers to the identification of the user (Man or Woman) of the product, and is of course only applicable where the sex concerned is obvious' – stocked (not sold) in the largest number of retail outlets, these outlets being weighted in proportion to the number of international travellers passing through them, or rather in front of them. So one bottle of *Soirée de Milton Keynes* sold (or unsold) at London Airport (11.7 megapassengers) outweighs fifty such bottles sold (or unsold) on the sturdy vessels of Nordisk Faegefart (MV Gelting Nord and MV Stella Scarlett) or a billion bottles on the SS Argostoli which has, according to the list on page 508, a passenger capacity of zero. ('Something seems to be wrong with our bloody ships this year, Anaximander', says the chairman of the board, dejectedly studying the balance sheets.)

What comforting names boats do have. The Bland Line of Gibraltar; SS Vergina, plying for the Stability Line of Libya; the Archaic, sorry the Achaic Line of Greece; and most delightful, SS Safe Christina of Sweden (laid up). Not a bit like her sister ship SS Dangerous Doreen, of which terrible tales are told wherever matelots foregather; I'm sorry to hear she's laid up.

This isn't how Yngve Bia sees it, of course. He says that there are good grounds to suppose, that the likelihood can be regarded as negligible, that it is safe to assume . . . that managers of these outlets will stock and restock what sells, and not stock, out of inertia or corruption or incompetence, what doesn't. There are definitions, explanations and justifications. There is a discussion of social utility – these folk have a conscience – which points out that while drink and fags can kill you, perfumes rarely, if ever, do. And, not being total idiots, the compilers of *B 'n' M in DFS* have assigned grades to all their data, omitting from the calculations the obviously insignificant, out of date, or unreliable, so we do not get told, as in some other publications with computer inputs, that Rockall is the healthiest place in the world because no one died there last year.

The not very interesting conclusion of all this is that Marlboro, Johnny Walker Black Label and Nina Ricci 'L'air du temps' are Terra's finest. (This is for 'lines'; I can also give you lashings of gen about 'brands' on the one hand, and 'products' on the other; for example that a seventy-five-centilitre bottle of Fernet Branca is stocked in only 9.8 per cent of these shops, so it's ten to one you'll have to keep your hangover.) 'Most' seems to mean most dear (or most cheap), which is much more entertaining for the average consumer, who can draw practical conclusions. Don't buy your Jim Beam Whisky on the Swedish Sessam line, where it cost $13.63, but wait until you get to Livigno airport, where it is only $4.57. Other things being equal, don't purchase your perfumery on the Silja Line (SSs Finlandia and Silja Star) but on Air Malawi, should they be covering the same route; if faced with a choice between Polferries of Gdansk and Air Garuda remember that what you save on Indonesian toiletries you lose on Polish Vodka, or perhaps the other way about.

There are also average price indexes which demonstrate, mournfully enough, that Manchester Airport Duty-Free is the least enticing, closely followed by other British Fly 'n' Save Bargainaterias, though all of them are philanthropic compared to some of the Scandinavian ferry services. Juba and Khartoum are the best stopovers, while Air Malawi simply gives the stuff away in bucketsful. All this is just the beginning. *B'n'M* is just an *apéritif* for COSSOP (Computerised Shop Statistics on Products and Prices) a personalized system that will provide whatever information you want whenever you want it, from sending you hourly listings of the price of everything everywhere, to giving you a tinkle when the price of a telephone-shaped crock of Bourbon ($28.68 at Helsinki Airport, $31.27 out in the Gulf of Bothnia) goes up or down.

None of this has any relevance to the literary world? Just wait for Computer Originated Criticism of UK Prose and Poetry. When COCUPP goes on line, the lot of you will be out on the streets, and the right place for you, I shouldn't wonder.

☆   *31.5.85*

I've been admiring the handsome publicity material for Stefano Bisconcini's lavish and definitive history of the cigarette lighter (*Lighters/Accendini*, Edizioni San Gottardo, 150,000 Lire). 'This is the very first book ever published in the world, dealing exclusively with cigarette lighters', they claim, but I'm sure it isn't. I remember one devoted to the history of the Zippo lighter exclusively: it may have been called *Prolegomena to an Outline Taxonomy of Early Pre-Classic Zippo*. But nothing is ever new: you could start collecting the slips that come from cash dispensers; mention your new hobby with shy pride to the chap you meet on a bus and you'll find he belongs to the East Essex chapter of the Society of Numismatopetalists, who are having their National Convention in July, and have been publishing a newsletter for years. (You can get it from the Hon. Sec., Mrs K. Despenser, Cowslips Cottage – a corruption of the Norman French Cashslips Cottage – Wall Bank, Salop.) You will also learn that Sotheby's have an important sale next Tuesday, starring a particularly fine run of the so-called 'Refusal Series' of the Flatbush Friendly Bank (1978-1983), including a near-mint 'Money, money, money, that's all you ever think of', a previously unrecorded '*I* should give *you* $50'), and three variant states of the rare 'Bug off, gonif', used only in the last two days of the Bank's existence. You will also learn that the prize of your collection, the 1865 'Argyroballistikon' with emblematic borders by Owen Jones, is almost certainly the 1984 restrike.

☆   *1.4.88*

I send you 2,850 short sentences!!

So, engagingly, boasts *The A.B.C. Proverb, or Pulpit at Home* (Liverpool, 1877) by George W. Johnson, 'Native African, Sierra Leone, Late Secretary of the Egba Government, Abbeokuta'.[*]

The boast is almost certainly correct. The sentences are numbered and the last is number 2,850: 'Z.Z may stand for Z and the last, – but if you and I pray Heaven will be our last, – THANK GOD!'

(pointing finger) 'He that hath ears to hear, let him hear.'

'I FINISH; YOU FINISH: ALL FINISHED, – AMEN.'

And the whole concludes with a fine woodcut of a steamer captioned 'The White Man's Question – When Will Black Man build a Ship like this? The Black Man's answer – We shall, if you will give us the chance', a song called 'The Beggar and the Christian'; some pages on the folding and use of the No 2 Creole reversible kerchief ('The first invention of our most worthy friend and countryman, Mr George W. Johnson, native African who had the honour of leaving his native country for England with Prince Alfred, on board H.M.S. Euryalus') and the semiotics involved ('third pattern, which is named "Deny Pattern" . . . signifies they are in a hurry and deny everybody on their way to be in time. Females going to society or sent in a hurry should always have on that pattern to prevent people stopping them on their way, either by shaking of hands, long how-do-you-do. We have known

---

[*] He was known as 'reversible' Johnson, writes a man from Abeokuta, and came to a bad end when the locals thought he was a British spy. But the Nigerian flag is based on his design. See also p. 212 below.

females to suffer by these humbugging by their husband for late cooking') and testimonials from satisfied users ('I met Mr Taylor, the talkative, on my way, and I was much surprised that he passed me by and never spoke a word'); likewise 'The Schoolboy's ABC'; a woodcut, 'White Woman Working a Sewing Machine'; a view of the Palatine Establishment, Liverpool; and sundry other matters including blank pages for entering Births and Deaths ('in order to do away with the usual words of our old Fathers that "Bor-Bor" and "Te-te" Age-Book "don, lose", Mr Johnson presents to all who buy this Book six ruled pages as follows which will answer the needful of a private registering of the names of your Family. GOOD LUCK'); some modest self-advertisement ('all order to Ladies and Gentlemen's clothing promptly attended to'); and finally (finally) a page headed 'THE END' that starts 'The end is the end' and ends with 'Goodbye! God Bless You at the end. Amen' but not before it has recapitulated the main themes of the preamble, the closing pages and the 2,850 sentences themselves.

The main text of the book is eclectic, or perhaps schizoid. Missionary pieties ('88: A good heart opens the Bible at all times') alternate with West African proverbs ('163: Break your glasses and you will drink water with calabashes'), with outbreaks of local pride ('156: Abbeokuta is the richest subscriber in produce for Lagos's Revenue'; '1691: King Dosumu of Lagos has given 5 of his sons, to the Wesleyan and Church Missionary Ministers in Lagos for Education') and autobiography ('1531: In our schoolboy days of 1848, there stood Josiah Brown, "now collector of Customs", Sierra Leone, the most quiet boy in obedience'). Velleity ('Good things never last') alternates with vigour ('No matter who, so long as you are a black man, you are an object of ridicule, by the dirty low class in England'). The occasional private reference has slipped in ('2287: Send your bill, and I will send your money. T. A. Williams, Lagos'; '2474: Will you come at once to arrange the payment for your ABC – Hurried Message from the Printer').

What we have here, plainly, is a new narrative form, alphabetized for easy reference, number-flagged for computer analysis (Johnson thinks it is for sending messages by telegraph to your friends who also have copies, but he built better than he knew), capable of infinite expansion, and transfinite flexibility. Towards the end, however, fatigue overcomes him. 2844, one feels, could have been better expressed:

> You schoolboys of my time and long before me, allow George to remind you of the sins we have so frequently enjoyed after school. Alas! to follow to stone 'Dow Dow' who I must say is of the offspring of Stephen of old; don't forget also of 'Partar Kupa' – and

'Brass-Cock-Hat' all those poor men are waiting in their graves for you and I to go to Judgment – *No laugh in this, my boy!*

And who are we to argue?

T

2557—"TEJUMO-ADE," or "TEJUMADE," is the name of the mother of the Author of this book, which means,—" Open your eyes upon Crown."—*(Name given to " Princess of Egba.")*

2558—The dead are covered over in iron safe until the day of resurrection.—*(Dream.)*

2559—Trouble passes trouble, sin passes sin.

2560—Trial in body is all that can be done to a Christian in this world.

2561—The wreck of the African steam-ship "Gambia,,' at "Cape Palmas," on the 17th May, 1877, was a heavy blow to the sharp merchants of Liverpool.—*(Letters lost! money lost!! passengers saved!!!–thank God.)*

2562—The world was made for man and beast.

2563—There are some flies which tease a man over and again more than others.

2564—The sun is a free fire for every body.

2565—The moon is a free lamp for every poor man in Africa.

2566—The dead will not speak, because they have plenty to speak in the day of Judgment.—*(Don't call it.)*

2567—This African book of A B C may do good in Europe, as it is expected to do in Africa.

2568—The way to Christ is always free and open to every sinner.

2569—Thessalonians 1st, 1 chap. 18 verse, that even the ministers of God, are sometimes hindered in the pulpit by Satan.

☞ " He that hath ears to hear, let him hear."

WHITE WOMAN WORKING SEWING MACHINE.

☆   7.11.86

We all do our best to preserve and at the same time enlarge the liberties of language, even if my own modest attempts at enrichment lead to accusations that I can't tell coacervate from butter (see *TLS* Letters, October 31). My courteous corrector, Mr George Heygate, says 'coacervate' is a transitive verb, when what he means to say is that *OED* only records transitive uses. (If I'd spoken, barbarously, of things coacervating themselves he would have no grounds for complaint.) 'To what purpose this coacervation of texts?' as someone asked in 1641.

The *New Statesman* columns are a good place to botanize among new demotic forms, some of which seem to be part of a political agenda. I'm not sure whether they muddle 'diffuse' and 'defuse', two rather different ways of dealing with a crisis (one way it blows over, the other way it doesn't blow up), but everyone else does; and this week I found the marvellous coinage 'fusillage' and the phonetic spelling 'vunerable'. 'Hetrosexual' has displaced 'Alsation' as the most popular misspelling, and is used as a mild pejorative. To me it has a louche, sexist, Gallic sound: 'av you sin *Hetrosexual*, a story of nautty capeurs at Londres hairport?'

☆   7.10.83

War correspondents in the Falklands had, I understand, their problems but most managed better than Burr McIntosh (strange first name, perhaps short for Burberry), one of the least gung-ho (gungleast?) of newshounds, and author of the modestly-titled *The Little I Saw of Cuba* (F. Tennyson Nealy, New York, 1899). The Spanish-American War, you recall, was made by newspaper proprietors for newspapermen; if so, nobody bothered to tell McIntosh.

The book's frontispiece shows him in Rough Riders' kit: Teddy Roosevelt hat, floppy-tie-and-moustache set, check shirt, mighty pistol, trousers stuffed into high hand-stitched boots; portly, but *sportif*. The jauntiness of the dress does not disguise the signals of anxiety: left hand gripping camera-case too tightly, right lost in the folds and dangling straps of his saddle-bag, and clearly in the act of fumbling unsuccessfully for something, a set of the jaw that says clearer than words 'Have I forgotten my lens cap/filters/chamois leather for wiping plates?' and replies, no less clearly, 'Almost certainly.'

There is a characteristic disclaimer:

> In presenting these pages there is in no way a desire to add to 'War Literature', or to attempt the slightest infringement upon the rights of various historians ... Fate having decreed that signal acts of success should not be accomplished, because of events having transpired as described, or because of absolute physical incapacity, no effort is made to lay claim to any performance of especial merit.

There follows a downbeat epigraph from Hardy ('It is only those that half know a thing that write about it') and an equally glum opener: 'looking backward, recalling the scenes and moments which seemed at the time to be filled with events of the greatest magnitude, one's mind and views cannot fail to be regarded as having been altogether out of proportion'.

Burr William McIntosh (who always writes in a style that suggests he is running uphill with too heavy a pack and a twisted ankle) arrived in Tampa on June 7, 1898, representing something called *Leslie's Weekly*, and armed with a powerfully-worded letter from the Secretary of War. In Tampa 'everything was found to be in a rather excitable condition'. He presented his credentials and was given the runaround, especially by the aptly-named General Shafter. 'Both he and Lt. Miles were about the last men in the world that one would wish to meet if seeking a favour or a courteous reply to anything.'

The book is of course full of McIntosh's photographs, mostly low in contrast and rather blurred: some have little black or white flecks on them. This section of the narrative is illustrated with a view of President McKinley's desk (in front of which he was kept waiting for several hours), a train (which broke down in central Florida) and the Post Office (which lost his mail). Eventually he got aboard the USS *Matteawan* with a box containing 'about 20 lbs of lemon wafers, some pickles and lemons'. There is a photograph of four hungry Rough Riders posed along the taffrail, the last photograph of Sgt William Tiffany, who died of medical malpractice aboard the hospital-ship *Olivette*, and Sgt Cook, an Englishman who stole McIntosh's boots.

They lay for days at anchor, set out for Cuba, returned and lay at anchor again. McIntosh was alternately seasick and starving, the lemon wafers all consumed. One day he hired a sailboat for a trip to Tampa: on his return he was nearly swept out into the ocean. The *Matteawan* sent a picketboat to rescue him but denied him succour when they saw who it was. After another week the fleet made the short crossing to Cuba, and hung about offshore. At last a landing was announced. It was also announced that only soldiers would be disembarked. McIntosh swam ashore, losing only part of his equipment. He dozed under a palm tree. Land crabs dropped on his head. He met some Cuban insurgents he didn't much like – they are called in his captions 'Cuban Soldiers(?)' or 'Cuban Warriors(?)' – and some corpses he cared for even less. None the less he took some moving photographs, but was so distressed that 'I must have gotten everything wrong', since nothing developed. He lay without shelter through tropical rain and missed the battle of Las Guasimas while 'a number of newspapermen who were sure to write things in the proper spirit were given the necessary tip'.

He returned to Siboney where he 'successfully cultivated the germs of yellow fever' and found difficulty in filing despatches as the telegraph department refused or lost most cables. His fever grew worse, but Mr Hearst arrived with two tons of ice. For several days he seems to have been in a semi-delirium, searching for peaches. He describes the search as 'fruitless'. He recovered sufficiently to take a side-trip to see if there was a negotiable trail through the mountains. There wasn't and he missed the next battle. He is there for the big engagement before Santiago and takes a photograph of the first shot fired by a heavy gun. Unexpectedly, the ground is shaking so much that it is out of focus. He takes a striking action picture of a man with a bullet through his knee, but it fails to develop. He watches the catastrophic manoeuvre with the observation balloon, and misses what is happening on San Juan Hill. He rides up the hill to find out what did happen, but his horse is commandeered. Later that day he messes with other correspondents and learns a lot of inside dope: 'it would have made one of the most readable books of the war if it had only been recorded'. There was more fighting, but he was 'too ill and worn out to enquire what was going on'. He got another horse, fell off, and staggered his fevered way back to Siboney. There he found that his films had been burnt and his cameras stolen. He met Sgt Cook wearing his boots: Cook said he would just go and change them, and disappeared. The boots turned up, very worn and without a thank you note, six months later in McIntosh's New York apartment, whither he returned when finally cured of yellow fever and malaria. The spare films, which had never got to Cuba, turned up about then too, but the undeveloped film was disinfected at the Quarantine station and all came out blank.

☆   *16.3.84*

I am not often stupent (G.B.S.'s word: Shavians must be eagerly awaiting the next chunk of the *OED* supplement to see whether it gets the official nod)* but I surely stupended during a recent television programme, a revisionist view of the Second World War, which maintained, among other daring theses, that soldiers were often frightened and occasionally ran away, that civilians grumbled, that courage, cheerfulness and resolution were not universal. A person who claimed to have grown up believing the Dunkirk Myth, which was apparently that the entire British Army was taken off the beaches by grown-up Swallows and Amazons (Cap'ns Nancy and Roger commanding) with a little assistance from the SS Saucy Sally, had now discovered that it wasn't. Such manipulation might have fooled his parents, he insinuated, but wouldn't do for (quote) 'the sceptical eighties'.

The sceptical eighties! Has there ever been since AD 999 a time of more credulous self-deception, a time when more kinds of contradictory occult rubbish have been simultaneously believed, a time when a public maddened by hard science was readier to be taken in by every spook, fakir, alchemist, mesmerizer, guru and shaman?

When there is software (save the mark!) for astrologers, when witchcraft is a sociopolitical option, when the cinema is given over to bloody fairy stories and wonder tales, when men believe that electron orbits are where you think they are, that you can fly or at least levitate by taking thought, that the Hoover Dam was built by interstellar piranha fish, that invisible lines of influence join our organs, our hilltops, our fates with distant astronomical bodies (or rather with the illusory patterns of those bodies): a carnival (mundus vult decipi) for the zombic, the Salemic, golemic, anomic . . .

But I am being unfair. We Scorpios are, you know, especially when the moon is in the fifth quarter, and a white cat walks across the comfrey, raising the prajña-vibrations in our Atlantean overselves, when the Iching is on the cake, the guilt is off the ginsengbread and the old Orgone shines down blue on Linden Ley.

My friend Ms Ge Potter, membership secretary of Succubi Against the Bomb, puts it all down to psi mesons.

---

* No, for the good reason that it was already in the main body of the dictionary: Carlyle was stupent before Professor Higgins. But 'stupended' crept in.

☆ *10.9.82*

I need to know more about the unfortunate N. Macleod, author of *Korea and the lost tribes of Israel with Korean, Japanese and Israelitish illustrations dedicated to Great Britain, America, Germany, France and the other Teutonic nations of Europe, the supposed representatives of the Royal House of Judah, and the seed only of the Royal House of Ephraim and the Children of Israel their companions* . . . (there's a lot more to the title but that is the gist of it), published in Yokohama in 1879, along with a curiously-illustrated guide book to Japan, obscure threats to his enemies, much self-pity, and advice to Japan on how to become a world power. (Adopt Christianity, fish freezing, scientific division of labour and the Macleod patent lavatory.)

Authorities distinguish him from other N. Macleods, for example the three Norman Macleods, of whom one was tried for high treason and later knighted, while the others were a pair of Scottish divines, father and son, authors respectively of *God's Mercy Manifest in the Expulsion of our parents from the Garden of Eden* and *Cracks at the Kirk for the folk of Kintra*, two splendidly plonking titles, one of them more or less responsible for the Disruption. The third Norman (editor of *Good Words*, by the way) did venture far enough from Caledonia to write *Peeps at the Orient*, but he seems never to have recovered from the rigours of the trip, and died in 1872, too soon to have been our man, who is identified by the British Library catalogue as 'writer of books on Japan', an admission of ignorance.

Macleod tells us a lot about himself, though intelligibility suffers from his and the oriental printers' unhandiness with punctuation, and his reluctance ever to finish a sentence. Macleod was a Macleod of Skye, apparently; 'poor Mac who refused £30,000 bribe to betray his prince, mima bimbo de gozarimasho, as it is too far north for the golden calf to travel, the navy is Britannia's wooden walls, but the Macs of Dunvegan . . .'

Most of his later troubles are described in the preface, one spectacular sentence, a six-hundred-word gallop from indent to full stop:

> Since the writers arrival in Japan in 1867 during the last shoguns reign he has devoted a great part of his time and all his available means to travel and researches . . . often without a single dollar in his pocket, when the exchequer was full, when necessary he travelled in state, tandem Japonicum with an extra outrider, the Japanese asked him if he was travelling at government expense, as if one could not travell pro bono publicum without having the credit of paying

for it . . . when the funds were lower he travelled by horse and kango, and when they were down to zero he strode shanks mare, the good steed King David rode when he slew the Philistine giant, twice he was deprived of the root of all evil, by fire and shipwreck the only times he was uninsured having allowed the policy to lapse . . . and when laid up in Osaka unwell, a few hundred copies of his first work were stolen from his publisher in Nagasaki, who left for Australia, and hawked in Japan by a foreigner at half price; and his booksellers write him that a heathen Chinee is doing the same thing with his last work in China, and to crown all he lately received the Job's comforting intelligence from his booksellers in Hongkong that they had come to grief after having made the best sales of his last three works . . . [307 words omitted] . . . this present edition . . . as good and ready a sale as its predecessors.

N. Macleod is also notable for his verse:

> King Davids seed, transplanted root of Jesses noble vine.
> Whose boughs spread forth to Caledonias rugged shore.
> Her fruit a race of Kings and rulers bore.
> Whose seed will sit on many a throne
> Reigning from the tropic to the torrid Zone.
> Her prosperous sons are found in nearly every clime.
> And will be to the end of time.
> And not till she her final cource has run.
> Will Judah's Royal banner sink beneath a never setting sun.

Then there's a lot of stuff about P and O and the prophet Ezekiel, and railway shares and mineral rights and the treasure of Solomon's temple found in Jin Mu Tenno's grave, and how to foster the fledgling Mitsu Bishi company and thereby 'grant both Japan and foreigners all that was required for their mutual benefit by which the sun would never set on the dominions of Dai Nipon, as well as cure her of a long standing foreign bowel complaint . . .'

The rising sun rose: I don't know about the bowel complaint; but I hope Macleod made out all right.

☆ *23.12.83*

I worry, sporadically, that one day the muddy but energetic stream of truly frightful, of sincerely hebephrenic/coconutty publications may dry up like a droughty wadi: no more syncretic cosmogonies by Huntingdonshire rectors with time on their hands and much on their minds, no more private grudges made spectacularly public in doggerel pamphlets, no more Utopias founded on the pyramid inch or comfrey soup. Today, I say fretfully, I may be able to tell you about *Love, Woman and Marriage* by 'Casca Llanna (Good News)', a choice exemplar with its stirring telegraphese dedication ('TO – MY DEAD MOTHER – God Bless Her! – whom I never knew – for she died when I was but a babe – but to whom I am indebted for the Courage, Love and Manhood in me! – courage to breast the fiercest storm and to strike for the Right! . . .'); with its Prefaces A, B and C, respectively in prose, verse, and musical notation; and above all with its remarkable advertisement for itself: 'the ablest and grandest book on Love, Man, Woman, the Laws of Affection and Marriage that ever fell from human pen. No description, critique or synopsis can begin to do justice to this mighty work, which ought to be bound in gold and be on the table of every man, woman and youth in the land and in the world.' There are advertisements, too, for other works, such as *Doula Bel, The Rosicrucian Symph*, and *The Disembodied Man* ('Chap VII – The Complexion Question in Soul Life – Negroes are not Black in Soul Land, nor do they have woolly hair – Our Names in Heaven – Sustenance, food, drink, curious – Very – 'Free Love' – Singular'); all the works of the notwithstanding-the-neglect-springing-from-the-rivalry-of-infinitely-smaller-men-world-famous genius Pascal Beverley Randolph.

Or tomorrow I may spread the word about my copy of *Hints on Husband Catching, or a Manual for Marriageable Misses*, by that multi-talented author, the Hon Mrs ——— (London 1846) with its strange New England marginalia. Can the same delicate hand that drew and lovingly shaded a stylishly sleeved hand pointing mournfully at the words, underlined and some doubly underlined, 'oh how bitterly recur to our bleeding hearts each word of unkindness, each hour of neglect that the departed one endured from us', possibly be the same gruff pencil that snarled 'O.K.' elsewhere in the margin ('O.K.' is first recorded, from Boston as it happens, in 1839, so *that's* O.K.), and wrote 'not so because of physiological and psychological reasons and infectious diseases'? Casca Llanna (what sort of a lexeme is that, by the way?) and the Hon Mrs ——— may do me for today and tomorrow, but next week? Next year? Shall I have to start writing my own *imbecilia*?

I need not have worried: here, on cue, comes proof that this rich spring will not run dry while the artesian sands of life do run. Here, dated 1983, is a book as awful as anything the heaped silliness of past centuries could achieve.

World Poetry 1983 maintains a high level from the title-page, 'Author and Edited by Kim Young Sam', with the holograph inscription 'Dear Poet; Alan Brown John' and the neat red hand-stamp 'World Poetry', to the last leaf of all, with the publication data: '25, January, 1983, Publised. $35, W25,000. prof KING YOUNG SAM Literature and Ethics, Chungbuk National University. World Poetry Research Institute. No 265–1 Sachang-Dong, Cheong Ju, Korea.'

The poems are printed in the poets' own languages (English, Spanish, French, German, Chinese, Japanese and Korean) each with a translation into Korean; the Korean poems are translated into English, presumably by Kim Young Sam himself. The preface makes his qualifications clear: 'With our whole hearts, we publish this world poems which is full of a high fragrance of poetic art wich makes the individual who eagerly desires liberty, equality, and love openminded, congratulating together let's unite our efforts quietly'.

The English language poets come not from England but from the USA, Malaysia, The Philippines, India and a place called Den Mark. I shan't quote any of the originals, though I am tempted by 'A Bettle Horse' by A. Chakrabarti, and would like to congratulate K.V.S. Murti on writing an English line that sounds Korean – 'beyond safe line in den so coy'. The poets seem decent enough persons, judging by their photographs, their poems are no worse than anyone else's, and I suspect that the contributors may have contributed to the cost of publication, in which case they have suffered enough.

Some of the English poems have the appearance of being translated, or not, from other languages: 'This world seems to be a skren of karagoz' writes L. Sami Alkalin of Turkey. (Karagoz is a satirical Turkish shadow play, like wayang.) As for the Korean poems, it is hard to guess whether they have gained or lost in translation. Is An Cho-Geun's simplicity real or deceptive, I ask?

> I wish to be a lighthouse keeper
> And to be a wild rabbit
> Around the small spring.
> I wish to live together,
> You and me.

I doubt if her conclusion ('now you are a teardrop/on the blade of a chrysandermum') could be bettered in Korean.

Is An Myeong-Ho as knowing as he sounds in English?

> While brushing baby-teeth
> A set of artificial teeth get pulpy
> And occupy good seat of Ondol room
> Between the eyelid hollowed out

> Go over the winding road.
> Is it a flutlering snowflake?

A great many Kims have offerings in this anthology (I think Kim is a surname, despite the Ks being indexed between John Tworoger and Lilian Hammer). 'Pleasant memories/let them be rept under rocrs', entreats Kim Dong-O; while Kim Yeon Sik urges the dreaming birds

> Fly Fly Fly in the sky
> Highly and imortalitily

'If you want your poetry is published in the special editcin, we will comply with your wishes', says the preface, and sure enough one poet – well actually it's Kim Young Sam – has taken advantage of the offer. What he gets are a number of pages in the middle of the book, with the words SPECIAL EDITION printed at the top of each page. Here there is, in addition to a quite adequate supply of Prof Kim's poetry ('You look unbeable to the dizziness/Caused by the wind./Loneliness is longliness?/Oh, you orchid'), a page of tiny photographs of his publications and achievements, from the *Virgn Poems* of 1953 to the receipt of the Anti-communist Literature Prize in 1977, the musical score of 'Balmy Breeze in May', a rhapsodic prose poem of infantile remembrances, like the opening of *Portrait of the Artist*, with a wonderful Joycean neologism or typo ('the deep dark night when the light had long been extinguinguished') and a strikingly favourable review of the above, on Jungian principles, by Jeong Gyui Yeong: 'I'll finish my comment before my wordiness about this poem lead me to a prejusic'.

Well my wordiness may lead me to prejusic, but I must quote in full the 'Love Song' of Jeong Tae-Mo, which provokes all kinds of Pierre-Menardesque questions about how many of its felicities belong to Mr Jeong, how many to the translator, how many to the compositor, and how many to chance:

> A small eyeball
> being looked at me
> sparkling sharply
>
> An eyebraw
> being looked as me
> else where
> I think
> Saw it ever before
>
> So as the cloud

being cruise
over the mountain range

Like a breeze
blowing milldly
onbamboo leaf

An evebraw
grazing by my soul

Calmly
and
softly

A certainmelody
feeling best
greazin by my earlap.

☆   30.11.81

I do not know how you spend the long evenings, but I have been wallowing in a choice clerical imbroglio, as recorded in *An Extraordinary Trial. A full report taken in shorthand of the extraordinary case of the Reverend H.B. versus the Revd Anthony Lefroy Courtney, Clerk of Donnybrook Church, for alleged defamation of character.* (John Bryan, Wellington Quay, opposite the metal bridge, Dublin 1833. Price 1s 6d. I have suppressed the plaintiff's name until I have secured the teleplay, libretto and pop-up rights.)

The Plaintiff deposes that he is a thoroughly respectable person, a clergyman of the Church of England (one gets the impression that some of the irreverent behaviour of the crowd came from persons who were not members of the Established Church). Settled in Donnybrook, he became acquainted with a Mrs Maguire and her daughter, whom later he married. The curate was also a visitor at the house and apparently a friend; they shared charitable duties. Imagine, then, the plaintiff's grief and shock when, applying to the Archdeacon for a licence to preach, he was interrupted by the curate with the words 'He is an improper person. He might as well be living in a common brothel as where he lives. Such a man might do very well to read prayers, but it would be an awful thing to hear such a person dictate the Word of God from the pulpit.'

Mr Holmes, for the plaintiff, as on many occasions speaking out when he should have held his tongue, says that his client is a decent man now, whatever he might have done with Mary Jones while he was at College ('urged on by the torrent of vice which too often surrounds the path of youth'). As for Miss Maguire, his client married her in Church in September 1831, and though it is true that she gave birth some three months later, that was all right because they had been secretly married all along. The ceremony had been performed by a Lutheran called Schwartz who had had no witnesses and kept no records; the Court was unimpressed.

Courtney's attorney then alleges that Mrs Maguire senior, so far from being given to piety and good works ('and by the by what had happened to the Parish Funds?' 'Objection.') is a retired London prostitute, who has been abandoned by her husband, 'a wild young fellow just returned from India', because of her extravagance, and now inhabits a splendid house in Sandymount: 'and there I am instructed has admitted colonels, majors, captains, nay my Lord if I am rightly informed, even some of his Majesty's counsel, learned in the law'. (Roars of laughter.)

Things begin to get rough when the evidence of an elderly artillery man is introduced. He had trailed the couple to Sandymount, out of idle curiosity, where 'they went up the tower steps into the tower, I then goes up myself and on my oath I saw him **** on top of the tower with the lady . . . as I belong to the Established Church I didn't wish to say any more about it'. This evidence is introduced to prove that they could not be secretly married, or they would not be doing it on top of towers in Sandymount, and the case is stopped shortly afterwards with expressions of revulsion on the part of the Chief Baron.

Dozing Joyceans among my readers may, however, have become aware that the events adverted to (and the asterisks are not mine) are taking place on a certain Martello tower where just seventy-three years later a stately, plump, medical student will find himself in need of a shave. I can't find a reference to this in the rather inadequate concordance I have to hand, but the themes of jurymen, loose ladies and sexual exposure ('some bugger let down the back of the omnibus, and he caught his death of the fusiliers') recur throughout *Finnegans Wake*. Have I unearthed another key?*

---

* Wrong again. I confused Sandycove and Sandymount.

☆ *26.12.86*

Epiphanies come in strange places. My last was in Fortnum and Mason's (sounds like a Christmas game: 'My first is in bowl, but not in basin; / My next is in Argo, but not in Jason; / My third is in hurry, but not in hasten; / my last is in Fortnum, and also in Mason; / My whole is the beginning of a word meaning "enormous"* in Serbo-Croatian.')

Well, I was wandering by the fish, game and wildlife conservation counter and I fetched up about half-way down a side of salmon pie. A thing I'd previously known as coulibiac, and I'd often mused about the little town of St Symphorien-en-Coulibiac, which produces a few bottles of a supple but oddly emphatic cru with a nose of kiwi-fruit, with a vine-covered tabac whose proprietor is the most notorious cuckold in Lot-et-Garonne, where the scent of wild myrtle and . . . (in the 1930s, columnists like Beachcomber, and especially D. B. Wyndham Lewis, now chiefly remembered for not being Wyndham Lewis, got paid for doing this sort of thing regularly); anyway there was a whole francophile *gestalt* triggered off by this word, I am getting drunk and sunburnt and goat-cheese-sodden just on passing the counter, and I see that Mr Mason or it may be Madame Fortnum – and what sort of a name is that, derived you may suppose from fortunatum, a late Latin euphemism for catastrophe, or the last sausage on a plate – Madame Fortenham has labelled it *kulib'yaka*. Not so much an epiphany but a diaphany or a paraphany or a neophany or a deuterophany. It was like one of those reversing staircase-stepped roofs that psychologists have in their houses (with a flight of Peter Scott duckrabbits on the walls too), a *gestalt* change, a paradigm switch, a catastrophe, a point of inflection, a passage from one or two metastable positions separated by a zone of instability, a phase change, a Damascus light. Gone are the vines and the gasconades, gone the scent of tarragon and boudin, the purple hills and the warm south. Instead there is pine and dried mushrooms and onion stew and onion domes and Ostyaks and Cossacks and polaxes and nunataks and pacamacs. For cognac read vishnyak. It's wild surmise time.

Uncertainty is infectious. Was I really reading about two intrepid journos hunting the Sumatran tiger with a team of Sea Dyak? Or were they hunting the taiga with a seedy yak? Sidi Yacoub? Did you say Yaqui or Yorkie? A C. D. Yacht?? Said ye what?

---

* ogromnoe

☆   *18-24.4.88*

I have before me *An Essay Explanatory of the Tempest Prognosticator in the building of the great exhibition for the works of industry of all nations, read before the Whitby Philosophical Society, February 27th 1851* by George Merryweather MD, the designer and inventor (London, John Churchill 1951). It is a substantial octavo of 64 pages, full of testimonials and substantiated prognostications and poetic effusions, and it is not until page 46 that we get to the crux:

> I made use of a simple contrivance, by placing a bell upon a pedestal, erected on the centre of a circular platform; which bell was surrounded by twelve hammers. From each of these hammers was suspended a gilt chain; each of which played upon a pulley, which was placed in a disk, that was a little elevated above the circle of bottles . . . one half of the metallic tubes was left open, so that the interior was exposed: across the entrance of each was placed a small piece of whalebone, which was held up by a small piece of wire attached to its centre: these wires were passed through the aperture at the top of each tube, and then hooked onto each chain . . . into each bottle was poured rainwater, to the height of an inch and a half; and a leech placed in every bottle, which was to be its future residence; and when influenced by the electro-magnetic state of the atmosphere a number of the leeches ascended into the tubes; in doing which, they dislodged the whalebone, and caused the bell to ring.

Dr Merryweather, if such truly be his name, tabulates his results for five years, speaks with modest pride of the benefits to mariners, and mentions the six different designs of the Tempest Prognosticator, 'the principle of which is the same in all, but differently ornamented; No 1, being the least expensive, to No 6, which is now in the Crystal Palace, the most expensive and adapted for any drawing-room'.

Can any semiologist, critical theorist, meteorologian, chronicler of Whitby or social historian, tell me, across the space of nearly a century and a half, whether or not Dr M is putting us on?

AN ESSAY

EXPLANATORY

OF THE

TEMPEST PROGNOSTICATOR

IN THE

BUILDING OF THE GREAT EXHIBITION FOR THE WORKS OF INDUSTRY OF ALL NATIONS.

READ BEFORE THE WHITBY PHILOSOPHICAL SOCIETY
FEBRUARY 27TH, 1851.

BY

GEORGE MERRYWEATHER, M.D.
WHITBY,
The Designer and Inventor.

———

LONDON:
JOHN CHURCHILL, PRINCES STREET, SOHO.
TO BE HAD OF ALL BOOKSELLERS.
MDCCCLI.

☆ *23-29.12.88*

A hurricane, a storm, a veritable tempest of letters from all over the North-East (two at least, and another from British Columbia, famous for merrie English weather), anent the helpfully-named Mr Merryweather and his trained bloodsucking campanologists, a team of leeches inserted into an apparatus so delicately planned that their asymmetrical wriggles, induced by climatic changes, ring bells to alert coastguards to an approaching storm. (This column, last month.) Merryweather wrote of his device, which he called the Tempest Prognosticator, and of his plan to have hundreds of them round the coast, in a tone of such smirking waggishness that I wondered aloud whether the whole thing was not an elaborate legpull, leechpull. Ha ha, say my correspondents, more or less, here is the purveyor of truths stranger than truth, the arouser of misplaced scepticism in others, hoist with his own incredulity. Doesn't he know that a magnificent specimen (the drawing-room model, presumably, with hispano-mauresque ornamentation) is preserved in Panneth Park Museum, Whitby?

They speak earnestly, but I am not to be fooled. In almost the same words H. G. Wells, at the end of *War of the Worlds*, remarks that Martian anatomy has been closely studied and that 'everyone is familiar with the magnificent and almost complete specimen in spirit at the South Kensington Natural History Museum'. For years I was convinced that it was there, perhaps in one of the many closed galleries full of enticing objects (like the full-sized model of a Kraken, *Architeuthis*, that I glimpsed behind scaffolding), or tucked away in a side gallery off the Blue Whale room, or hidden in the gloomy *souterrains* of the New Spirit Building or perhaps evacuated for safe-keeping against Hun invasion or Russky nuclear attack in some titanium cave under a Scottish mountain. It seemed likely enough: the Museum was a Wellsian place in those days; especially the New Spirit Building, which, when I finally wriggled in, turned out to be full of dead old animals preserved in rather old spirit, though no doubt the building and the spirits and the animals too come to think of it were once new. The very name is a Wellsian joke, like 'Can I have the key to the absolute?' from 'A Slip under the Microscope', a story set just round the corner, in the Science Schools, and published, curiously, in *The Yellow Book*, though H. G. is hardly the first name one thinks of in relation to *fin-de-siècle* exquisitude. The slow hard acknowledgement that Wells was only kidding (no wonder they lynched him in New Jersey) was one of the first of the griefs of my growing up, but we get strong in the broken places, in the words of Mr Hemingway, that American newspaper gentleman with a thing about bulls and what he called Cahoonies, an Irish family I suppose, would that be one of the Wicklow Colquhonies I once asked him.

I am not to be fooled again. It may interest my so-called correspondents to know that I have worked quite closely with leeches in my time (them and me were like that) and they could never predict the weather worth a damn. Many's the time I've asked their advice before popping off for a weekend in my yare little ketch the *Virginia Wolf*; and many's the drenching their counsel earned me, bad cess to them.

☆   24.12.82

Well-intentioned persons who observe me spending profitless weeks alternately hunting for the book I have just offered someone and the address of the someone to whom I have just offered a book, suggest frequently that I should equip myself with a business computer, one programmed to find customers, write catalogues, read other booksellers' catalogues (transmitted by landline from *their* computers) and order books and adjust bank balances accordingly. The difficulty is that if you make book-keeping a thing of the past, you may make books a thing of the past. In seasonal terms, if you're a turkey, don't cultivate cranberries.

☆   18.5.84

Nothing like an old book for bringing history to life, I always say, and here, slithering into the hand like a short length of venomous snake, the age of appeasement comes alive with *Adolf Hitler* (80pp. George G. Harrap, London 1935).

Textually it is selected posies from *Mein Kampf*, compressed and diluted, if such a thing is possible, and the authors are Kurt Schulze and H. E. Lewington, the former, you will observe, being one of their chaps, Oberstudiendirektor in Magdeburg to be precise, while the latter is one of ours, actually German Master at the John Ruskin School in Croydon. It is one of Harrap's 'Plain Texts in German', a venture which aimed at 'producing booklets in the reading of which pupils will require no coercion'. Coercion? Dear me, no, hardly the thing for healthy British boys and girls, fresh-faced and glowing from a rough-and-tumble in the playing-field (not together of course), all the more ready to enjoy yarns about a German lad with lots of grit, yarns that describe him giving bullies short shrift, acquiring admirable work habits, and sniffing out the moral shortcomings of various assemblages of 'Jews, Social-Democrats and November-traitors.' There are cheery pictures by one C. H. Drummond, whose work I seem to have come across in other boys' adventures of the period, showing der kleine Adolf glowing with precocious leadership qualities, patriotism and general zest. Drummond has a nice line in snarling working men in peaked caps with red stars on, a clear give-away for the unmasking of Foreign Agitators in many a Bumper Fun book; here the agitators (referred to as a 'rote Mordpest') are having fun bumping off Horst Wessel, 'einer der besten und unerschrocksten', says the text and by George he looks it too! 'At the subsequent trial', the notes explain, 'it was alleged that the crime was actuated by jealous motives over a certain woman and the criminals received comparatively light sentences. However in 1934, under the National Socialist régime, justice was finally done and three persons executed.'

The grammatical exercises at the end rather spinelessly avoid any political commitment, restricting themselves to the events of the first few pages and Hitler's early years: 'Setzen Sie in Plusquamperfekt', they request, ' "Young Hitler carefully studied all the pictures of battles." ' They might so easily have chosen 'The international Judaeo-Marxist Conspiracy is the cause of all Germany's woes' as something snappy to be tried out in the future perfect, the aorist and the plusquamwhatever.

But stay! Looking again deep into young Herr Wessel's aryan eyes, we become aware that something is not quite, how you say, kosher. On his sleeve he proudly sports the Party brassard; but the Swastika is the *wrong way round*! At once it becomes clear that the note about the trial is ironic, the drawings subtly subversive, the reference in the preface to the text having been passed by the new special Censor's Bureau in Munich is not a boast but a nudge. H. E. Lewington, and perhaps Kurt Schulze with him, is laughing up his sleeve at the little braggart, in a polite but fearless fashion! The Dunkirk spirit was abroad already! Who do you think you are kidding, Mr Hitler, when you say old England's done?

☆ *10.9.82*

Now here is a book-list:
Naran, J. *Teach Yourself Indonesian*. (EUP 1976).
Burgess, A. *Earthly Powers* (Penguin, 1972)
Finucane, R. C. *Appearances of the Dead: a Cultural History of*

Ghosts (Junction, 1982)
(Joyce, J.) Collected Ephemera anent Bloomsday, 1982
Byron, Lord G. *Childe Harolds Pilgrimage* (Virtue, 1845, 'with engravings by the best artists')
Rodenberry, G. *Star Trek: The motion Picture*
Anon, *Henrietta's Heartaches or the Futility of Family Life* (n.d.)

If this seems omnivorous, that is right: it is part of the diet of a six-month old Borzoi called Bronze (he was to be called Boris, but this is too like the Russian *bris*, a sound used to shoo away importunate dogs, which might have caused him confusion if his racial memory is functioning). His mouth being on a level with the middle shelf of the standard bookcase, and having, it seems a *horror vacui* tends to draw books to itself as a lamp flies (as a crow flies, as butter flies).

But since (as those of my household who oppose my proposal to have his mouth amputated are quick to point out) there are thousands of books about the house that he hasn't eaten, it is a matter of some urgency to determine which way his teeth will turn next. When he had eaten only the Burgess and the Byron, I deduced that his method was alphabetical, and inductively hid the Cabala collection and the six copies of Cabot Lodge's *Memoirs* (as new); and when he ate the anonymous *Henrietta*, I wondered if he was giving me a hint as to the authorship (Joyce Cary, Cabeza de Vaca, Dr Cabanès?) But his next meal (marking and inwardly digesting) was Steinbeck's *Cannery Row*, (a suitably puppyish book, you might think, boisterous, goodhearted and a bit soft) which only made sense if he was working through some kind of canine index which cross-referenced titles and authors, like the old joke about Mill on Liberty with Ditto on the Floss, which members of the Society of Indexers (did you know that there is a Wheatley Medal for an Outstanding Index?) assure me never happened, dismissing it as a mere canard (see Canard, Enchaîné; ditto, mere *see* Lake Duck; ditto, orange, à l') or Old Wives' Tale (*Old Wives' Tale, The* see Bennett, Enoch Arnold; *see also* Peele, G; Hubbard, O. M., Dame.)

It is perhaps relevant to mention that *Cannery Row* was the first London (1945), rubber-stamped 'colonial edition' on the rear free endpaper, and with the ticket of The People's Bookshop, Johannesburg. This makes it a genuine, uncommon (if trivial) variant, which I had been hoping to sell for a non-trivial sum to a Monterey completist ('completist' is booksellers' euphemism for 'monomaniac'). Of course the absence of a dust-wrapper might have deterred him (I mean the putative Californian, not the Borzoi, who is demonstrably indifferent to the presence or absence of wrappers, having done his Baconian best – reading maketh a full dog – on the Finucane, new and wrappered, and on the Byron, jacketless from birth, though otherwise a particularly fine and fresh example – maybe the freshness attracted him – of early Victorian glt. cloth dec.).

Well, some books are to be tasted and some few to be chewed and digested; but I was most hurt – and so was he – by the damage to *Henrietta*, a pretty little parody of the actress-memoir *genre* with tipped in illustrations in the style of Du Maurier, which I have found in no catalogue or bibliography. It has, I should add, a 'Hail and Farewell' by Hugh Walpole, and is presumably entirely by him* and would thus be an exciting acquisition for a Hugh Walpole collector, if there were such a thing.

By the time the habit is conquered (we are trying powdered dogsbane on the spine and electroshock on the paws) there should be an impressive if eclectic list, and I intend to issue a catalogue with the title 'slightly dogged'. Friends in the trade (or 'friends' as I prefer to think of them) suggest that I should describe the remainder of my stock as 'books the dog wouldn't touch'.

☆ 5.9.86

O ye poets of these latter times, profit from the example of Joseph W. Sault, sweet singer of Welwyn. In *Garden Citizens of Today and Tomorrow (New Freeman*, St Albans, 1937), now generally recognized as his *chef d'oeuvre* (see *Fifty Years of Sault Studies: A Festschrift*, practically *passim*) the poet-chronicler of the New Towns, compatriot of Shredded Wheat, sometime editor of *the Welwyn Garden City and Hertfordshire Pilot* (before it was incorporated into the *Welwyn Times*), commits himself boldly to a poetry that speaks for Everyman (to say nothing of every man) while remaining profoundly rooted in a sense of place, a poetic for which no occasion was too sublime or too mundane.

Garden Citizens of Today and Tomorrow will stand comparison, up to a point, with Crabbe. *Spoon River Anthology* likewise springs unbidden to mind. Sault has attempted nothing less than a diachronic and synchronic directory of Welwyn, its history of hopes, its traumas and its triumphs. The Founder (the late Ebenezer

---

* Wrong. Only the foreword was by Walpole, the rest by some forgotten hostess he wished to please.

Howard, OBE) stands first, of course: 'Your plans to check gross ignorance/In building towns,/Now seem such simple, commonsense,/But, well we know the human mind/Is blind'. After him, what a colourful pageant of characters! There is Councillor W. R. Hughes ('the English gift of compromise/here functions at its best,'), Councillor George Lindgren, CC ('and now he mingles with the mighty/to rescue poor old Blighty'), Councillor E. D. Pinner ('Building good roads was your task/When Welwyn first was founded') and Councillor Jane Pinner ('Sound Democrats must pass,/Alas'), to say nothing of Councillor C. B. Purdom, the Urban District Council Staff, Mrs Richard Wallhead (Widow of the late Richard Wallhead MP), Francis H. Burn Esq of the *Welwyn Times* ('A thankless task some men refuse/for Welwyn boils with extreme views'), the Police, the Railway Staff, and Jesus Christ, King of Welwyn.

But Sault doesn't stop there. After a brief excursion into prose to discuss the topic of municipalities issuing their own banknotes, a subject on which, as on so many others, he can only be described as Welwyn-formed, it's back into poetry for twelve pages of adverts, a brilliant and I suspect unique way of financing the publication. And the adverts, it must be admitted, inspire him more than the local worthies. If his praise of Mrs W. E. August is a little hesitant ('Your plays in Welwyn woods/have never been excelled'), his acclaim of The Welwyn Stores is unstinting, not to say rollicking:

> We give you hearty welcome to the famous Welwyn Stores
> With sixty-odd departments and its ever open doors
> For drapery, good food and drink, for household goods galore
> For milk and fruit, for cheese and teas, come straight to Welwyn Store;

which doesn't prevent him doing just as well by the London Stores ('If you need a kitchen cupboard/Or linoleum for the floors,/Take a bus to St Albans,/and . . .'); the Bridge Restaurant, Barcley Corsets ('Directors and the staff all know, from John o'Groats to Dorset . . .'), Lemsford Garage ('Why worry, when we've careful men/to keep your car smooth running;/Ring WELWYN GARDEN 390,/Enjoy your Sunday morning'), and the sombre elegance of the Harkness Roses Ode: 'Time has proved that Welwyn's soil/Is suitable for roses,/Visitors from foreign shores/Admire the streets and Closes'. In 'Hitchin Laundry' he excels himself:

> So, 'phone the HITCHIN LAUNDRY,
> And don't forget to mention
> You saw the laundry's name
> Mentioned in these pages,

> The versifier needs his hire,
> Like most, he lives by wages.

It may not be immediately obvious what is happening here. Joseph Sault is getting the advertiser to pay for an advertisement for his services as a writer of advertising verse, the advertisements subsidizing his less lucrative poetry of social value. (I have not even considered the possibility that he got a sub from the councillors.) If this catches on, there is a new glittering supply-side future for poetry. We could even dispense with the Arts Council – the end of civilization as we know it.

☆   22.7.88

Oh, good! Here's the book I've been looking for for *ages*! It is probably just the ticket for your little problem as well, since it is, says the title-page, 'A master-key to Universal Knowledge, Achievement, Wisdom and Morality', several of which we are both short of. The book is out of print, which is why the world is in the state it is; but the title – if that's the right word – is: *The Radio-Orbicular (Spider Web) Process of Thought, Based on a New Philosophy of Equal Compensation, Discovered by A. A. Braun* (London: The Postal University, Drury Lane, 1922). It is always inadvisable to summarize a master-key to universal knowledge, achievement, wisdom and morality – and there is no way of telling, I have just realized, whether the achievement, wisdom and morality are universal, or only the knowledge – but it would be neglectful not to draw attention to the author's modesty, rare among discoverers of new philosophies. 'Weigh not my words,' says page 2, 'words are ever inadequate vehicles of thought. But through words the Spirit gropes His way to perfection.'

'Groping through inadequate vehicles'; a nice description of most persons' daily activity, but I doubt if it would stand up in court.

But there's a stronger proof of humility in this particular copy, which carries an inscription in the author's holograph: 'I am told there is a great deal of tosh in this book.' Would Plato or Paul or Buckminster Fuller have confessed as much?

The RADIO-ORBICULAR
(SPIDER-WEB)
PROCESS OF THOUGHT
BASED ON
A NEW PHILOSOPHY OF
EQUAL COMPENSATION
discovered by A.A. BRAUN

THE MASTER-KEY TO
UNIVERSAL KNOWLEDGE, ACHIEVEMENT, WISDOM AND MORALITY.

LONDON
THE POSTAL UNIVERSITY
37 DRURY LANE, W.C. 2.
(1922)

☆ *17.2.84*

WHEREAS divers persons, including my editor, a reader and the family systems analyst have expressed the opinion (being persons proper to express an opinion) that my prose is hard to follow and I share their difficulty; and whereas it is the first duty of a communications person to communicate, as it is that of a media person to meditate and a columnist to what d'ye collum; and notwithstanding that poetry can communicate before it is understood, as T. Eliot stated and must have wished he hadn't, thereby opening the lid of Pandora's stable door onto a veritable Augean mares' nest; and considering the fact that those who live by the word are in danger of perishing cold isn't it, and those who waive the rules may be not waiving but drowning; and inasmuch as a major source of obscurity is parenthetical proliferation or bracket-busting; NOW THEREFORE I resolve that my thought-patterns as far as any pattern is discernible shall be elucidated, clarified like ghee and made transparently perspicuous by the immediate adoption of an alphanumeric polychotomously ramifying deweydecimal paragraph-indexing, thus:

1. (*More about rotten foreign poetry*) or

1´. (*More about foreign rotten poetry*)

1.1. 'In its youth, I confess, this column thought sausages were funny', wrote Nathaniel Gubbins of the *Sunday Express*, a 1940s humorist (see **1.1.1.**) now overdue for critical re-evaluation but not, hopefully (see **1.1.2.**), for republication, which might prove as embarrassing as listening to Tommy Handley of ITMA whose indefatigable merriment helped to steady us and lighten our hearts through the dark days of et cetera.

1.1.1. Eg 'For saying dot, Hans to der contzentration camp haff gone'; 'No, it's Vi (see **1.1.1.1.**) that can't eat eggs and Flo (**1.1.1.2.**) that can't eat fish.'

1.1.1.1. What does Vi stand for, or how do you say it: is it Vigh for Violet or Vee for (duhduhduh*doom*) Victoria? And if so what happened when Lady Violet Bonham-Carter was first introduced to Mrs Harold Nicolson?

1.1.1.2. I think it was Leonard Woolf, at the publication party for *The Journey Not the Arrival Matters*, who inadvertently sent Robert Louis Stevenson to the Cevennes. Stevenson, who had booked a fortnight's holiday at Benidorm, was mournfully anticipating the incivility of the Guardia at Alicante. 'Cheer up', said his interlocutor, 'Air Castile's (see **1.1.2.1.**) in-flight service is a by-word and its stewardesses miracles of Iberian grace. The arrival lounge will be the only bad part of the trip. The journey itself, hopefully, will be much better.' 'Yes', mused poor old R.L.S., misunderstanding as usual, 'to travel hopefully is a better thing than to arrive.'

1.1.2.1. 'Castile's in Spain! Castile's in the air!' was their advertising slogan; 'Il ne manque que style' was proposed but rejected.

1.1.2.2. There was a similar misunderstanding later when Stevenson told us he'd hired a horse for the trip, and Ralph Waldo Emerson suggested he'd be better off on his ass.

1.2. The whole question of the innately funny, the *ens ridibundum* or *lachstoff*, remains a subject for intense academic speculation and experimental effort. Geloeometric trials have been undertaken with sets of separated monozygotic twins, subjected under control conditions to carefully calibrated measures (see **1.2.1.**) of culturally neutral (ladders going through windows, bums) or culturally determined (beautiful downtown Burbank, Cyril Smith, the Emu totem) sure-fire hilarifiers.

1.2.1. Humour is measured on a logarithmic scale, one jest being the intensity that will raise the angle of the percipient's lips by 45°, at standard temperature and pressure. For everyday purposes the decijest, which is one-tenth the perceived funniness (see **1.2.2.**) is a more useful unit. Other relevant measures are the unit of humorous duration, the millijest-second, or yuk, and its multiples and submultiples such as the kiloyuk and milliyuk; the unit of source-jocularity or humorous flux (one microallen produces a level of one yuk at a distance of one hundred metres); the unit of capacity or total joke-content, the wag (Klein's *Tables of Shear Angle in Prestressed Concrete* is used for standardizing, the third edition having less than 1 nanowag/page, though the fourth edition has a wry footnote after the Acknowledgements); the gaw, or inverse wag, which measures the resistance of an audience to a three second 1-decijest wit-dose (this is the International Standard Gag, not yet officially adopted).

1.2.2. Because of the logarithmic relationship between source and sensation (the Weber-Fechner or Psychophysical Law), a joke must be one hundred times as funny to produce ten times the laughter, smile or other observable response in the jokee.

1.3. There exists not even the beginning of a consensus as to whether the joke originates in the percipient, the percipiend or in their interaction. The search for the absolute joke, the joke which is funny when there is no one to see it, is a piece of Platonic whimsy by the Hilariopostdeconstructuralists, whose *cahiers* (*Deconnerie; Écrire/Sourire/Fourire*) deserve to be better known.

1.4. J. B. Fryer, leader of the English school of empirical or stand-up humorologists, writes: 'For every person at least one topic produces uncontrollable amusement. But there is no way of knowing if this topic is determined by the genes, in early childhood, or an instant before you read this.'

1.5. In my case it seems to be Albania.

1.5.1. Look, I'm sorry about this. I'm as opposed to racial generalizations as the next man, and if I had my way all racial jokes would be about Etruscans or Elamites.

1.5.1.1. There would be no theoretical objection to using both, in the general format 'One fine day/rainy evening/moon-festival an Etruscan and an Elamite met at the baths/market/launderette.'

1.5.1.1.1. For multipartite jokes, the categories of North/South/East/West Elamite (or Etruscan) are recommended; these can be subdivided as required, *viz* North-East Etruscan, South-West Elamite etc.

1.5.1.1.1.1. It is not recommended that this paradigm be used for joke-situations involving more than twenty-eight protagonists.

1.5.1.1.1.1.a. I seem to be trapped in a regressive index.

1.5.2. Obviously there is nothing risible about any language *per se*, even one which owes its grammar to 'the well-known Albanian Primer' of Naum Veqilharxhi.

1.5.2.1. What a boon he must be to Albanian Scrabble-players! Especially if his followers were denounced for crypto-veqilharxhization (triple letter points for q, x and z).

1.6. I have been getting a lot of childish amusement out of Koço Bihiku's useful *Outline of Albanian Literature*, which was put about by the Naim Frashëri (see **1.6.1.**) Publishing House, Tirana, 1964. It is translated by Ali Cungu into sober but unidiomatic English, curiously reminiscent of the flat, fluent, confident and totally foreign enunciation of the English newsreaders on Radio Tirana (see **1.6.2.**).

1.6.1. 'Naim Frashëri spent the early days of his life in the naturally beautiful environment of his home village, an environment that left deep, unobliterated traces in the tender heart of the poet to be.'

1.6.2. I can just hear one of them uttering the words: 'Bardhi's work is permeated throughout with the author's love of country and national pride. Basing his arguments on undeniable historical facts and presenting them with the consummate skill of an able dialectician who has full command of language and wit, F. Bardhi invalidated his opponent's theses (see **1.6.2.1.**) and called them historically unfounded.'

1.6.2.1. His opponent, needless to say, was a Bosnian Bishop who doubted Scanderbeg's Albanian ancestry.

1.7. The main theme of Albanian poetry before the establishment of socialism seems to be commiserative, thus:

1.7.1. 'Now Albania how are you/Like a tree felled out of view' ('O Moj Shqypni' by Pashko Vaso) or

1.7.2.
Never has Albania been
Topsy-turvy in such mess;
Never have Albanians seen
Ugly deeds of wickedness.

1.7.3.
And when the firing ceases
And banners have been brought home
Albania chopped in pieces
Will flourish and be handsome.

1.8.
Sang Naim Frashëri:
Poor Old Europe at that time
Plunged it was in great despair
But it started up to climb
When Rousseau came and Voltaire.

1.8.1. That was before the foundation of the league of Prizren.

1.9. Ndre Mjeda's patriotic lyrics became more and more outspoken and actual:

Hie hence you vile perfidious dreg!
Albania has discarded you:
To Asia fly and pull the leg
Of those you like so much to woo.

1.10. But Mjeda's masterpiece is his lyric and epic poem 'Andrra e Jetës'.

1.10.1. The theme of the poem is the simple and touching story of a poor family whose life has been reduced to the barest means of sustenance.

1.10.2. Mother and daughter have no other pretensions than to have what to eat and to be left in peace at that remote corner where their cottage stood.

1.10.3. But misfortune knocks at their door. Tina, the girl who tends the goats, is afflicted with consumption and dies away. The other girl, Zoga, goes off to marry. Poor mother is left alone and helpless.

1.11. We pass rapidly over Fan S. Noli, Foqion Postoli and Migjeni.

1.12. The young mountain woman who expects a baby soon must also live on cherries. The peasants inside an old shabby hut have built a huge fire round which they try to warm themselves. Later at night they make room for their cow around the open hearth. Towards dawn they find that the cow with its bulky body has weighed down upon the little youngster of the family. Thus in order to save a cow which provided them with milk, a principal food product for these mountaineers, the parents became unintentionally their own gravediggers (Migjeni: 'Fatal Beauty').

1.13½. Since the establishment of the socialist order of things brilliant achievements were attained also in the field of culture. Comic works mostly make light of the negative manifestations in present-day life.

1.14 and last.

The dawn has cleared all gloom,
The fields are all in bloom
The teams have joined and plow
Collective farmlands now.
New life has dawned, hurray!
For you at Myzeqë!

SALUTATION

The CURTAIN now falls on this STAGE of vivid imaginary MYSTICS — each ADVENTURE having PAINTED a PICTURE for the Reader's VISUALIZATION.

As LIGHT follows DARKNESS — when the SUN arises in the EAST — may the unfoldment of these stories be an ENLIGHTENMENT INTERLUDE to fulfil Mankind's need for RELAXTIVITY — from the Clouds of Gloom — to the SUNSHINE of a LIFE worth LIVING.

Bizz-Quizzy—W.R.B.

☆ *23.5.80*

It's all the fault, as I'm sure you realize, of the British and Foreign Bible Society. I mean, any fairminded person will admit that the root of the world's ills is that booksellers' overheads are so high, with the result that folk who in happier times would be entirely occupied collecting Elzevirs or the scarcer Goldsworthy Lowes Dickinson are obliged instead to take up promiscuity, irredentism, crime, banditry and distress of nations.

Consider. In 1971, on the morrow of decimalization, books sent to America by reduced rate parcel post (and the North Atlantic secondhand book trade is the very lifeblood of our export drive, I mean the very camshaft of our export drive) cost one and a half new pennies for the first four ounces and a further 1p for each quarter-pound. So a parcel weighing, let us say, 2lb 3½oz (a very proper weight for parcels) would have cost 9½ pence. Now, thanks to inflation, metrication and the simplification of weight steps ('easier-for-them' as Kingsley Amis's Jake snarlingly puts it), the same parcel would cost £1.15 and next year may rise to £2.60, a hairsbreadth less than a stunning increase of 40 per cent per annum for a decade.*

If parcel rates do rise next year it will be because of UPU (Universal Postal Union) imbalance payments. When UPU began, it was agreed that everyone would deliver parcels from foreign parts without making any further charge, and would keep all the revenue from parcels going abroad. But after a while a certain murmuring was heard from the handful of independent non-Christian states like Persia (as it then was) and Afghanistan (where I am told, postmasters would bite the corners off stamps to postmark them); they complained that various evangelical societies in Europe were economizing on missionaries by posting the Word of God to the benighted, thereby obliging the authorities to hire hundreds more postmen to trudge the dusty roads to Bander Abbas or Jalalabad, and these men had to be paid out of exiguous postal revenues since the benighted Persians and Afghans were not in the habit of posting vast quantities of heavy Korans to the giaours of Ferangistan: could not something be done about it?

It was: the system of periodically adjusted equalization payments. *Hinc illae lacrimae*, and perhaps the time has come for a really massive missionary and charitable effort in Europe by the Muslim world. No expense should be spared in this endeavour.

---

* Now, nine years of alleged low inflation later, £3.30, a further increase of 14% p.a.

I do not want to point the finger at the British and Foreign Bible Society, who publish my favourite book. No, no, I am referring to *The Gospel in Many Tongues* which prints (1954 edition) John iii 16 in 826 languages from Abor Miri ('Depe emnam de Ishor bui tani amo . . .') to Zulu.

Since 826 squared is a large number, there must be lots of pairs of languages which have never been systematically compared, and there is surely the possibility of a wonderful new theory of ethno-history, based on the discovery of a close kinship between Jorai of Indo-China and Jukum of North-East Muri Province, Nigeria or between Madan and Mandingo, or between Basque and Burushaski (that one has indeed already been suggested, on the grounds that each language is spoken by a tribe of sturdy mountaineers with no known relatives and that there is a 'b' in both). I met a man at Land's End whose grandfather met a man who had known Dolly Pentreath, last speaker of Cornish (the last listener outlived her), and he knew a Welsh sailor who had encountered this speaker of Syriac or Assyrian in a Beirut bar, and they communicated happily. Welsh scholars used to claim theirs was the oldest language (after Enochian, the tongue of angels) and the same as Hebrew. Like the Welsh for a path is 'chaered' and the Hebrew is 'derech', but you have to read the Hebrew back to front, isn't it?

☆ 22.5.87

Ran into a severe case of Brit-USan incomprehension the other day: what you might call linguistic dispareunia but probably shouldn't. Happened at a mainly-for-truckers stop on Interstate (he died interstate, I should like to have it said to me) 95 in Pa. I was sitting there reading the small ads in *Movin' Out*: '45ft SB–1 Thermo–K. 161', 290, 10spd. Both 80% rubber. Will split. Super Sharp'. I was already pondering semantic divergences ('Female College student desires driving position. Certifiable') and wondering if what I really needed was a pair of Politechnics 'Protector' Sap gloves ('Incredible power: Inconspicuous, Guaranteed'). And wondering whether to take the Behaviour Prediction Test ('in less than an hour discover an applicant's attitudes and tendency toward safety, drug abuse, violence and dishonesty'). I read the comforting words of Chaplain Jack and Chaplain Glenn, muscular Christians both: The Reverend Jack's office hours start at 4am at the little chapel at All-American Truck Plaza, PA; not a place, I dare say, where incense burns invisible and dim and pustular acolytes clutch piaculative pence. Talking of pence, there must be an awful lot of nickels weighing down the pockets of James Chirk (not his real alias), coinbox raider, for Ohio Bell to want him so badly: they will pay $15,000 for him.

While all this was going on – not much really – the waitress moseyed up ... she more sort of sashayed ... offered me the menu, full of trucker food ('toss salad and hard roll with fired eggs'). But I wanted to know about the special, which was a Pair of Whimpies on a Hard Bun. 'Like a Sloppy Joe only sloppier', she explained, without a pause for thought.

'And a Sloppy Joe is...?'

'Where is this guy *from*?' she demanded, not rhetorically. The food was only passable, but the restaurant used a better scriptwriter than Alice's; bringing in a frozen rice pudding (not at all what matron used to make): 'They tell me,' she offered with an enviable detachment, 'they tell me it's relatively fresh.'

☆   *10.8.84*

We all snatch at distinction wherever we can find it, and the other day I was gently preening myself with the thought that I was perhaps the only person in my corner of London engaged on the crossword (16 Across: Rectal Injection, 5 letters) in the Winter 1929 number of the *Bloodless Phlebotomist*, a magazine published by the Denver Chemical Manufacturing Company (of New York, curiously) in the interests of spreading about the globe (Drogueria 'Standard', 2 Strada Zorilor, Bucharest; Muller and Phipps [Malaya] Ltd, 26 Gang Passer Baroe, Batavia) the Good News about Antiphlogistine. Antiphlogistine was a sort of dove-grey therapeutic artificial mud, with which sufferers from divers ills were comprehensively poulticed, and had little to do with Phlogiston, except that today both are equally unfashionable (nothing is so powerless as an idea whose time has gone), except again that while Phlogiston never did exist, never rising above the rank of postulant postulate or apprentice hypothesis, Antiphlogistine demonstrably did and I still bear the scar of an over-zealous dose. (It looked, come to think of it, rather the way I've always imagined *hyle*, the primal matter of the Aristotelians; a universe of medicated clay is no harder to imagine than a universe of quarks.) 'Bloodless Phlebotomist', I suppose, is a good thing to be, even if it does sound like a rather refined term of Parliamentary abuse.

My interest in the crossword, an early example of the form, petered out when I realized I was ineligible for the prize of a clinical thermometer, but I noted with relish – we snatch, as I said, at whatever distinction we can – that 19 down BIN was, for surely the only time in history, clued as 'Bismuth Subnitrate (abbrev), 3 letters'.

☆   7.12.84

I'm just back from a most invigorating triplet to Mexico: not the Mexico of cactus and cowpat, but a southern, non-Spanish, tropical forested Mexico, of papayas and pyramids, eerie Mayaland. And what, or rather who, makes Mayaland mysterious? Almost single-handedly (and I am not forgetting von Däniken, I am not forgetting the sterling contributions of the 'Villa Maya' nightplace, with its 'forniture of caved wood and deerfur' and morris-dancers on the steps of a styrofoam ziggurat) it has been mystified by José Diaz-Bolio, laureate of Mérida, who has something approaching a full Nelson on the Information Services Industry in Yucatán. José has published 'ten books of poems in prose and verse, some of them in Mayan style', he is the author of *Teoria Sobre lo Bello* and 'thousands of articles, many on Sociology and Aesthetics, and a Spanish guitar method in which are given more than 400 tune positions'. But mainly he is the author of a theory. In 1942 he became aware that the Yucatán Rattlesnake (*Crotalus durissus durissus*) has a pattern on its back which resembles that of many Mayan friezes, and also that the rattlesnake's rattle was the main religious and calendrical symbol of the Mayans, because it grows a new rattle every year. (It doesn't, Diaz-Bolio readily admits, but the Maya thought it did and think so still. 'This is the oldest idea I have been able to trace on the American Continent.') Since 1942, Diaz-Bolio has worked on his theory, and now recognizes that Mayan art, Mayan architecture, Mayan calendars and textiles, Mayan religion, Mayan and indeed everyone else's geometry and mathematics all spring from the back and the rattle of *Crotalus durissus*, 'the first Pythagoras a very long time before that Greek philosopher lived'. He has diagrams to show how the repeat-unit of the diamondback pattern, a crossed square which he likes to call 'The four-vertex canamayte', gives rise to the circle, the pentagon, the Mayan profile, the cosmogonic square whose eight petals represent the moon's phases, the vault, the pyramid, '14 parallelisms with the sun and no less than 16 axes of symmetry', and the first American flag. It also has the gratifying consequence of making the Mayans older and more original than the Aztecs, Olmecs, Incas and Egyptians.

And this is what you get when you innocently buy the *Guide to Uxmal (Only one containing the theory of Mayan Civilization)*. It is also what you get if you buy the *Guide to Chichén-Itzá* the *Guide to Tulum*, the *Guide to Copán*, or the *Brief Encyclopaedia of Mayan Civilization*. It is as though all guidebooks to Stratford, Saint Paul's and the Geology Museum were written by Baconian, Satanist Flat-Earthers. It's hard enough to disentangle the rubble of pre-Classic, Classic, post-Classic and Toltec ruins, without Diaz-Bolio inventing new names: 'Archaeologists erroneously call this frieze Dead Serpent, a name that shows how far is Mayan archaeology from its goal ... Only a person who has never seen the vertebrae of a rattlesnake can commit this mistake.'

He has a similarly cavalier way with zoology – 'the tails and ears of the jaguars have rattlesnake traits' – and even with measurement: 'Size: approximately 216 feet by 150. It is a question why the plaza did not result a perfect square.'*

Nor is this all. Sitting in a bookstore, idly reading a newspaper story about unfortunate Police Constable Jesus Puc Puc, who, while trying to arrest the notorious disorderly, La Lepra, was surrounded by La Lepra's friends, jostled and stripped of his insignia of rank, I noticed a Mayan Grammar, the very thing I had been looking for for a while. I bought it; later I read in it. The author's preface, by one Zavala, exhorted everyone to learn Mayan, as it was a primitive language, and primitive languages were more perfect than advanced ones like Latin and Greek, having had less time to depart from the standard of perfection set by God when he created the language. This didn't seem to accord with the very latest transformational theories, and when I turned to the list of other publications by the same author (*Teoria Sobre lo Bello, Method of Spanish Guitar, Guide to Uxmal*) it dawned on me that the diabolic José had republished a nineteenth-century grammar in facsimile. Likewise, the Brief Compendium of Yucatán History extends only as far as 1910, and contains more lists of Apostolic Nuncios than are now considered fashionable, and the Explanation of the Mayan Calendar reprints three fifty-year-old articles. If you want to know what the chaps with computers and radio-carbon have done to decipher glyphs and stratigraphy, you had better get your reference sources in London or Mexico City.

---

* Should you discover that these lengths are equal to $6\,(6^2) \times 6\,(5^2)$ feet, or $6^2 \times 5^2$ fathoms, or very nearly the ratio of one to root two, please communicate with José Diaz-Bolio, Apdo Postal 155, Mérida, Yucatán.

☆   *25.7.80*

You'll forgive me, I'm sure, if I return to the ever-interesting topic of postal charges. I wrote to POUNC, the alleged Post Office watchdog, whose name apparently stands for Pusillanimous Otiose Unctuous Nerveless Collaborationism, asking did I have the right figures for the price of a parcel now, then, and in the future. They replied denying everything, and even invented some much higher rate for postage in 1971, to show the increase wasn't so great, until I checked some old invoices and they said yes, maybe their records weren't as good as they might be, but there were no plans to increase the rates and where did I get that information? From a POUNC paper on higher charges, I replied. 'That's very interesting, we'll have to look into that.' And later I received a letter saying that as I probably knew (the flattery bit) Post Office Imbalance Payments were due to rise from 1.5 to 5.5 gold francs per kilo (I had thought they were paid in moidores or Maria-Theresa thalers), but while it would be unrealistic to suggest that this will not affect postal charges (exquisite euphuism), Postal Headquarters had given POUNC (better called FAWN or CRINGE) an assurance that rates would not rise by the full 150 per cent. As my Cassandroid shrieks had been about a threatened increase from £1.15 to £2.60 for 2 Kg, which is a rise of 126 per cent, the assurance that the increase will actually be less than 150 per cent brings us naught for our comfort, yea naught for our desire, save that the post gets slower yet, and the cost rises higher.

☆   *13.3.81*

Just returned from a brief visit to San Francisco, partly to investigate Dental Revivalism: 'CAN GOD FILL TEETH? Ten dollar donation. Bring flashlight and mirror to see evidence of His handiwork.' I went downcoast to La Jolla, of which I had, derived from John Steinbeck, the clearest and most inaccurate image: a cove full of baby octopi and nudibranchs as delicate as short stories, just a truckstop and a handful of philosophical Mexicans collecting abalone at the hour of the pearl. It turned out to be a deal more citified than I had been led to believe, being the utmost part of San Diego; and San Diego itself is so much where it's at that it makes LA seem as oldworld as one of the less trendy Aberdeenshire herring ports. 'I love San Diego because the consciousness level is so high and because of the number of committed people', says the Reverend Terry Cole-Whittaker, described as 'La Jolla's Guru of entertaining Enlightenment' by *Southern California Seacoast*, a magazine of impeccably tomorrow consumerism and high-rent ecology; advertisements offer Hele-skiing with Con-tempo Travel, and complimentary hair analysis from Nexus 'Nature and Earth United with Science'.

The Reverend Terry, who has excellent credentials – 'I have done actualizations, Burkland Business School, Transactional Analysis, Transcendental Meditation, gestalt, Science of Mind training and classes, body work, Rolfing, rebirthing, yoga breathing and I turn upside down a couple of times a day in my new anti-gravity machine' – predicts, quite earnestly as far as I can tell, Heaven on Earth by the year 2000, brought about by lots of synergy, and members of Congress becoming egoless. 'They will do processes. They'll get into alignment'. I didn't see a lot of synergy, or if I saw it I didn't recognize it, nor many nudibranchs either, the cove, though urban, still being there, but the tide in, as I was informed by several exceptionally amiable surfers and loafers, some of them so laid back you could only see the soles of their feet.

Meanwhile, folks at SRI International (once Stanford Research Institute, not part of Stanford U; Uri Geller got his imprimatur there) have a 'multimillion dollar ongoing project studying American values and lifestyles', which has just registered a change in generally accepted success symbols. Out go fame, being published, rare foreign cars and a five-figure salary; in come 'oneness of play and work, easy laughter and unembarrassed tears, being in touch with self'. 'And the bucks are good too', as this admirable magazine (it has some superb photographs of nudibranchs) points out in an advert for staff. (They're looking for excellence and significance they say, but in my application I've asked if they wouldn't mind mediocrity and triviality instead.)

What with all the synergy, or lack of it, and plastic kelp at Del Mar, I was tempted still further south by the *Welcome Amigos Guide to Ensenada* (Ma Luisa Arrendondo, English Redactor, Martha Angellica R, Desing). It has a slightly threatening manner ('Did you help Amigos guide on your travel yes or no') but makes the most of the city's amenities and services:

> A taste of Mexican tamales in Mary flavors. Doctor Daniel Barba Garcia Ears Nose Troat. Auto Servicio 'Car Was Service'. Doctor Julio Gongora Garcia Ear Nose Trost. Get a Good conduct letter from your Local Cheriff. Shot guns and arrows got preference for hunting purposes. Doctor Mario Ortega Cora Urinary Conduits.

But the fear of a Lowryesque end (Malcolm, not LS, mescal not Newcastle Brown) drove me back north. That and a fearsome advert by Calpini Optical: 'Quality and Tradition in Eye Care all over Mexico'. Traditional eyecare, I have the feeling, involves obsidian knives on the tops of Aztec pyramids.

☆   *15.5.81*

'SPECIAL DELIVERY': do not the words still conjure images of pert, biddable street-Arabs ('trust me, guv') with mufflers and bicycles, despatch riders grimacing like T. E. Lawrence ('Just scoot over to the Wingco with this chitty, will you, Ross?'), men in souwesters, maewests or thermal vests, administrators in crisp kit, the night-mail crossing the Border (its wheels going Wystan Hugh Auden, Wystan Hugh Auden), MBE'd post-mistresses trudging the moors spongy with ling and sphagnum, loud with the harsh churr of the ptarmigan and the low chunter of the bannock? Dismiss such evocations. Banish them into the time-blurred limbo of rain-grey documentaries. Special Delivery is the worst of the many bad bargains offered today by the Post Office (or Interdatumco-GB, as it probably prefers to call itself).

I realized this when I started getting envelopes aglitter with urgencies that had taken slightly under twenty-four hours to gallop the ten furlongs from Gray's Inn Road. Studying leaflets on postal services (a curable addiction), I found that the Post Office (or EuroPost-Albion) had performed just what it had promised, thus: first-class mail, posted before the specified last time of posting for delivery first post the following day, may be delivered first post the following day. Or it may not. But pay an extra fee of £1.25, post before the specified time for posting for delivery first post next day, and it may very well be delivered first post next day. Or, again, it may not. But in that case, and this is the lure that drives men wild, makes them ready to fight and die for a handful of green labels, in this case the post-office will give you your money back. (Only the £1.25 of course, not the first-class fee, even if your vital document arrives a month late. It couldn't be all that vital, or you wouldn't have sent it by Fearfully-Up-To-Date Communications Corporation in the first place.)

Do they make any additional effort to get your special delivery specially delivered? OGPU-Brit protest that they do, but they have no financial incentive. Like so many of the services with fancy names and exorbitant fees (Datapost, Swiftair), special delivery offers as an expensive privilege the level of performance that used to be taken for granted. If the posts are running well, first class will do. If the mails are fouled up, then Special Delivery will arrive no sooner. Either way the odds favour the horse, putting British Snailmail in exactly the same moral position as the tipster who says 'Send no money now (but give me a third of your winnings, if any'). Well not exactly, because they take the money in advance and they decide the outcome of the race.

☆ *29.10.82*

Admiring the colours of autumnal foliage is probably the most harmless, indeed the most *moral* hobby of Western Man, even though smartass signboards in Bennington, Vermont say 'Welcome, Leaf Peekers', which slyly suggests that one is a sort of vegetarian voyeur. (Kew Gardens comes to 42nd Street: peep at the peas without their pods! Watch the almonds getting shucked! The all-nude green show! The Brussels sprout lets it all hang out!) But it isn't so: I mean I know it's an intimate physiological process we are watching here, but where there is no flesh there can be no carnality. So, in an arc from Northern Pennsylvania, through Maine and Quebec across the Laurentian Shield, where short bright hot autumn days encounter frosty dry windless nights, nature's paintbrush goes entirely bananas, or rather strawberries, oranges and tomatoes, for about two weeks a year, but not every year, and not all at once, so there are foliage advisory bureaux, Good Leaf Guides to warn you that the maples didn't turn in Maine, or the tamaracks are blighted in the Berkshires, and everyone should head for the Green Mountains or the White Mountains or the Finger Lakes and breathe deeply and glut his eyes and consume pumpkin pie and fresh (nonalcoholic) apple cider and stuff like that. It's a very unAmerican, indeed a very Japanese thing to do, and if there was a New York-style *sushi* bar in Vermont, everyone would live for ever.

But it must be one of the planet's most extraordinary phenomena, probably our only three-star attraction in the galactic Baedeker:

> *Earth* (Sol 3): primitive, but by no means unspoilt. Dominant native species (bidepal, aerobic) rapacious and xenophobic. Climate uncontrolled. Music and insect life good. Food and sanitation poor to indifferent. Frequent *wars* (qv).
> ✻✻✻Fall foliage in NE N America.
> ✻Coral reefs, Angkor Wat, Hermitage (holography prohibited). Interesting *mating rituals* of several species (three-spined

sticklebrick, European Royal Families). Nearest Astronautical Association Garage: Zeta Eridani (11 parsecs).

In fact the region was quite anomalously crowded, and I suspect that many of the cars with out-of-state licence plates were ringers, ready to zip into hyperspace at a word from their couriers. Often local newspapers contain editorials that can only be explained as coded messages to extraterrestrial tourists.

☆ *2.9.83*

'Computer to Run Marathon', jested the evening paper, evoking an image of a plucky British Acorn (with salt-caked software) struggling gamely on, its little legs going 19^{12}, only 14K but all heart, while foreign mainframes of doubtful polarity are crashing around it or being disqualified for illegally interfacing with a bus. Or the cybernetic pentathlon: chess, overcoming design hurdles, hurling the floppy discus, the sprint print-out, and carrying the can for human error. But all it really meant was that the Grand Viziers of the London Marathon have decided to abolish the pre-marathon Marathon, and its prize of an entry for those who guessed which pillar box to queue in front of. This year a computer will evaluate the million or so replies to a questionnaire, designed, says C. Brasher (starting-pistolero-in-chief) grimly, to keep out the comedians – this time, definitely, no one dressed as the front legs of a centipede, no hoppers or hang gliders, no one campaigning for proportional representation or Etruscan Rights, no exofficio novelists, pop cellists or singing waiters. I have seen an advance copy of the questionnaire. Name? Age? Sex? Number of miles per day in training? (I said per day, not per week.) Best time over twenty-five miles? Do you realize that you will be competing against people about twice as fast as you? Do you intend to become paraplegic between now and the start of the race? Do you intend to wear a tee-shirt with a vulgar advertising slogan? Do you intend to wear running shoes with a distinctive tread? What other hobbies do you have (choose from the following): a) running in other marathons b) walking long distances extremely fast c) sprinting d) ultra-marathoning? Have you run in a marathon before? If yes, do you suppose this gives you any special claim? If no, do you suppose that this gives you any special claim? Now complete the following sentence: I deserve, above all, to run in the London Marathon because . . .

Apart from an occasional jog at speeds I should remember to call gerontological rather than geriatric, staggering along London's canals from Limehouse to Southall (a full Thames to Thames trot would be just under twenty-six and a quarter miles and does that suggest anything to the GLC's Office of Pastimes and Pleasures?), my own pleasures come from reading about it. Running books and magazines represent a kind of wholesome pornography, with the same combination of physical explicitness, fetishistic concentration on a single function, the encouragement of fantasies of endurance and achievement, the flinging of others into stereotyped submissive roles, excessive competitiveness, and a lack of appreciation of the whole person.

There is a notable difference of style across the Atlantic. US marathon mags are full of soft-focus photography, free verse using biochemical terminology, advertisements for high-tech, high-fashion, high-cost foot apparel and unexpectedly complex training gear; personal stereo to play you inspirational words and music, digital pulse takers so you'll be the first to know if you drop dead. There are in-depth interviews with Alan Sillitoe, and the revivalist fervour of Dr George Sheehan, a born-again track-basher ('when I began running in my mid-40's, I rewrote my life-story. It has become a biography of pain'), who believes that athletes' sweat smells sweet, unlike the guilty apocrine sweat of the nervous sedentary. There is a genial polysexual sexiness about it all (compare and contrast *Personal Best* and *Chariots of Fire*); according to a survey, American long-distance runners, not only fantasize about sex while running, they also fantasize about running Marathons during sex. British magazines on the other hand are less glittering, less faddy, less designed to stimulate expenditure, and largely given over to explanations of the English team's poor performance in various international events.

Flanagan's Run by Tom McNab is the Bible, or rather the *Pilgrim's Progress* of the ultramarathoner, the one who thinks of twenty-six miles as a reasonable lap length. (A Classical and athletic purist is planning to supersede the Marathon with the Spartathon, on the grounds that Herodotus doesn't say anything about a run from Marathon, but he does say that Pheidippides ran from Athens to Sparta and arrived on the second day with enough breath to orate.) *Flanagan's Run* is a factualized account of the fictitious 1930 Los Angeles to New York race, and is stylistically remarkable as the only novel I know of that gives, every few chapters, a full list of the chief characters' placings and times. Other novels could do the same. At the end of forty chapters it's Moby Dick (Whales) eleven thousand miles in the lead, Ahab (USA) in second place just a harpoon's length ahead of Queequeg (Fr. Polynesia) with the united Arab Emirates team still waiting to make the break. Jay Gatsby leading by a toe on the East-Egg – West-Egg leg, with Nemesis coming up fast on the inside.

Long-distance running is one of the most dashing Patton-like thrusts of the feminist advance: until a few years ago women were barely tolerated, like lady undergraduates at Oxford before the War; now they are equalling men's record times of a decade or so ago and any moderately optimistic projection, especially one based on the last Boston Marathon, shows them overtaking men before the turn of the millennium. There may yet be a macho backlash; but the admirable and combative Anna Coote was mistaken in attributing to sexist resentment the cat-calls that followed her around Hampstead Heath when she trained, and complaining about this in the *New Statesman*. I am neither female nor nubile, but I encounter on my runs a deal of conversation, much supportive, but much not. (Small boys shout 'Get those feet up'; small girls, curiously, cry 'Got a light?' or ask the time.) A comrade from *Time Out* put Ms Coote right, attributing all jeering to fat envy: then he had to face ludicrous criticism from what might be called the Wide Left, whining that all exercise was a bourgeois diversionary tactic, to encourage consumption, self-absorption and competition, and come the revolution there will be neither fat nor thin, fast nor slow. From each according to his faculty, to each according to his speed, says I.

☆   31.5.85

I completed the London Marathon, that is the London Marathon TV-watching Marathon, in a personal best of three hours, forty-five. Throughout that time my gaze was remorselessly fixed upon the screen, while bystanders commented on the smoothness of my elbow and epiglottis action, eating up the coffee and biscuits as though they were coffee and biscuits. You couldn't but notice what the stress of the event did to the speech of those describing it: but then the London Marathon is an event 'which some people would give an arm and a leg to enter' according to an organizer, evincing that felicity of expression which ... At one exciting moment a commentator wondered aloud 'Why isn't Jones alongside him, running eyeball to eyeball?', an image that almost disturbed my steady, flowing, viewing movement. 'Mother Nature has proved a formidable foe' threnodized another, showing, I thought, a singular lack of respect for the old lady. As the pace hotted up, so did the commentators. Excitement rising in his gorge like last night's Cheddar, one shouted 'And now Stephen Jones has put his foot on the carburetter'. After that, it was all down hill.

☆ 26.9.80

At a bookstand recently, I was drawn to the *North Frontenac News* ('serving North Frontenac since 1970') by its crossword. 1 Across was ' "I think . . . therefore I –" (2 letters)', and I got that fairly speedily, with some help from the Down clues; but I was intrigued by 47 Across 'hypothetical word' and frankly baffled by 47 Down ' "— you!" (3 letters)'. Had I stumbled here, in what might legitimately be called the backwoods (at least as compared to South Frontenac), on a new trend in puzzle compilation, where proper, improper and purely hypothetical answers interwove as in a Pynchon novel?

I couldn't think of a five-lettered type of rabbit, so I had to buy the paper, which was full of reports of discontent around Ompah at overcropping wildrice, new kitchen cupboards in the Oddfellows Hall at Snow Road, and a day-long workshop at Sharbot Lake on Building Self-Confidence through Interpersonal Communication ('topics to be discussed will include self-concept, self-disclosure, assertiveness, and relating to others – not simply in theory, but participants will also be involved in the practical application of these important skills'). Rural Women also would have a workshop, and Stan and Florrie would like the three flags stolen from their cottage return with no questions asked. I'm perturbed by this last item, and wonder whether it represents simple anomie or something more sinister: were the flags perhaps blasphemous, seditious (the flag of North Frontenac Irridenta, with claims to the Eastern Marches, the Snowy Foothills, and the oil-rich Gulf Islands) or merely hypothetical? Or have I misunderstood, and are they seeking the return of flagstones, flag irises or (see *OED*) 'a piece cut out or pared off the sward; a sod', 'a blast or gust of wind', fourpence ('from MLG *vlegr* coin worth somewhat more than a Bremen groat') or 'an opprobrious term applied to women . . . *sic fartingaillis on flaggis als fatt as quhailis*, DUNBAR'? No wonder Stan and Florrie don't want any questions asked.

I did the crossword, which was rather a disappointment. In addition to the standard complement of monosyllables – REP,

OPTS, NO and HO ('Santa's word (2 letters)'), there were some duplications like 'Same as 46 Across' which represents new ground in weary desperation. They both turned out to be IT; the type of rabbit, as I should have guessed was WELSH, which made 47 HEY, and the hypothetical word was, alas, IF. In all, a disappointment, and not a patch on my favourite crossword, composed by Violet Elizabeth Bott for *The Outlaws' and District Times* (see *William in Trouble*, by Richmal Crompton, 1927). That, you will recall, had two clues only, 'Oppossit of cat' and 'Wot you hav dropps of' the answers of course being DOG and COF.

☆ 12.5.84

Relentless in pursuit of the perfect book, I went last month to Malta. It wasn't there, the perfect book, but besides the megalithic and baroque splendours (Maltese architecture, like some somnolent cactus, flowers every five thousand years) I was unexpectedly charmed and bewildered by linguistic and semiotic strangeness.

For Malta is one of those curious blind countries where a highly literate people is daily confronted with a world of alien texture, a land where the idiom of the people is scarcely represented by the printed, screened and transmitted word.

You need to live in a fairly remote hedgerow in England not to be wrapped in language – the words of posters, packets, instructions on the can and guarantees on the sauce-bottle – while the Londoner or the New Yorker must have millions of words a day reinforcing his vocabulary, pre-empting any other sensory input (which is perhaps the reason city dwellers have no sense of smell).

But in Malta I had again that sad, weird sensation of disjunction that you get in Welsh Wales, in the Basque country, in the wrong parts of Belgium, in Quebec, though less now than ten years ago, the sensation that the eye and the ear are tuned to different programmes.

Of course, all Maltese speak English; but they do not talk it. So while one listens to a charming and unfamiliar Semitico-Romance Mid-Med medley, one sees only Persil and Brillopad and Major Road Ahead and Computer and Video News and This Way Up and Please Knock.

Of course there are fields where Maltese dominates: religious and political announcements, for instance, Church and Government in alliance for once (though the opposition press refuses to print the radio and television schedules of Xandir Malta), poetry, folksong and countless newspapers, official forms, police and parish notice-boards, elementary textbooks, even one comic (called *Il-Komik:* Klang! Heqq! Ayma! Jaqaw!), the occasional monolingual xenophobic 'wet paint' sign (ABJAD FRISK if I read aright).

But despite modern low-cost duplicating methods, letter-heads and shop signs, invoices, road signs, wipe your feet, adjust your dress, remain in English only. Why couldn't Leyland, when they were furbishing the plucky little buses that run everywhere like green corpuscles ('buses leave Hal Far every hour on the half hour') find a bilingual sign-painter to translate Only Three Standing, Box For Used Tickets? Some, I discovered later, do have the latter: it's KAXXA GHALL BILJETI WZATI give or take a few diacritical dots and dashes that the *TLS* doesn't carry, any more than most local typewriters, another of the burdens of being a minority language. Spoken, it's more comprehensible than it looks.

All of this is plainly a newcomer's reaction; the Maltese don't in general feel linguistically colonized or neo-colonized: English is our language too, they insist. At the theatre this week *Deathtrap*; next week Emlyn Williams's *Il-Lejl jasal Żgur*. If the bus-drivers wanted bilingual or monolingual NO STANDING signs they would have made them, with a fraction of the effort that goes into installing and decorating the shrines or Madonna-grottoes above each driving compartment: VERBUM CARO FACTUM EST picked out in a handsome rounded script, a blend of *lettre bâtarde* and Greengrocer's Full-serif Swollen Gorblimey; the few pagan drivers had HAPPY FOR EVER or MANCHESTER UNITED or indeed just LEYLAND, similarly calligraphic. On one windscreen I counted twenty-five stickers with spiritual, commercial or sporting exhortations in English, German, Italian, Latin, wordless (Tottenham Hotspurs group photograph), even two in Maltese.

I took with me, for protection and as conversation-starter, Joseph Aquilina's impressive but visionary *Teach Yourself Maltese* (English Universities Press, 1965 and later); by exercise 4 we should be able to say 'the man is cruel and quarrelsome, but his wife is bashful and diligent', and form diminutives like *zappuna*, a small mattock. I made very little progress.

Like the islands themselves, the Maltese language takes its superstructure from the north shore of the Mediterranean, its geology from the south. The rocky grammatical base is Semitic (though the great overhanging mesas of verbal paradigms have been worn down to rounded hillocks), while the vocabulary commemorates every European who blew in and out as conqueror or merchant-Catalan and Sicilian, the borrowings of a century and a half of British rule, millennia of the Roman Church. There is a widespread romantic belief that the Semitic core is not Arabic but something earlier: Punic or proto-Canaanite or some Hamitic tongue, Ancient Egyptian or Libyco-Berber. After all the Arab Conquest lasted only from 870 to 1090, when the Muslims were expelled or at least subdued by Roger the Norman. (And what did he speak, by the way? Sicilian? Old French? Norse?)

Modern Libyans stress the arabicity of the language to the sceptical Maltese; Europeans will find a mixture of the familiar and the unpronounceable. Good Evening, Thank you, Please are respectively Bonswa, Grazzi and Jekk Jogħgbokk; a restaurant offers Timbale, Ravjul and Ross-il-forn; there is a poster appeal about the 'importanti suġġeti: Il-Budget' from the Assocjazzjoni tas-Self-Employed.

The cadences of the language are almost wholly Italianate. Arabic gutturals are reduced (except of course in Gozo, as Stephen Potter might have said) and all those q's and għ's (the h has an extra crosspiece, which in our case we have not got) which make written Maltese look so ferocious, are silent to the English ear and only inserted for fun, like currants in a currant bun. Thus *q'ghed* is just Ed, or rather glottal-stop-Ed, and all kinds of entertaining sight rhymes and non-rhymes are possible. Luqa Airport, the first stop unless you take St Paul's route (shipwrecked in Mellieha Bay), is the starting point for limericks less indecent than I had supposed, thus

> There was a young Lady of Luqa
> Whose beauty made men wish to scruqa
> Her lovers grew fuqa and fuqa.

The additional lines (which might contain some reference to making a Maltese cross) should present no difficulty.

(Enter Ms Ge Polter, wrath): Why are all your limericks, nay all limericks, preoccupied with the verbal or physical abuse of women?

Myself (sheepishly): Don't blame me, but the genius of the English language, which provides innumerable rhymes for 'her' or rather ' 'er', employing the neutral vowel or schewa, thus ... *(dreamily)*

> I once knew a young lady called Schewa
> Who was charming and fetching and clever
> *Ms G. P.:* That's enough
> Of this chauvinist stuff!
> *Me:* I think I could go on for ever.

Perhaps with something about the Archbishop of Gozo. But you can't change the ever-interesting topic of the limerick, any more than you can change human na . . .

> *Ms G. P.:* I'm starting a group for persuading 'em
> That Women (with righteous men aiding 'em)
> Could stamp out this form
> Whose role-model norm
> Is exploiting or elsewise degrading 'em

But the silent q gave me my most magical moment in Malta, which came when I was being given a lift back up the stiff climb from the Inland Sea (more like an Inland Pond, actually) in a truck with two large native dogs. 'Nice dogs', I said insincerely. 'Yes, I use for hunting.' 'What do you hunt with them?' 'Whales.' '??????' 'Yes. 'uails and duffs.'

There was a similarly surreal linguistic moment concerning marine mammals provided by the *Times of Malta*, though the credit should probably go to wire service. This was a report that an animal liberation movement had broken into a Hamburg laboratory and released 500 or maybe 5,000 porpoises. I had a wonderful image of an endless column of cetaceans (*Phocaena communis*, actually, and thereby hangs an epigram) flopping porpoisefully seaward through St Pauli, terrorizing the brothelkeepers and their clients all down the Reeperbahn, until a suspicion dawned that the German for 'porpoise' and the German for 'guineapig' were teasingly similar.

The local archiepiscopate categorizes foreign films as admirable, acceptable, partly or wholly harmful: 'skabroz', 'diskutibbli' 'lingwaġġ volgari'. It addresses believers in Maltese, tourists in their vernaculars: 'Personnes vetues de bacon correcte, evitando assolutamente abiti indecenti, ebensowenig hot-pants.'

The ancient stones are silent too: if the perplexing new dating is correct, they are a thousand years older than the earliest Sumerian. What would those splendid sedate Great Mothers, with their sturdy shoulders, inflated thighs and absurd doll's peg-legs, say to us, and in what language, if they could speak? It would surely be something polite, for they don't look in the least like fertility symbols, and one of them is without question Queen Victoria, imperial Indian sash and all. Others lie on couches: are they dreaming, meditating, transmigrating, or simply votive offerings with nasty diseases? There's one the Archaeological Museum calls, precisely enough, 'Irregular Object On Couch', while Michael Ridley (*Megalithic Art of the Maltese Islands*, Dolphin Press) calls it 'Carving of Fish on a Bed'. Likewise, Mgr Dr Anthony Gauci, author of *Gozo* (St Joseph's Home Printing Press, Hamrun, 1969), who is stronger on menology and ecclesiastical interiors than on dendrochronology, seems to have special sources of information about what went on at Ġgantija: 'in the two depressions on the ground they washed the white doves used for the sacrifice'. White doves, Monsignor? That's in the passage which leads to the chamber with the snake (Ridley: eel) now in Gozo museum; Gauci supplies a surreal inventory: '3. On a shelf in the corner. a) A shewolf suckling Romulus and Remus. b) A grecoroman artistic head of a youth. c) a very old bronze leg. d) An inscription of unknown age.' I asked about the very old leg, which seemed to be absent, and the guardian articulated clearly the sound 'Plouf', with an expressive shrug: but I don't know what it expressed. Perhaps something along the lines of 'You know how it is, sir, these old bronze legs have a habit of walking.'

Perhaps the explanation of the great plethora of ancient temples – if temples is what they are – is the primeval working of the emulation effect, or the Xewkija Factor, the mysterious dynamic that drove the inhabitants of Xewkija (say it 'Choux qui'l y a'), a largish village in Gozo, to beggar themselves for decades to build a church vast beyond their population or their needs, but with a dome bigger than that in Mostar, a smallish town in Malta with the third, now the fourth hugest-domed building in Europe, if not the known universe.

But who has put flowers in the ancient stone bowl at ruined Mġarr? And what was meant to go there? Has anyone analysed that smeary incrustation in the underground temple at Hal Saflieni to see if it is dried blood, wine or fermented hallucinogenic mushroom? It remains infinitely diskutibbli.

And what about perfect books? Well, no. There were books, mostly theological, mostly recent and mostly incomplete, mostly stacked inaccessibly in the back rooms of antique dealers: but the bookworms, I mean the genuine bookworms, had a 200-year start on me, reducing everything remotely desirable to macramé. The book I most wanted to find was a new one, *Gozitan Wit and Humour* by N. E. Atkinson, author of *Insure My Legs, Please*, which was annihilatingly reviewed in the local *Times* ('most jokes fall flat and many seem lacking the punchline ... no redeeming social value ... incredible number of typos, misprints and unnecessary question marks ... seems to have been translated through many languages'), but the new-book sellers of Malta (and Gozo too, to be fair), when they had stopped laughing, denied all knowledge of it.

☆   *23.8.85*

The above was not composed on an Apple, an A.C.T. Apricot, or Kiwi (first down-under computer), nor yet a Texas Instruments Strawberry ('Texas Strawberries bring a new flavour to word-processing'). It was not processed by WORDSTAR, SCRIPSIT, ERATO (Error Reduction And Text Over-write) nor yet CALLIOPE (Colloquial, Algebraic Literal Language I/O Poetic Equivalent, nicknamed 'Merry-Go-Round' from its bug-infested tendency to drop into iterative sub-routines). Nor yet was it run off by a daisy-wheel, dot-matrix, laser-guided inkjet nor by thermal transfer on to the kind of paper which scrolls resiliently into tight rolls, entrapping the reader's finger (come to think of it, Calliope is usually represented holding such a scroll, a Parnassian print-out).

It should have been so composed, though, and I have spent an entrancing week learning a miracle-working apparatus with a one-handed, five-key, micro-miniaturized keyboard, which mysteriously turns one-to-five finger exercises into letters, punctuation, or commands to the machine, swift and silent and ideal for using in the British Library.

Unfortunately a slip or so of the thumb – and I was all thumbs – turns letter j into GO BACK TO LAST DOCUMENT SEPARATOR, turns capital K into PROCEED BACKWARDS THROUGH TEXT AT STEADILY INCREASING PACE WHILE IGNORING PANIC-CRAZED FINGERTIPS DABBING AT EVERY KEY IN TURN and turns MWMK (*'mwmk*, ancient Egyptian for turtlegrease as well as acronymic for MAILER WASHES MUMMY'S KA, a tetragrammaton constantly on my lips) into OBLITERATE EVERYTHING I HAVE WRITTEN, the Hi-tec equivalent of Lady Isabel Burton or J. S. Mill's fire-kindling housemaid.

So it's back to the clay tablet and wedge for me, with exclamations of *Savitry!* and *Carancho!* whenever I make a mistake, and no place on my ort-strewn desk for the twenty-first century. But I do have room for a sweet-scented cylindrical calendar, inscribed with various symbols indicating the omens for the day. Unfortunately (*Indrisy!*) the text is in Batak, an outmoded Indonesian script that looks like birdtracks in the snow, if it ever snows in Sumatra, but fortunately there is a mimeographed sheet of explanation in trade-English. Still more fortunately, I don't know how the Batak calendar interlocks with the one I use, so I have to ignore its advice, most of which is aposematic, or off-putting: 'This is the pair of the pincers of scorpion. We must not organize the celebration on this day, as the scorpion is sure to catch the organizer with it's pincers.

This is the scorpions' belly. We must not organized a celebration on this day. Only those born on scorpion-days may do so. This is the scorpion's tail. We must not undertake anything on this day. Not even the following day.' Nor does getting away from the scorpion make life easier: 'This is 'alasungsang' (i.e. antipode of scorpion). (on the days indicated this sign) We should be extremely careful, as they are murtured.' Then there is the checker-board sign ('this is the sign of the fish day, i.e. host shall five his guests fish to eat. If he offers them meat he will have to face the ill-effects of his dee, his castle shall be killed in great number'), the desperate double fish-hook ('this is day which death. Everybody who undertakes anything shall die, according to the *datu*'), and the scarcely less distressing sun-setting-in-cave (or igloo-underneath-flyover) sign: 'He who undertake something shall have stomachache.' But most of my trouble, I now realize, comes from doing things on single-kidney-bean days: 'This is day in favourable of incompleteness; anything done on this day will only be done incompletely. Completion will only be possible when a parsili is offered.' Pass the parsili, Mabel, and make sure it's well murtured.

If you want to read more about computers, turn to page 95.
If you would rather read about *Indrisy*! and other interjections from Madagascar, go to page 98.

☆ *18.5.84*

The fields of lexicography and grammar are full of hairily indignant caterpillars ('three inches is a very good height indeed') who are convinced that correct speech is the stuff that comes out of their mouths and that any change is for the worse; and there has been a great quantity of fruitless waggling of prolegs at the resistless spread of the new use of 'hopefully' as, if I have this right, an adverb qualifying not the action of the main verb, but the sense of the whole clause, giving it a pseudo-optative tinge. Greek and some Amerindian languages do it with a special form of the verb (the moods of the verb in Menomini, a language more spoken of by linguists than spoken by speakers, express, as moods should, the speaker's feeling about the probability and desirability of what he is reporting); other languages, Melanesian for argument's sake, do it with a particle (imagine 'Melanesians do it with a particle' as a bumper-sticker); English is beginning to do it with 'hopefully'.

Myself, I welcome it, having long felt the need of an optative for expressing shades of meaning like 'let's you do it'. But has anyone pointed out that 'mercifully' has traditionally been used with this sort of meaning? If I say, for example, 'Mercifully, Roger Scruton has not written an article in today's *Times*', I am not suggesting that the quality of mercy in this instance inheres in Mr Scruton, but in God, an almost entirely different Person. 'Mercifully' stands for '. . . and that's a mercy', as 'hopefully' stands for ' . . . at least that is what I hope', and as 'gratefully' is beginning to be used to mean 'and that is something we should be grateful for'. I heard someone say, recently, 'thankfully, she married the curate'; but I have no idea in which sense they were using it. Man on the radio, talking about how to interrupt the iron chain of circumstances that leads people to get drowned (stay as far away from the water as possible, was his major recommendation) said something like 'thankfully, she was rescued', a profitable bit of ambiguity. (He also said 'water is with us to stay', but that's another story.)

☆   10.8.84

Ès ou sav la ni pli moun en Karayib-la ka palé Kwéyòl pasé Anglé? You probably don't sav any more than I did until recently.

    Whenever I get feeling elderly, whenever there is a damp November in my soul, as Melville says, I rejuvenate myself by learning a new language, whaling voyages being a little harder to come by than they used to be.

    Or rather, by starting a new language, because I never get beyond Lesson V ('More about Interrogative Pronouns'), or on exceptional days, Exercise VII ('Preterites in *iš*. The use of the honorific *pung*'). Often I overmatch myself completely, like trying to study some language just recorded by MIT graduates from its last living speaker, a centenarian hammock-weaver from Yucatan; but studying a language from a transformational grammar is like trying to get Hellenic local colour from a study of Athenian municipal budget proposals, or amorously embracing a skeleton.

    This year's language was new indeed, scarcely recognized as proper language by those who speak it, only sporadically written down, its orthography only agreed in 1981. This is Kwéyòl or Patwa (the spelling 'patois' marks you as a neo-colonialist), the current speech of the ex-British Colonies of St Lucia and Dominica, and the French Overseas Départements of Martinique and Guadeloupe. Throw in their far more numerous neighbours in

Haiti, and you have some six million speakers, more than Norwegian or Danish or Periclean Greek, more people than speak English in the West Indies (see opening sentence). The ambitious include Louisiana Cajun, the speech of Cayenne and even of Mauritius. And there are a few thousand speakers in Tower Hamlets, London, which is why the local authority is backing the Patwa Project, not designed primarily for frivolous linguistic kibitzers like myself, but for English-speaking children who want to know what their parents are saying, for parents who are perhaps only semi-literate because they haven't been able to make the double leap from speaking one language to writing another, for writers and poets who want to use the language that their history has shaped.

Patwa's vocabulary is French, its structure – perhaps – West African: it has, obviously, diverged in the officially Anglophone and the officially Francophone islands. And I'm having a wonderful time as the native speakers struggle with their memories and the systematizers try to create order, while I battle through reports of maritime disasters ('twibilasyon péchè') in bilingual 'Balata' and hold my tongue when Dominicans and St Lucians disagree.

Is this all a left-wing plot, under the banner of multiculturalism, to undermine the English language and English notions of propriety? Yes, if French is a plot to subvert Latin, and English, a creole dialect if there ever was one, simply ungrammatical Anglo-Saxon contaminated with a lot of exotic slang. At first sight Patwa may look like abraded French, but things are not what they seem at first sight, or as we Patwans say, 'dlo mouchas pa lèt' (cloudy water isn't milk).

☆   *31.10.80*

'Twenty shelves, five long shelves per side, cover all the sides except two; their height, which is the distance from floor to ceiling, scarcely exceeds that of a normal bookcase.' (From J. L. Borges, *The Library of Babel*, translated by James E. Irby.)

'Twenty shelves – five long shelves per side – cover all sides except two; their height, which is that of each floor, scarcely exceeds that of an average librarian.' (From J. L. Borges, *The Library of Babel*, translated by Anthony Kerrigan.)

'Twenty-five shelves, with five long shelves on each side, cover all the walls except one. They cover the wall from the floor to the ceiling and are about the height of a normal librarian.' (From J. L. Borges, *The Library of Babel*, translated by G. R. Coulthard.)*

☆   *23.8.85*

I've always had a soft spot for Madagascar, if only because the people are called Malgache, which sounds as if it ought to mean a soft spot ('I was abseiling down the bergschrund when I dropped my karabiners into a malgache'), and because of the soft musicality of their language. 'Tsaroako ny tsikin'ny androko omaly/Izay manjary aloka foana, indrisy!' sings J. J. Rabearivelo in *Love Song*, which may be rendered (courtesy K. Katzner, *Languages of the World*, Routledge and Kegan Paul) 'I recall the joys of days gone by/They waned alas to flit away!'

But when I read that an armoured division of the Malagasy Army had been called in to destroy the *dojo* of an intransigent karate sect which had been terrorizing peaceable tourists (or, according to others, brutally to extirpate the only democratic opposition) I thought it was time to be better informed. So I bought *Aretina Sy Fanasitranana* by Dr Andrew Davidson (Antananarivo, 1876). This is evidently a medical text (there are sections on Beriberi, Skrofula and Aretiny Addison) and, judging from the preface and acknowledgements to, among others, 'Dr Warburton Begbie, Indrisy!', it was written in Malagasy by Dr Davidson of Edinburgh and the NY Friends' Foreign Mission.† This must be one of the first Western medical texts in a sub-Saharan language (I'm not counting papyri on the therapeutic applications of *'mwmk*) but is none the less unintelligible for that, even the manuscript bits in English on the interleaved blank pages:

> Joseph Rampur, formerly an attendant at the asylum. His habits were not intemperate, but he occasionally took too much *rum*. Guarding cattle on 'Chanane' estate in Black River, which is a

---

* I've checked the first and second Buenos Aires editions, and the geometrical blunder, tactfully corrected by Irby and Kerrigan, is the author's. (You can't construct a library, or anything else, of linked units, if each unit has only one link.) As for *librero*, my dictionary says *bookseller*, not librarian; or ('in Mexico, Colombia and Paraguay') *bookcase*. It doesn't mention Argentina.

† E, O, Ray! A blunder as clownish as Sonnerat's (see below). The imprint 'NY Friends Foreign Mission' has nothing to do with Big Apple. Ny = the.

malarial locality. He got his wages one evening and he and two other companions bought a 'chopine' of rum each. He drank his own share, was intoxicated, and

... rapidly developed into that maddening physician's cryptography ... which denies us the end of the story, although the word dysentery can be made out, likewise enteritis and either 'succumbed' or 'recovered'.

So I hunted up a copy of G. W. Parter's *Concise Grammar of Malagasy* (Trubner 1883); proceeding backwards, I have only reached the last chapter, which deals with interjections. *Endray!* (ah! oh!) *E, O, Ray!* (Eh! Ho! Ha!) *Endra!* (Oh that! Would that!) and *Indrisy!* (Alas!). *Indrisy!* (Alas!), although by now familiar, is a bit of a problem, because *OED* says it means 'Lo, Behold!' or possibly 'He is over yonder!' and it tells the story of Pierre Sonnerat (*fl* in Madagascar *c*1780) ambling through the tropical rain forest when a new species of lemur swam into his ken. 'Indri! (Lo, Behold!)', or possibly 'Indri izy! (He is over yonder!)', cried his faithful Malgache tracker, whereat the Gallic juggins wrote 'Indris = espèce de lémur' on his shirt-cuff. We all know that what he had seen is in reality called a *babakoto* or babacoot (*Lichanotus brevicaudatus*), but a lie or a misunderstanding can go around the world while the truth is putting its boots on, especially if the truth is a lemur, noted for its sloth. The sloth ('or ai, from its plaintive cry') is Latin American, not to be confused with the Malagasy aye-aye, which goes aye-aye and sounds like a Latin-American dance. Computers have AI, different again. I could go on ... but *'Sanatrìa!'* I hear you exclaim (Forbid that – !). The interjection *sanatría* had 'perhaps' (I am quoting G. W. Parker) the following mode of origin: it is a plant used medicinally by the Malagasy; it is also the name given to an earthen pot daubed with streaks of coloured paint in accordance with the directions of the incantation worker. The pot is carried to the place where the disease had its origin and is believed to attract the disease to itself, and is consequently left there, the person who leaves it exclaiming *'Sanatría!'* (May it – i.e. the disease – be *sanátry!*)

I turned to *Curiosities of the Vegetable Kingdom* (SPCK 1849 or thereabouts) to find out more about the plant, but the only Malagasy vegetable which figured was the tanghien tree, a poisonous plum used to test for witchcraft or other crime. The accused is made to eat as much boiled rice as possible, followed by three pieces of chicken skin 'about the size of a dollar'. He then drinks the tanghien scrapings mixed with banana juice, is ritually comminated by the *panozondoha,* and made to drink large quantities of rice-water 'till the stomach rejects its contents; when if the three pieces of skin are found all is well, the party is pronounced *madio*, legally and morally innocent'. If they are not, he is incontinently brained by the bystanders, using the very rice-pestle involved in the rite. A fortiori, if he dies without vomiting, he was even guiltier, and serve him right. (Compare and contrast with the philosophy of English witch-finding ordeals, where the victim's death proves innocence, tough luck, lass, but we'll give you a grand funeral.) A skilful *panozondoha* could select ripe or unripe fruit according to his personal feelings, and the accused person's means. It was observed that the rich were hardly ever found guilty by the tanghien-test. If I add that it was customary to seize a few bystanders to serve as experimental controls (poor persons, by and large) and submit them to the test to show that the poison really was poisonous and there was no possibility of corruption, you may well wish to perform *mifady ahitra*, the adjuration of the grass. Do this by plucking a piece of grass from the ground and hold it up, as to express 'May such misfortunes be far from us as we would avoid treading on the very grass of the village where such sorrow dwells'. Or you might prefer to take your chance with the karate team.

☆ 5.9.86

I listen to radio speak-persons with gusto. The other day, one got the weather report from something he called the Bureau of Climactic Research; and during a phone-in about spelling difficulties, a phonic-in, someone remarked 'Before I took that course I was practically dickslectic'.

I was in a dickslectic deli the other day and there were two delicacies sharing a plate: they were labelled *truffles* and *triffles*. That, I thought, was a poser for transformational grammarians, who will surely look for the shift in meaning represented by the fronting of the vowel, or whatever; the same shift as in butter/bitter, puzzle/pizzle.

☆ 23.8.85

Went to the Zoo to examine their Indris, but was lost in admiration for the unsung heroes of the Adopt-An-Animal Scheme. Not the popstars and multinationals who fund gazelles and lions and giraffes, but the homely folk who put their pennies behind the Undistinguished Flycatcher (*Muscivora subfusca*) or the Lesser Grey Newt. A modest lady had adopted a sea anemone; Bumble the Cat has sponsored an Octopus, which is cheek; some people called Turtle (Myrtle and Bertil, since you ask) claim to be backing a Turtle; a locksmith is funding a kea; Class 3T are fostering a school of piranha. The whole scheme is rich in moral ambiguities, pregnant with opportunities for projection, introjection, abreaction, acting-out and generally acting up. . . . Fostering-suitability interviews in the Pangolin House. Candidates wait here please.

'Like to adopt an animal would you?'

'Only if it is entirely convenient, my Lord.'

'Come for your pound of flesh-eater, have you? Lion or tiger?'

'No, no, Sire, an ounce will do. Or a serval, a wolverine, a polecat, a stoat, even a bad-tempered vole.'

'Why you whey-faced bean eater, what claim have you to such an aristocrat of the animal kingdom? Half share in a hedgehog is more your mark, I warrant you. Coming in here with your sweaty half-crowns, imagining you can get custody of a cassowary, camel rides of a weekend, droit de seigneur over (though I says it as shouldn't) a rather attractive dugong, whose breasts have maddened generations of mariners . . .'

There's a sign near the Birds of Prey that looks like entries for the Booker Prize: '*Razorbill* by Felix D. Brunt. *Raven* by Jacqui Pitts and A. Nordmark.'

But no one has adopted the Carrion Hawk, *Polyborus Plancus*, the carancho or caracara. I always thought *carancho* was an obscenity frequently on the lips of the guttersnipes of Saragossa, while the *caracara* is a mournful keening *gauchesco* song, much heard in the Borgesian bars of the *Banda Oriental*, where, supping a lucent *borracho*, a eucharistic potion at once frugal and stupendous, we become aware, in the momentary chink of the indifferent bartender's change, that we share in the libations that doomed Iphigenia, in Falstaff's sublime and evasive *crapula*, taste to the bitter dregs the self-accusing cup of the supernal and necessary traitor. In that late afternoon, under the leathery sun of the pampas, we are one with the headache that drove de Quincey to an alternative at once rational and oneiric, we share the hemlock-cephalalgia of Keats and Socrates, the temple-pain of doomed Sisera, the branded forehead of the first fratricide. In the moment of hangover each man sees in the mirror surface of his drink that he, finally, is Cain, his brother. (From 'Doña Alvarez and the Cup', in *Narraciones*, Buenos Aires, 1943.)

☆   22.7.88

Lonely Planet Publications of Yarra and Berkeley, who publish guidebooks to Zanskar and Rarotonga and the Galapagos, also undertake a series of phrase-books that render articulate the parts of the planet other manuals do not reach, tourist vade-mecums (or komwizmees) in Ladakhi and Sinhala and Korean and more.

I resisted the Thai book, even though it taught me wonderful things about the use of polite particles: ('every sentence in this book is to be thought of as followed by an invisible *khrap*'), but couldn't live without the Tibet and the Papua New Guinea phrasebooks (112pp and 92pp, £1.95). The books are prettily produced and linguistically literate. For all their compactness, they find space to teach the correct manner of sounding retroflex consonants (as in *driy* 'female yak') and the difference between *long* and *bilong*, to tell you where to hire bicycles in Lhasa and to regret that the well-waters of PNG Pidgin (NeoMelanesian) are becoming polluted. Contaminated with English, if you can imagine such a thing, producing a hybrid hybrid, Ponglais or PigPidgin. *Tok bilong yupela baimbai kamap olsem long Inglis tumas* as you might say. Conversely, the purest Pidgin, a perfectly proper notion that takes some getting used to, is spoken in Manus Province, *Virginia Water bilong Nugini*.

John Hunter's *Papua New Guinea Phrasebook* (also described as a 'language survival kit') teaches post-colonial linguistic etiquette too: don't refer to yourself or fellow tourists as *Masta* or *Misus* ('still in use in remote areas'). There is a worrying chapter on travel into the interior (*bas i go long bus*) and scary messages (*Sapos mipela no kambak* . . .). Towns offer more familiar perils: *Mi kol, mi hat, mi kros, mi hangre, nek bilong mi drai, mi laikim rum igat ples waswas, mi got pekpek wara* (diarrhoea).

The Tibet phrasebook is by Melvyn C. Goldstein, 'assisted by Gelek Rimpoche and Trinley Dorje'. Tibetan, which is usually intimidatingly full of huge consonant clusters, becomes far more accessible in their transliteration: 'one, two, three', in my old textbook *gchigs, gnyish, gsum* (with various accents) are here *chig, nyi, sum*; 'seven, eight, nine' rubs down from *bdun, brgyad, dgu* to *dun, gyay, gu*. The grammatical section recalls childish pleasures. This is a yak. The yak is black. Is this a yak? Are there yaks here? There are yaks in Tibet. There are many yaks in Tibet. This is not a yak. This is not a polaroid camera.

There are universal phrase-book expressions like *I want two pens* and others reeking with local colour, like *Hey-male-slightly-older-than-oneself, take me a little way up the road in your cart*. The first phrase translates *nga nyugu nyiy gaw*, which sounds positively yakkish.

There are phrases also in Tibetan characters, so you can point and ask for things you cannot pronounce, like *kokoko la* which looks like three palm-trees with seagulls circling over them, accompanied by a water jar. It is almost a pictogram: there may be no palm-trees or seagulls on those snowy heights, but they still need refreshment: in the haunts of the yeti, Coke is It.

☆   10.9.82

Deep offence has been caused by volume III of the Supplement to the *OED* in the palm-fringed paradise of Andhra Pradesh, choicest stretch of India's coral strand, where there is a heartfelt welcome for the weary traveller. 'A heartfelt welcome for the weary traveller', say the tourist bureau signs, in English as well as the local speech, Malayalam. Malayalam, a Dravidian language with an attractive script that appears to be applied to the page with a cake-icing bag, has given us copra, teak, and possibly mulligatawny, and is clearly not a tongue to be sneezed at, a risky activity at the best of times. The Andhra Pradesh Tourist Bureau ensures the accuracy and colloquial vigour of its English-language announcements by employing a special corps of translators who check the text by rendering it back into the vernacular. Such a person is properly known as a remalayalamer, and may be said to know his job backwards and forwards. They are, or were until unfairly neglected by Oxford, one of the chief attractions: 'Visit Cochin, home of the world's largest palindrome'.

☆   29.2.80

Wandering resentfully through the London Underground – not the trains but the stations, which should be stately pleasure domes and are instead horrid irrational ratmazes, aimless blind alleys and meandering gutters, that twist and climb and sidestep to avoid the roots of trees, snuffling furtive Mrs Tiggywinkle corridors that may by smug serendipity lead to an underground council chamber, an exit, a hidey-hole, a store-cupboard or even, on a good day, a platform – I have often puzzled over the identity of the builders, who apparently took a pre-existing system of barrow graves and sewers and laced them together with a warren of tubes and runnels and bolt-holes and back entries, adding (certainly as an afterthought) a few trains to connect the outlying portions.

Hobbits and all their furry self-satisfied precursors have had a hand or hairy foot here, of course, but the grand design can only be the work of someone who likes nothing better than simply messing about in moats – our perspicacious friend and architect of all that's most English, the mole.

Or as Topsell calls him (*History of Foure-footed Beasts*, 1608) 'The Mole or Want'. (So what we call a little gentleman in black velvet, country folk think of as a long felt want.) Topsell quotes Isaiah, as translated by Munster: '*In that day shall a man cast away his goods of silver and gold into the holes of Moles and Bats . . . By S. Jerom it is translated thus A man shall cast away his Idols to worship Moles and Bats*'. It is a superstitious conceit that 'if you whet a mowing sythe in a field or meddow upon the feast day of Christ's Nativity (commonly called Christmas Day) all the moles that are within the hearing thereof, will certainly for ever forsake that field, meddow, or garden;' and pagan to believe what 'all the ancient Wise men and Magicians did hold, that this beast was capeable of Religion . . . a whole town in Thessaly was undermined by them. Almighty God endoweth them with skill to defend and wisely to provide for their own safety, but also planteth in them such a natural and mutual love to one another; moreover at every small step or noise or almost breathing, they are terrified and run away and therefore (*Pliny saith*) they understand all speeches spoken of themselves'.

Altogether a fine beast, and deserving a place as our national symbol. Away with your Lion, away with your Unicorn, the Royal arms have new supporters now; sharp of snout, blunt of sight, blunt of claw, *two moles sable, fossant* the Jubilee line.

☆ *24.12.82*

I must not confuse Andhra Pradesh and Kerala, as Mr Guptara (Letters, October 10) courteously points out. It was a mere slip of the cortex on my part, for I had a linguistic atlas in front of me when I wrote and was indeed on the point of making a knowing pun about Cochin and its suburb Mattancheri ('Bonjour, Cochon', something along those lines) when wiser counsels prevailed. By way of penance I have been studying Tamil. It is true that Tamil is not spoken in either Andhra Pradesh or Kerala, but my only source for a Malayalam grammar is rather dismissive, describing it condescendingly as 'sanskritized Tamil with the personal terminations dropped', though it admits that 'remains of them are said to be found among the Moplahs of South Canara'. (There's a divinity that shapes our personal terminations, rough-hew them how we will, and the Moplahs, I discover, are Malabari Muslims; readers of John Buchan may recall the Bright Young Things disparagingly called Moplahs in *Three Hostages*, though, it transpired, they had sterling qualities of character under their strident exteriors.) This was discouraging enough, and still more discouraging was the specimen – parable of the Prodigal Son – with a literal back translation: 'But this thy brother dead-man had-become, again revived; not-seeing goer had-become, seeing-reaching-being-because we having-been-merry to-feast-wanted-being-is-it-not? is'.

So I am postponing Malayalam until the arrival of the long-awaited volume in the Teach Yourself series, by Professor Ramakrishna Margolo of Cochin U. The provisional title is *Ram. Margolo's Malayalam solo Grammar* (Palindrome Press 6.89).

I didn't get on much better with Telugu, or Teloogoo, as my Victorian authority prettily calls it, though it is one of the specimens dissected by Thomas Prendergast (formerly of Madras) in his *Mastery of Languages or the Art of speaking Foreign Tongues Idiomatically*. His chief dogmas are: Don't Go Abroad, Don't Read Grammars, 'avoid seeing or hearing one word in excess of those which you are actually engaged in committing to memory'. Children don't use grammars, Prendergast reasonably observes, and illustrates Telugu, without straining the reader's memory, by the reasonable but plainly mad device of attaching Telugu endings to Latin words. (Tu misina librum non vidi.) He then offers three everyday sentences, one of which is 'Tell the horsekeeper to take away my horse to the stable, because by your carelessness I have been prevented from going out to ride this morning.' The words are all numbered and a handsome chart ('the labyrinth diagram exhibiting the evolution of sentences') shows how very many sentences, many of them fresh and meaningful, you can make, *simply by shifting the words about.*

'A palaeoChomskian generative deep grammar!' I hear you cry? Indeed, and in an appendix Prendergast speaks of his friend Mr Long, who has made 'a machine of singularly ingenious construction': an apparatus which when turned on its axis exhibits an 'endless succession of the variations of four sentences each of twenty-one words'. Not content with this Laputan computer, Long loads his machine with musical phrases and invents the first synthesizer, a sort of Ur-Moog.

That left Tamil, and passing over a book gnomically called *Inge*

Va or the Sinna Durai's Pocket Tamil Guide ('go to the river bank and cut three hundred bushels of mana grass') I came with relief on the genial Mr Jegtheesh, author of *Tamil in thirty days though English*. Mr Jegtheesh explains that he didn't really mean to write the book at all, gives some not very helpful pronunciation hints ('ae as in elephant'), and then races to the list of everyday words: water, fruit, must, tank, thief, pial, army ... pial? look it up in the Tamil-English section, yes: a pial or elevated veranda. Jegtheesh's list of birds and beasts is calculated to sow confusion (*cheval* a cock, *koku* a crane, *poule* a tiger), but his fruit are engaging: mango, grapes, fig, quava, melan poma-granite, wood-apple, pumple.

Pumple is the English for *puppallemaasa*, which excited me, but the *OED* is very scathing about people who imagine that this is the local word for grapefruit, rather than a South Indian corruption of Dutch *pompelmoes*, of which the first half probably means pumpkin, while the second half is the Dutch transcription of the Old Javanese distortion of the Portuguese version of 'lemon' (but you probably knew that). So pumpkin-lemon becomes pompel- (or pumple- or pample-) moose or moss, or moes or mus or mouse, 'which our sailors commonly call pumblenose' to say nothing of pummelnose and pimplenose, which have clearly gone far abeam. (And 'grapefruit' is almost too recent to get into the main *OED* at all, scraping in as a curious American way of saying 'forbidden fruit', or of course, pampelmouse.) Meanwhile back at *Tamil in thirty days*, we are put through some brisk imperative exercises: Put the Flower; Give the Pen; Close the Eye; Help the Poor; Shew a Shirt; enough, with the next lesson on sentence structure (the stars twinkle; the sea water is saline) to generate a wide variety of simple poems.

In the conversational section ('learn these sentences, even if you get them by heart. Then you can go round Tamil Nad talking to the people') we get guidance in etiquette as well. Will you share the lunch with me? Here is Iddli, take them. Iddli is specialized food item in Tamil Nadu. We Americans know the high culture of Tamil Nadu. What luggages have you? There are two suitcases and one bed. I am glad you take much interest in Tamil Language though you are a foreigner.

Said foreigner, knowing what is good for him, does not stint the praise: 'O What a beautiful Beach. A Magnificent building. I have heard of the fame of this University.' At Mahabalipuram he lays it on a little thick: 'Yonder. I see an elephant. How did it come here? It is not a true elephant, it is a monolithic sculpture. My eyes deceived me, the deftness of the hands of the sculptor is something marvellous. My eyes are drinking deep in their beauty.' Consistent flattery gets the tourist invited home ('My wife is a graduate. She is an adept in Cookery also.' 'You are a fortunate man'), where he surpasses himself. 'What is your opinion about the Tamilians?' 'The civilization of the Tamilians will not die as long as the world exists.'

And now it's time for revision of the hundred most important words ('loudly', suggests Mr Jegtheesh). So I'm wandering the streets in a Coromandel dream, shouting Cheetha Patha, Valeppu, Thalavale (Dysentery, Fit, Headache); Marrpohr, EE, Muthalalle (Wrestling, Fly, Capitalist); Alle, Challe, Kolllu (Lily, Phlegm, Horsegram . . .).

Scouring obscure shelves for Tamil Grammars was a profitable exercise, for it brought me a refreshing sight of one of my favourite reciters, P. Hately Waddell's *The Psalms frae Hebrew intil Scottis* (Edinburgh 1882): 'The Lord is my herd, nae want sal fa' me; he louts me til lie amang green howes, he airts me atowre by the lown watirs . . . Na! tho I gang thro the dead-mirk dail; e'en thar sal I dread nae skaithin . . .'

I also stumbled over *Rubajatet e Omar Khajam-it*, a translation of FitzGerald into Albanian, by Rushit Bilbil Gramshi. M. Gramshi (or perhaps M. Rushit) preserves the FitzGerald rhythms (which would no doubt be recognizable in Martian or in Betelguese); there are guessable notes ('Omar Khajami cfaqet krejt Hedonist') and wonderful exclamations like Ngrehu! or Zgjohu! I thought I'd sold it long ago and whenever Khayammists approached me and asked for anything, no matter how obscure, I'd say casually (as booksellers will, it's surprising how few are murdered): 'I've just sold the Albanian translation, I bet you'ld have like that.' Now that I've found it, of course they will complain that it is the wrong dialect, Gheg when they only collect Tosk, or Tosk when all they are after is Gheg.

☆ *18.2.83*

I swear I am not and never have been a member of any organization devoted to the subversion of meaning and order and their replacement by palindromic anomie. I have here a list of 155 members of ICTEPETCI, the International Conspiracy To Encourage Palindromes Everywhere Through Continuous Iteration, and its front organization WORDROW, Wielders of Reversible Dicephalic Reflexive Omnidirectional Words. Among the ringleaders, if that is the right word, is Paul L. Kebabian, PhD, whose book *Letter-*

square Palindromes (21pp. $3.50) has just reached me from the Abababba Press, 308 N. Bradford Street, Dover, Delaware (funny, I thought they were in Oihio or Alabamabala).

SATOR AREPO TENET OPERA ROTAS, remarks Dr Kebabian, who knows the value of a strong opening, and observes that although 'Arepo' doesn't mean anything, the form is elegant and until now the English language has lacked lettersquares. 'This need', says Dr Kebabian, 'has now been met.' (This what, Dr Kebabian? This need? Doctor of what precisely?)

The need has been met in a fairly elementary fashion. Any combinations of letters of the form abcdcb will yield a lettersquare (but you knew that already), so it is merely necessary to make sense of what is produced. Thus XMASAM yields

```
X M A S A
M X M A S
A M X M A
S A M X M
A S A M X
```

which he interprets as a message from Santa Claus ('Xmas Am') signed X. You will now be ready for

```
M A R A F
A N O N A
R O T O R
A N O N A
F A R A M
```

which he construes as 'Mar a fan on a rotor. Anon far am'. Wild onagers (or tanagers or dowagers or teenagers) would not induce me to repeat the little historiette which Kebabian posits to set this phrase in its context, nor to tell you about the one that begins 'Mid ad I Maya, dad'.

Kebabian's are mostly of the masculine poor type where words and lines do not coincide: English versions of the full feminine rich form are restricted by needing 'rotor' or 'radar' or 'level' or 'madam' or indeed 'tenet' as the middle term. I shyly proffer:

```
R E M I T
P A R T S
R A D A R
S T R A P
T I M E R
```

which makes an approximation to sense, and I recommend to other obsessives selim/miles, and repot/toper. But shouldn't this whole thing be stamped out now?

☆   7.12.84

In moods of profound depression and inadequacy I cheer myself with the reflection that I can always get a job as a compositor with Mistic Products of San Juan, Puerto Rico.

I've no experience of the printing industry, it is true, but I think that still puts me slightly ahead of the present team at 2463 King Edward Blvd, San Juan, or, as they put it on one of their less successful days, 2463 Kin Edwart Vizd.

Mistic Products of San Juan are in a business that may be unfamiliar to the closeted, rationalist readers of this column. They are one of a number of specialist enterprises that put up unidentifiable powders in small packets with interesting graphics, with instructions as to how to get the best results in the way of suppressing gout or guilt or gangrene, winning lotteries, favours, eternal life, stuff like that. These circulate in market places and *botanas* throughout Central America, and uptown Manhattan.

Packet One (red scythe and sickle surrounding skull, red fist with decisive thumbs-down gesture) contains 'Polvos Legitimos de "La Guadaña Juzgadora",' which they translate, accurately for all I can tell, as 'Genuine Powder of the Judeing Scythe'. 'Blow it any way the air is blowing', they recommend, 'saying; just like I disalve and blow this Powder of the Judeing Scythe, go away from my presence every man or woman that in any are my enemies.'

So far so good: no doubt the more sensitive men or women that in any are your enemies will take a powder if urged so pointedly; but on more intimate matters, I have to say that Mistic Products loses its typographic head entirely. This is how they translate Packet Two, 'Legitimo Polvo "Yo domino a mi hombre" ', with a sturdy lady in a *fin-de-siècle* chemise and black stockings, stomping a muscular but supine chappie who seems to be trying to guide her right foot up his left nostril:

GENUIENE POWER
I COMAN MI MAN Putt this powder on your bady yo Will coma dy our men he will almays be your lover obediente and satifled nothing *w*ell ever hin *aw*ay MISTIC PRODUCTS.

☆   15.2.85

I am intrigued, you are absorbed, he is obsessed. He is Andrew Belsey of the Department of Philosophy, University College, Cardiff, author of *A Short Treatise on the Art of the Palindrome*, and copies can no doubt be obtained from him except that if I read the limitation correctly as eleven copies they probably can't though perhaps he can be persuaded to print another fifty-eight or one hundred and seventy copies to keep the total palindromic.

I would be churlish indeed not to salute Mr Belsey, who kindly recognizes my own feeble essays in reversibility: but he has taken the subject light-years beyond what I might aspire to. Palindromic theory: genuine palindromes, perfect palindromes, genuine imperfect palindromes (NIL LEWD I DID LIVE, EVIL DID I DWELL IN NY LLEWELLYN). Genuineness, in the Belsey terminology, means the symmetry of punctuation and diacriticals; perfection means the symmetry of word length (which makes, of course, for strange robotic cadences). It follows that there must be some happy tongues, including, obviously Chinese (but I would be glad to be proved wrong) in which palindromes are inconceivable. Belsey then considers palindromic cores (ON NO, TENET, EMIT TIME) pairs and semi-pairs (AMORAL AROMA) and the theory of palindromic squares and grids, which make his pages beautiful but obscure. There are a number of end-stopped fifth order magic squares, but none in English word perfect, terms which I could not bear to explain: DEPOT EMU, HO! is how one begins.

There are many pages of examples; reading them one dreams about the mad land of Palindromia (Capital: Dragograd; population 80008) where Wagga Wagga nestles under Ararat, where lamas tend llamas, where they munch on reed deer and sup regal lager, where they build spools and sloops and rotors out of gnu dung and other set animal laminates, where the economy is warped by golfers who reflog deeds . . . which is the last straw, or rather the last straw-and-non-dna-warts. . . .

I have been thinking about the classiest classical palindromic square, SATOR AREPO TENET OPERA ROTAS, which has beauty, symmetry and indeed everything except meaning. It occurred to me that if you were to write the square in a circle and repunctuate (the idea has been ridiculed, I must say, by some of the most eminent classicists in the land) you might get SAT. ORARE. (Enough of prayer!) POTENET OPE, RARO TASSA (Let him persist in the work, by the rare chalice . . .). The theological and historical significance of this will escape nobody,* and that dictionaries fail to record the verb *potenare* simply shows how extensive the conspiracy must be.

But Belsey, for all his scholarship, fails to quote the ur-palin-

---

* There was a man who had a cosmo-conspiracy theory about chalices, grails, and secret brotherhoods.

dromes of the Thracian satirist Sotades ('noted for coarseness and scurrility', *OED*, thrown into the sea by Ptolemy Philadelphus) (that's Ptolemy Philadelphus 285 BC–247 BC, a fine bibliophile but – like so many fine bibliophiles, alas – 'his private life and relations do not exhibit his character in as favourable a light as we might have inferred from the splendour of his administration', Smith's *Classical Dictionary*). 'Sotadic', indeed, may serve as a synonym for 'palindromic', ('Sotadicall verses: that is verses backwards and forwards' John Healey, 1610); when, that is, it does not mean 'catalectic tetrameter composed of Ionics *a maiore*' or 'coarse and scurrilous'. A Victorian sexologer, Burton perhaps, published maps charting the Sotadic Zone, the regions (carefully cross-hatched) of erotic irregularity, a sort of homophile tropic or isogay.

Sotadics, and much else, are to be found in Tony Augarde's rich but rational *Oxford Guide to Word Games* (240 pp. Oxford £6.95) which is readable, recherché and literate: well, Augarde is an Oxford lexicographer; but the topics invite extravagance. He covers the more obvious – spoonerisms, puns, limericks, lipograms and rhopalics (we label 'rhopalic' utterances exfoliating polysyllabic sesquipedalianisms); and also hangman, concrete poetry, rebus (rebi? rebusim?) chronograms (My Date aCCurate, Cogent, eXaCtLy eXpressed VeXes no one) and Scrabble, though there he fails to give full credit to the achievements of the astounding W. Poole, Esq, recorded in the *TLS* in 9 December 1977. (So also does Gyles Brandreth, whose *Scrabble Omnibus* (222pp. Collins Willow £8.95) is almost everything a scrabble omnibus should be.)

But back to Sotades.

> Roma, tibi subito motibus ibit amor,
> Si bene te tua laus taxat, sua laute tenebis,
> Solo medere pede, ede, perede melos

may not be perfect, in Belsey's terminology, but is none the less impressive for the third century BC – apart from being in Latin, a common failing of the time. Nearly 1,900 years later, English took its first tentative step backwards, with John Taylor (*Nipping or Snipping of Abuses*, 1614) offering 'Lewd did I live & evil I did dwel', blushlessly employing an ampersand as a hinge and proposing: 'This line is the same backward as it is forward, and I will give any man five shillings apiece for as many as they can make in English'.

Palindromes at 25p a time should be carefully wrapped and sent to The Water Poet (1580–1653); c/o St Martin-in-the-Fields, Trafalgar Square, London, and not to *The Times Literary Supplement*.

☆ *31.3.85*

Top of my late-1980s agenda, my agendissima: THE WAY FORWARD IS NOT THE WAY BACK. STOP THINKING PALINDROMICALLY.

Fact is, I never have thought what you might call progressively about them, and my creations only work with lots of elision, stammering, nonce-spellings, abbreviations, and the proper names of people like T. L. Ufficid. Forty minutes' hard rumination only produced LOOK! O SO KOOL! which has a sort of Janet-and-John naivety, though of course in Palindromia children learn to read with Otto 'n' Anna. That's a special category, a palindrome of palindromes, a dual palindrome, say ... AH! A DUAL P ... PALINDROME! MOR'?: D—N! I'L APPLAUD, AHA. I'm afraid that's about my level, I mean my LEVEL.

But I have a lot of news for you. Did I say there were no Chinese palindromes? There are, of course, and letters from all over tell me so. Dr Sarah Hart of Paris has a thesis, at least a chapter of a thesis, about them. They are ancient and elegant and some are shaped like lattices and springs and wreaths and mazes and water buffalo. And Professor Sansone of Illinois, apart from courteously pointing out my tendency to confuse Latin and Greek, marshals evidence against Sotades, I mean against Sotades having written palindromes. What he wrote were sotadics, catalectic tetrameters frequently on indecent themes, in a metre that lent itself to various kinds of playfulness. It was other sotadics, later and in a different language, who thought it would be fun to make them go backwards. When the Greeks did get round to reversification, in Byzantium, they spoke of *karkinoi* or crabs.

And Hutchinsons have sent me LID OFF A DAFFODIL, an amphisbaenic book with reversible pictures, and each page stuffed with palindromic phrases. At first I feared it was actually a palindromic book, defying all the laws of entropy, that would tell one life history one way, and the other would tell how Mom had one day undied (passed back, sold the farm, been kicked by the bucket), got up off her sickbed, growing younger and watching her children ... 'Don't you know that Time's arrow has only one point?' I wanted to ask the author, John Pool. LOOPY POOL we used to call him in the Retroscriptic and Exotic Speech Training Unit at Locksley Hall College of Uttoxeter U. (That's UTTOXETER (LOC. COL.) RET. EXOT. T. U.)

Next week Pasitropisms, which read forwards, backwards and upside down, and are ideal for saying no to the son of Ixion in a blend of Greek and middle low Spanish. With inverted queries and exclamations too! FUN ENUF, you may think.

☆   1.4.88

J'accuse by Emile Zola,
Emile Zola by Jack Hughes.

This pair have haunted me for years and I have wandered the earth looking for others of the clan, like some mad haunted Gothic monsterfancier; and I have only come up with
Morgan Forced Her by Howard Zend
Up, Dyke by The Witches of Eastwick Collective.

And I will go to any lengths to find a suitable context for this pun also:
   'Me and my friend 'ave learned Portuguese so we can get jobs as barmaids in Madeira.'
   'Yes, or Azores'.
   'Ooh, cheeky!'

☆   26.7.85

There's no longer any possible doubt: the friends of INTERPAL are after me, led by Otto Evil, Live Otto Evil that is. Their mysterious graffiti ('Radar Boob!', 'Dud Nun', 'Sanatas e morte: retro me, Satanas') appear on hoardings around me, scrawled in the dust of Tube-train windows, muttered over the intercoms of taxis I do not recall hailing. And by every post, it seems, I get notification of more and more outlandish achievements. Every time I say I'm going off palindromes, there is a universal shout of Oho or Aha or Heiotohotoieh. First there came, anonymously and by a circuitous path, a play script. Only about eighty words of actual speech, but pages of stage directions, justification and critical apparatus. The truly dreadful thing about palindromes is that you know how they are going to end: 'In my beginning is my end' as T. Eliot, top poet, did not mean to say in *Not Ron, T. N. Rub*. So the moment the curtains rise and a character called THEOLOGIAN observes 'Drat such a stressed dog!', you know, with a profound and horrible surety, that sooner or later, after several pages of tense dialectic ('Sin is Bad' remarks the theologian), with entropic ineluctibility, someone is going to say 'God! Desserts . . . ah, custard . . .' as the curtain falls.

Then there came a brief billet-doux from a man in Philadelphia with a natty line in Hebrew Word-Squares ('the bee found in the honey must be set afire and burnt', unusually lucid for the genre), and then a letter from a person signing as Tohu W. Bohu, which I have reason to believe is an assumed name. Ms Bohu is, alas, one of an increasing number of correspondents I cannot correspond with, as they follow the North American etiquette of only giving the address on the envelope, and I follow the British custom of opening my mail at the breakfast table and throwing the envelopes away with the kipperskins and fermenting marmalade. As I also follow the British custom of then doing nothing about my mail for at least a week, the address is by then trash-compacted or recycled. T. W. Bohu quotes at length from Page's *Further Greek Epigrams*, telling me fascinating stuff about the palindromic epigrams of Nicodemus of Heraclea, the isopsephic ones of Leonides of Alexandria, and the lipogramic *Iliad* of Nestor of Laranda, composed so that Book 1 is alpha-less, Book 2 beta-free, Book 3 gamma-deficient, Book 4 has zero delta-content and so on. The cream of the jest, the cream of the nut of the jest, the jest nut cream, is that the Greek for one, two, three and four, is alpha, beta, gamma, delta; so Book Gamma is agammic, Book Delta is disdelta'ed, Book Epsilon is Epsilon Minus (after Epsilon it gets too complicated to go into).

☆ 2.8.85

Worse was to come. Worse came. Worse was *Satire, Veritas* by David L. Stephens of North Carolina, published by Word Ways (Monograph Series 1, 1980, n.p. but California), and sent to me by the obliging David Sachs. *Satire, Veritas*, if Mr Stephens can be trusted, and who would doubt it, is a palindrome of 58,795 letters. It will be sufficient to quote from the non-palindromic, explanatory, justificatory preface:

> These lines were found on the desk of Giles Selig Hales, the young editor of an avant-garde literary journal, ready for mailing to his friend Eton Harrison. The letter purports to be a sample of manuscripts from his desk . . . some of the writers are, apparently, not quite sane, and some are assuredly, at least drunk . . . Eva, Giles' frenetic and bibulous friend, writes obscure verse, conducts interviews with deceased (?) celebrities, and is obsessed with the idea that dogs are taking over the world . . .

The preface also contains an indelicate medical note about the disease of *koro* or *shook young* (a curious condition of what might be described as extreme if local reticence which affects Asian males, and with which William Burroughs, Snr, has also been much preoccupied). Given all this, you will not be surprised to learn the text begins

> Sir, I stratified a mix, I made notes, mots to Ms, Eton. Giles Selig Hales' Saga. Ecce Homo, Saib Eton. On hubris asleep . . .

No more please. Things are getting worse. Yesterday I bought a manuscript nineteenth-century jotting-book, and a slip of paper fell out: it contained a musical palindrome, an invertible canon. And I have just read the astrophysical trend-theory that the Big Bang is winding down not to the heat-death of the universe, which I was quite looking forward to, but to a superdense black hole engulfing galaxies, which will implode in one great eructation that sends time spinning backwards and the scattered atoms back to GNAB GIB. Life is a palindrome, my friend, and I, ma, am I in the middle.

☆ *15.3.85*

'Hey, I have something from this same guy's library', remarked a well-endowed Manhattan bookperson to me recently, pointing to an eighteenth-century Book of Common Prayer in red, rubbed morocco, with the Divine monogram inlaid on the upper cover, 'I.H.S., have you any idea who he was?'

I played the perfect Englishman. 'Yes, I do know, but I'm not claiming, actually, that it's His own copy.'

I've had this terrific insight into the genesis of the picaresque-travels-in-USA genre, the English pilgrimage to the Occident. Travelling from the Old World to the New (that's east to west, deasil, sunwise; the opposite direction from west to east or widdershins, the way we go when we return from Phoenix to Farringdon Road), we are going laggingly (unless we are very rich) with the sun, thereby outMarvelling Marvell: though we cannot make our sun stand still yet we can make him run more slowly. The effect of which is an increase in subjective day-length (except for fly-by-nights), eight hours to California, five to the Big Apple. And the effect of an increase in day length, an endocrinologist might tell you, is to kid the hormones into believing (melatonin does the trick) that it's spring, suddenly, with all that that entails. So the moment he steps off his big-bodied jet – how alluring the words sound now – at JFK or SFO or LAX, a young man's fancy and so's a young woman, and old birds see the world through a livelier iris. This of course only affects the carnally-minded and would not be expected to influence academics, bibliophiles, or literary persons.*

Winging angelically over Greenland's icies, I had a double sense of pilgrimage, because I carried in my pocket, and sporadically open on my lap, a copy of *Itinerarius Terrae Sanctae* by Bartholomaeus de Saligniaco (Lyons, 1525), ready at the drop of a comment to translate with spontaneous fluency certain carefully prepared passages to anyone fool enough to come within range. (I always have the hope that someone will lean over and say 'That looks extraordinarily interesting. I don't suppose you would know where I could – ah, *purchase* a copy?')

It lists the vaut-le-voyage sights of Venice, Rhodes and of course Jerusalem, with plenty of magic wells and flying fish and warnings against incredulity ('non mox nasum suspendas') on the part of those who haven't been anywhere and don't believe that cabbages grow anywhere but in their mother's gardens ('credens nuspiam nisi in horto materno Brassicam crescere' – can I have got this right?) Some cabbage-headedness is certainly provoked by a story about the canine sentries at the Castle of St Peter in Rhodes, who patrol the ways by night, sniffing out infidels, whom they promptly chomp ('moxque dilacerant'), while snuffling approvingly at Christians whom they caressingly conduct wherever they wish to go – 'a beautiful and irrefutable argument for the truth of the Christian faith'. Bart and his friends took three months and a lot of travail, tempest and general discomfort to get within sight of the Promised Land, at which point an understandable clamour broke out aboard; 'groans, sighs, tears, shouting, psalm-singing like crazy' (velut amens). And here are we, many thousands every day, floating over places where twenty years ago only a few explorers and unlucky Eskimo had trod, so blasé that we need to be entertained by tapes of brainstorming sessions on management problems and opportunities or the best of Norman Wisdom. (Didn't he write the *Ancrene Wisse*?) Most amazingly, this costs about two weeks of a mean industrial wage: say about a shilling of a craftsman's money by the standards of 1525. And nobody sang

---

* HRIW: Melatonin is now blamed for jetlag and injudicious decisions by planet-hopping politicians.

gaudetes when we landed (well I was going to, but there was this immigration person looking at me . . .).

It was quite an incident-full trip apart from that, what with a potentially damaging brush against a CHiP – no micro-chip he, but an oversized California Highway Patrolster with a laid-back voice and a bulging holster ('just git over har boy') while his partner covered us with enough lethal hardware to produce a mild case of fear-and-loathing-in-Vegas paranoia (we were headed that way) in two only moderately gonzo British bookmen ('what if he finds my stash of appetite suppressants?'); what with a rich encounter with the notorious Berkeley Ethnopharmacological Circle and its beauteous and learned chieftainess, who told me amazing things about the role of toadstools, tadpoles and stingray spines in Mesoamerica, and under which step of the pyramid of Teotihuacan to hunt for the lost codices of the Aztecs (but I am sworn to silence); what with a date with a Date in Indio and two brutally disappointing blind dates with nostalgia.

It was Writers' Week at the University of California, Riverside, and though I'd missed Maxine Hong Kingston launching an archaeological campaign for the start of the Year of the Ox at the site of Chinatown, I was in time for Ken Kesey. 'An evening with Ken Kesey' said the signs, and there was a glass of stale Kool-Aid perched as if by accident on the noticeboard. The evening was anything but electric. 'The largest and ruliest crowd of the week' applauded delightedly when Kesey came on in a Tom Wolfe suit and hat, and read a published piece from a shortly-to-be-published novel, *Demon's Box*, that tells the Sixties Like They Was. The episode described a delegation of California freaks on an embassy to Swinging London, and the famous party at Apple Corps where John Lennon (described throughout in the reverential tone most of us reserve for Jesus or Kim Il-Sung) stopped, by sheer magnetism, a brawl between Yanks and Limeys (not my phraseology). There were gloomy comparisons with the present day (punks don't have the fun that freaks did) and an elegiac refrain that turned to Villon in my head:

> Semblablement, où est Janis, où Mamma
> Cass, où Brautigan?
> But where is the snow of yesteryear?

Occasional shafts of understatement pierced the elderly murk, but when an ex-Prankster ('O Jesus the times we have seen') complains of the spongers, boors and crazies who bother him in his rural retreat, and talks of freedom, 'including the freedom not to take Welfare' it gets clearer than ever that mind-changing drugs never changed anything, least of all anybody's mind.

After the reading there was some unplanned street theatre, when a local CND group staged an updated mummer's play on the steps. (The rough Middle English rhymes were nicely transposed: 'with my moxie/I can cure apoplexy', boasted the Doctor, but in vain: the moral was that the dead stay dead.) The performance encountered some opposition: 'They are fucking up my schedule for the Chancellor's Meet-a-Writer Reception', someone behind me mourned, 'Why don't we call the cops?'

I had a much better time at the Indio Date Festival ('the only comparable event is the Arabian Nights Festival at Opa-Locka, Fla') which celebrates the $30 million agri-industry with Queen Scheherazade and her attendant Princesses Danielle Smit and Manjit McKinzie ('she'll autograph anything you want . . . she's just as nice a girl as you can imagine'), with a midway and freaks (a letdown, mainly, except for Fat Peggy – 'takes four men to hug her and a box car to lug her') and foot-juggling and ostrich races ('can't fly a bit but those suckers can jump six feet') and camel stampedes, where the unfortunate if sporting girl from the Orange Julius concession, unstirruped, un-hard-hatted, was promptly unhorsed or rather disencamelled to sympathetic groans.

I spent a day – not a Sweet Thursday but a sour Sunday, at Cannery Row. Cannery Row, I have to report, is no longer a poem, a stink, a grating noise, a quality of light, a tone . . . It is a bright-painted, rehabilitated, fun-consumption, upwardly-mobile, odourless and well-lubricated grave. Those stories that were so delicate that they have to be left to crawl on to the page: they have been bashed by economics and battered by progress and blasted with dollars and they are gone.
 I'd better explain how it was between me and Cannery Row.
 Me and Cannery Row were like *that*. (That's me, yearning from five thousand miles away.) *Cannery Row* (a paperback, a poem, a nostalgia, a habit, a dream) travelled everywhere in my blazer pocket, along with *Hassan* and *The Thirty Nine Steps*. A shrewd (and probably cynical) English teacher, blessed be his name, had recommended it, and, smothering a sense of disloyalty at liking

anything approved by authority, I fell for it hook, line, and can-opener. I was going to be a marine zoologist, a poet, a drunk, a Californian, a bum. We sat around in places (mostly waiting for girls who didn't turn up) and took turns reading it aloud. (I'll tell you about reading *Hassan* aloud sometime when I'm feeling less shy.) We thought of Steinbeck as this terrifically tough, unsentimental writer, like Hemingway. (We thought of Hemingway as tough and unsentimental.) That was where we wanted to be, collecting with dreamy zeal the curious creatures of the tide-pools, getting drunk, laid, into fights (perhaps we could avoid fights).

I very nearly became a marine zoologist but that's as far as it went. The canneries closed (they were already closing by the time I started reading *Cannery Row*), the sardines and the people went away, and somehow I never got to Monterey: the car crashed, the road was closed, the Queen was visiting, some such thing. So this year I made it, thirty years too late, and I wish I hadn't. There are rusting boilers, but only in the Cannery Row Memorial Park: otherwise it's all designer kites and four hundred and eleven flavours of fudge, fine dining in sea-food eateries that wouldn't be seen dead with a sardine, and fun drinks in Pepita's (once La Ida) and the Ole Doc Ricketts Lab Saloon. There are arcades and markets and a Steinbeck Memorial Room and depression glass at non-depression prices: if Bartholomaeus was disappointed with Jerusalem he doesn't admit it.

But all is not utterly lost; above the rocks by Western Biological, where I planned to collect anemones and tunicates, one of the canneries has been turned into simply the best marine aquarium I have ever seen. Technology developed for displaying sharks and killer whales is here used to show the far more romantic lives of seaweed and invertebrates. A sixty-foot tank contains a forest of giant kelp standing as tall as oaktrees; anemones the size of gorse bushes, chambered Nautilus, for once an animal and not an ash tray: and there is even a touch pool where I was allowed to handle (we all have secret pleasures) chitons and sea cucumbers. (I've had this deep relationship with sea-cucumbers since I was adolescing; what it feels like is a small semi-rigid dirigible about half-full of sago. To me it was a creature from an old dream, and almost reconciled me to the absence of the stink, the grating noise, the quality of light.)

Don't sneer, you lot, sitting in Dartmouth Park or Ladbroke Grove, dreaming of Kathy Acker and the East Village. By the time you get there, in 2020 or thereabouts, it won't be the vision you have now.

☆   15.2.85

I have seen the future of fiction, and its name is Mud. That's MUD. M.U.D., the Multi-User-Dungeon, is state-of-the-art compu-fantasy, and arguably the most important development in narrative technique since the stream of consciousness was dammed to turn the hydroelectric wheels of literary industry (see my forthcoming *No Beavers on the Liffey*, where this metaphor will be developed at nauseating length).

A Dungeon is the locale, or at least the locus, in which one-to-many players, each guiding one-to-many characters, act out quests, run mazes, engage in combat or commerce, encounter benign or maleficent creatures, realistic or fantastic, the rules being elaborated during play, the game having no discernible winning-post or time-limit, the whole supervised by a non-playing bardic umpire, the Dungeon-Master, and the outcome of the various battles and meetings determined by the fall of dice (to complicate matters, the experts prefer seventeen-sided ones). The original and type version of the game (I imagine all of this is news to three readers in Sikkim) is Dungeons-and-Dragons, invented by someone who may or may not be named Gerry Gyax, but the same principles may be applied to space-opera, cops-and-robbers, cowboys-and-Indians, entomologists-and-butterflies, or even novelists-and-nymphets. A precursor is the programmed, interactive, semi-aleatory, multiple-choice story-book: 'If you decide to sleep with the pharmacist, turn to page 88; if not, return to Charles Bovary, page 63.' 'If you decide not to throw yourself under the train, return to page 1 and start again.' 'Your signals are spotted by a passing Dutch merchantman, which rescues you, thereby aborting what would have been a very educational and allegorical experience for a group of young British lads.' Other forerunners are the panto, the audience-participation game, the People's Movement for Democratic Drama (HE'S BEHIND YOU! OPEN THE BOX! AGAINST STRANGLING DESDEMONA: 68%).

For those who find the rolling of dice too physically demanding, or for simple technomanes, the whole enterprise can be packaged and fed to a computer, which will then present you with a sequence of situations, and a series of options:

YOU ARE AT A FORK IN THE PATH IN A GHOUL-
HAUNTED WOODLAND
ONE PATH LEADS TO AN ELF-RIDDEN SWAMP
ONE PATH LEADS TO A DEMON-INFESTED GLADE
YOU HAVE: AN AMULET OF DOUBTFUL EFFICACITY
SOME ARROWS OF DESIRE
A PHILLIPS-HEAD SCREWDRIVER

Literary Dungeons are also available, or if not available, at least imaginable.

YOU ARE STANDING AT THE TOP OF A MARTELLO
TOWER
A STAIRCASE LEADS DOWN
INVENTORY: 1 SHAVING BOWL
1 FEARFUL JESUIT

The repertory of things that you can do is limited by the machine's capacity. GO E, GO W, GO UP, GET, DROP, FIGHT, SLAY, ENCHANT, that sort of thing. The more parochial machines get quite pompous if you transgress their petty boundaries: CAN'T GO THAT WAY, DON'T UNDERSTAND THE WORD 'LEVITATE', THERE ISN'T A 'STUFFED' HERE SO I CAN'T GET IT.

But MUD has done away with this fancy-cramping narrowness of mind. Instead of the pitiful 16 or 128 K of your private memory, you can now, for the cost of a telephone call, log into some gigantic mainframe somewhere which has the capacity to create a playing space the size of Essex, and to manipulate as many players as choose to join in. You will come across these other participants during the course of the game. There is no way of telling (don't blame me, blame a chap called Turing) whether the other characters are 'real' persons, or simulacra controlled by the machine. Except that when one of the other players puts the phone down and goes to lunch, his characters, presumably, disappear from the plot, which must be nerve-wracking for all those other characters whose stories impinge on theirs. The novel which stops while the author has coffee! The ultimately untrustworthy narrator! The confusion of first and second order narration! Calvinist determinism meets Calvinoist indeterminacy. Pirandelloid confusion, Borgesian subtleties. It is the nightmare of *Tron*, Dodgson, Sartre and Milton, the nightmare of being trapped in a subset of the real universe: indeed the basis of all nightmares, including this one.

☆   23.12.83

My local constabulary – or possibly Interpol – are mounting a campaign against shoplifting and kindred seasonal sports, a campaign which features a sort of hairy pear called the 'stealybug'. He lounges in a hammock sipping a julep, resembles one of the more elaborately ciliated animalcules, or the popular image of a fairly benign bacterium, let us say the one responsible for dandruff or Caerphilly cheese. 'Don't let the stealybug take things easy', 'help cop the stealybug', 'let's get the stealybugs out' . . . such is the general tenor of the message.

    Well, well. Those who do not know their history are condemned to repeat it. Anyone of a certain age, or anyone who does know history, will recognize the stealybug as a clone or bud or spore (I'm not sure how these things reproduce) of the Squanderbug, an ill-considered creature of the National Savings Association. Some time in I suppose the late 1940s these beings turned up in schools, I mean in shoals, though they turned up in schools, too, in herds and flocks and mobs, on the back pages of magazines like *Picture Post* and *Razzle*. The Squanderbug looked dirty, sly and jolly, like a favourite Uncle. He slipped into pockets and handbags and purses and scattered coins and notes, which he spent gleefully on all the little indulgences that the British had been denying themselves for years.

    His very name, which was intended to excite fear and loathing, was in fact full of the most enticing overtones. To public school persons (we still had social classes then) bug evoked their favourite pursuits of sodomy and entomology; for the proles he was slummy and cosily unhygienic. His appearance, which was meant to be offensively unshaven, villainous, and with a faint whiff of racial undesirability, suggested instead delightful anarchy and unmilitary nonchalance. He presided over an enormous outburst of heedless extravagance. He was replaced, I think, by the Fritterbug, doubtless on the advice of a consonantal psychologist who had decided that things beginning with 'sq' were cuddly and pneumatic and probably smelt of vanilla, while fricatives suggested rancid cooking fat or pagan culture heroes with undesirable habits (Frithibeog's Saga). The wave of desperate spending (I think sweets had just come off the ration, but I may be conflating) continued, with results that we all know about. The whole campaign was a classic WWII bummer, along with the odious 'Billy Brown of London Town' whose priggish recommendations on Tube trains nearly brought about a collapse of morale in those who had enjoyed the Blitz, or the ineffable 'YOUR courage, YOUR cheerfulness,

YOUR resolution, will bring US Victory', which just about summed up the decade.

Well there you are; Interpol or the Metropolitan Police are condemned to repeat it. Hang on to your handbags. Far more likely to succeed, because it is near everyone's nightmare nerve, is the poster with 'Why are they talking to my mother?' spoken by a forlorn moppet who is being comforted by a woman policeperson. This has already provoked raucous graffiti (fill in the blanks yourself) which shows it must be working.

☆ *14.8.87*

The BBC has an estimable programme called *What the Papers Say* (it seeks to tell you what the papers say), which these days reminds me more and more of Joyce Grenfell awarding prizes at a nursery school art exhibition while resolutely ignoring the fact that the entire schoolroom is disfigured by gigantic obscene and subversive graffiti. They tell you what this paper thinks about the Sunnis and the Shia and what one thinks of constitutional issues in the Philippines and how they are practically unanimous in their concern with M2 money supply figures and you sip your coffee and think my! what a responsible press we do have, our constitutional freedoms are safe in their hands. Meanwhile in the real world two-thirds of the newspaper-buying, the daily-printed-material-buying public subsists, perhaps by choice, on nothing but vicars' knickers and royal romps and loony lesbian moors monster bingo fun. The river of information is pumped and desalinated and facsimilated and satellite-bounced around the world, but high up in the mountains the source is polluted by the same old dripping excrement, the same old dead sheep.

The foreign press, by contrast, has an unerring sense of news values. I have by me – as who does not? – a recent issue of *La Semana al Servicio del Pueblo* (The Weekly Public Servant? A Week's Devotion to the Popular Cause? Seven Days of Doing Good to YOU?) of Tecate, Baja California (where the beer comes from), which leads with a story of universal appeal: 'INHABITANT OF TECATE INJURED BY SHOT AS HE DESCENDS FROM HIS AUTOMOBILE TO URINATE'. The opening paragraph of the story is a model of journalistic explication: who? (José Ramón Uribe Paredes); when? (22.30); where? (corner of Avenida Mexico and 17th Street); no, where? (sorry, in the left arm); additional information, material but also picturesque, enabling reader to identify with subject of story? (to satisfy a physiological need).

The remaining paragraph is succinct. The injured person presented himself to the IVth Sector of the PJE (Simón Abitia Torres, Secretary) to make a report of his own free will. He accepted that he had made a human error but was driven to it by fuertes dolores in the estomago which obliged him to search for a place to ir al baño, notwithstanding (sin embargo) on lowering his pantalones he heard the detonation of a firearm and discovered that blood was running down his arm, because the bullet had struck him.

And there, admirably, without trivial detail, spurious background, vain speculation, or any species of lily-painting (ITS WHOOPS OLE AS JOSE SPENDS PESO) or refinéd-gold-gilding (BATHROOM BANDIDO BRINGS PANIC TO PUEBLO), we leave our hero, with a firm grasp of his stomach, his trousers, his bleeding left arm and the senseless cruelty of the universe.

☆ 9.8.86

So I thought I'd write about Albania again. Had thought of going there, but suspect it would be more fun to let the travelographers do that for me.

I've got two of them working on it. One's a recently rediscovered document, *Travels with Zenobia*, edited by William Holtz (University of Missouri, 1983). Zenobia, I blush to tell you, is the name of the car, and Professor Holtz of U Miss or rather U Mo (as in 'Me Curly, Him Larry, U Mo') has scholarly thoughts about when people stopped giving names to their cars – when they stopped representing horses and mules, more or less. With Zenobia there travelled one Rose Wilder Lane, recently in the *TLS* as author in 1916 of a fictional autobiography of Charlie Chaplin that was stylistically ahead of its time and suppressed by the unamused Chas, just republished by a professor at Indiana U who unfortunately wasn't let in on the joke, and one Helen Dore Boylston, who went on to write *Sue Barton, Student Nurse* (1936), *Sue Barton, Senior Nurse* (1937) and *Sue Barton, Staff Nurse* (1952) to say nothing of *Clara Barton, Founder of the American Red Cross* (1955), a striking example of a prequel. These were typically indomitable Yank ladies of the endless prelapsarian summer days before the fall of 1929, whose hearts were undoubtedly young and who had conceived this strange yen for the land of Skanderbeg, and took terrific risks in the countries of that nice Mr Mussolini ('the whole country surges with hope and pride') and that nice Mr (later King, later Mr) Zogu; they arrived in Durrës with nothing but the clothes they stood up and sat down in, only one decent hat (something mind-bogglingly called a hat-trunk was lost in transit) and – of course – lashings of money.

There is more to be gleaned from Zef Muzi's *Liber Bisedimesh Anglisht-Shqip* ('8 Nëntori' Publishing House, Tirana), which stands ready to talk one through a trip from 'Good Morning! Hallo! Goodday! I have come to the People's Republic of Albania as a member of the Workers' Delegation/Sports Delegation/ Women's Delegation/Cultural Delegation' all the way to 'I hope to find you even better next time with even more advanced industry/ with your agriculture still more modernized and mechanized.' We look at farms ('Can we see a cowshed? It is really nice'), museums ('This is the pistol of the martyr', 'There are the clothes of the People's Hero', 'This is a fascist officer killed by the guerrilla units') beauty spots ('This is the building of the CC of the PLA') and schools: 'It is organized on the basis of three components: lessons, productive labour, physical and military training, all of them run through by the Marxist-Leninist ideology of the People.' We do not however see any churches or mosques. ('Let us go on an excurssion. Shall we go outing. Do you have any churches or mosques? All churches and mosques were closed by the people in 1967'). To compensate for this we go to a bookshop ('Have you the works of Enver Hoxha?') and to a bar ('Let us drink this toast to your leader, Comrade Hoxha'). We are encouraged to ask questions: sensible questions like 'what is the average wheat/maize yield per hectare?' and silly ones like 'It is very tasty. What is it made of?' We ask questions that provoke answers like 'On no account. No way' ('Në asnjë më-nyrë') and others that evoke answers like 'In the 1980 European Shooting Championships Ermira Dingu won first place in the rifle event.' 'Are there any artistic activities?' 'The lecturer is at your disposal for three hours.' We are even given the linguistic tools for a modest but principled protest about conditions: 'I want to make (I have) some complaints. I get no water from my tap. There is no light in my room. The window doesn't shut (doesn't open). The fuses have blown. The tap drips. The toilet won't flush. The WC is clogged up. No, it was very nice indeed.'

It is health problems that make me anxious. We start with some straight naming of parts: faqe, the cheek; bërryl, the elbow; fytyrë, the face – 'mots de son mauvais, corruptible, grosse et impudique' as Kate remarks in the course of a similar anatomy lesson, *Henry V*

Act II. But at the first sign of illness among the visiting delegation, Mazi gets rattled. Strip to the waste and lie there. There is nothing to worry about. Appoplexy. Asthme, diphteria, skin-abrazion, exocoration; contussion of the brain, conjunctivitis, meazles (fruth), tubérculosis, smoll-pox, sun-troke, vertigoe. Stop the machines! switch off (Ndaloi, Ndërprisni!) I'll stay right here.

☆   23–29.9.88

There isn't much future for any blueprint of society that doesn't leave a bit of space for the Spirit of the Market Place (which has as much to do with market forces as Courtly Love has to do with Chastity Belts).

It's a notion that recurs as often as more obviously romantic fantasies, like the happy peasant or the contented craftsman. Science fiction is full of it, that *Kim*-like pageant of the many-hued folk of Empire, cheery bumboat-women with stems of yellow fruit, costly stuffs and rare roots, the eager chaffering parrot-sellers, the dignified, hooded thoat-dealers from desert lands far to the South; so are my dreams. (I don't know about anyone else's, obviously – yes I do.) It is a Liberty-pattern image of mercantile virtue; we've all glimpsed it: the gift of a handful of figs, the man who cut a generous tester of watermelon and showed me how to judge ripeness, the Bulgarian farmer (it was in Toronto, not Plovdiv, but why not) standing shyly between two waist-high black radishes just like the ubiquitous icon of the Master of Animals, or the infant Hercules strangling two serpents . . . insert your own cherished holiday snap.

Here is the market of Neverland, the trim stalls with the fruit of marvellous unknown local varieties, all priced in bulgy baroque numerals, the wooden toys of extraordinary skill and originality, homebrews of surpassing strength, homeknits, homespun, homegrown, homereared, homefried, homecurdledurdled; unboxed, ungraded, freshcaught, dewpicked, unpasteurized, unsophisticated.

Sexy too. The cosy dream is exotic and erotic. For a market is one of those ambiguous spaces, neither private nor public, at once indoors and out, an intimacy without shame; they are all doing it in the same square or souk, under the same arcade of marble or cast-iron: a public agape or gangbuying.

And cheap. That's the core of the fantasy that makes us pay hundreds of pounds in fares in order to save a few bob on gherkins.

It is a consumerist longing: getting one ahead of you lot, and getting it cheaper and fresher. No one has reveries about *running* a cheap vegetable stall in the market at Nuku'alofoa or Diyarbakir. In the dream, we are Just Visiting. When the market becomes routine it might as well be a supermarket.

The worm in the golden apple is the price ticket on the bird of Paradise. All that bargaining is not picturesque but desperate, the wooden toys imply an inadequate industrial manufacturing base, the piles of cheap paw-paws speak of monoculture. In the real world, Second, Third or Fourth, markets are miserable affairs: they sell soap-powders and used medicine bottles and plastic sunglasses and babies' dummies and coffee substitute and milk substitute and tin toys with sharp edges that run off unobtainable battery sizes, transistors shaped like clocks and clocks shaped like transistors, napkins in traditional patterns of extruded polystyrene and endless T-shirts, with hearts as verbs, I (heart) Brobdingnag. I (heart) cultural imperialism; I (heart) pictography. I wonder what the Aztecs would have made of it, with their practical knowledge of the ins and outs of the human heart: could you find in Teotihuacan market place – until the spoilsport Spaniards came with their own marginally more humane death-cult – cotton T-shirts that displayed blood-dripping Tezcatlipoca: 'I (heart) hearts'?

There's a supercharged Gresham's Law round here: plastic drives out wood, the moulded drives out the carved, the T-shirt drives out the sari or the huipil or the sark or kamiza, eeze-squeeze ketchup drives out the handful of dark green aromatic leaves. What's left of local art has lost all locality, leather and brass knick-knackery from the vast Interpeasant factory on the Moon.

And the T-shirtification of language is the market leader, heading the rush to leap over the cliff into the ocean of Pedesperanto, or rather Paleneo. (Paleneo was a design for an international pictographic language invented by the man who wrote the 'Saint' books, and hands up any of you who think I made that bit up. It's Hodder and Stoughton 1972, and now do you promise to believe implicitly any far-fetched thing I tell you?) But Charteris's language was quite elaborate, with signs for 'investment', 'memory' and 'useless' (£ + $ in box, brain-return, square wheel); while the new Interslobbish, Huliganese, Headbutt Pidgin, is a language with about seventeen nouns – symbols representing the seventeen cardinal virtues of Vandalia: lager, flag, tits, heart, suntan, chips, burger, porsche, dosh/bread/roobledooble/loadsa/sponduli, bulldog (beaver, eagle, totemic animal), willy, swastika, hash/acid/ecstasy/glue/meths/ sterno, boot on face. (That's fewer than seventeen and I'm scratching about already.)

You could write the grammar-book entirely in symbols, like Interglossa:

Flag or Totemic sign = I/we/us/ourlot/superior/pure/masterfully

Heart = admire/support/believe in/trust

Fist = sign of the negative/against/disagree/oppose. Examples:

Union Jack Fist Swastika Union Jack Heart Lager. (*That was a most enjoyable and sportsmanlike game against Ajax Düsseldorf: let's go and have a quiet drink somewhere.*)

Fist Heart Fist Plate-of-Spaghetti Willy Tits. (*Thank you, but I should prefer to continue my conversation with this couple from Rimini.*)

Willy Eagle Fist Swastika Union Jack. (*My country 'tis of thee*).

Willy. Willy Tits. Union Jack Loadsa Burger Loadsa Lager Loadsa Gluesniff. (*This dear, dear, land.*)

☆ 25.1.85

Cardiff, Los Angeles, Washington, Tel Aviv, Tirana, Cork, Phoenix. Can you spot the odd one out? You can, of course. All of them – except for Tirana where the Liga Enver Hoxha Umoristik i Popullit Shqiptarë has proved uncooperative – have hosted or will host International Humor Conferences. (I adopt the American spelling *passim*. I do not say [sic], as I do not make *sic* jokes.) Last year's, in Tel Aviv, was also the venue for the so-called First Colloquium on Jewish Humor (I thought that was Genesis XVII, 17, 'and Abraham fell on his face and laughed'); this year's will be in Cork at the end of June, with a special Symposium on All Aspects of Irish Humor, and if someone doesn't sponsor me as a fraternal delegate, *someone* isn't going to find anything very funny for a long time, I assure you.* Phoenix has to wait until 1987, but then Phoenix, or more precisely the Tempe campus of Arizona State University, has the annual national WHIM conference, and the English Department at ASU publishes, every April 1, *WHIMSY*, the *Western Humor and Irony Membership Serial Yearbook*, a forced acronym if there ever was one. *Whimsy-II* has just reached me (jokes travel more slowly from west to east than sunwise, following a little-known physical law) and with it an application form for this spring's WHIM-IV where PEOPLE

---

* They didn't. I didn't.

YOU WILL MEET include Harvey Mindess and Amanda Bender (described in the dedication as 'funny psychologists from Antioch U.', and co-designers of the Sense of Humor Inventory or SHI-test); Red Bilodeau of Creative Lunatics, and Nathaniel Thaddeus Bullneck III; Robert Skoglund the Maine humorist, a retired Judge from Los Angeles, and Dale Lowdermilk of NOT-SAFE, the World's Most Sarcastic Org. Why, I can hear you chuckling already! And when I add the names of Virginia O. Trooper of *Laugh Lovers' News*, Ms Goodheart and Mr Goodman of Laughter Therapy Organization and *Laughing Matters* respectively and the euphonious J. Olowo Ojoade from the General Studies department of the University of Jos, you will hardly be able to restrain a full-throated chortle, will you?

Whimsy-II is a substantial quarto of 300-odd pages with almost as many contributions: from Vampire Metaphors in Selected Works of Henry James to Contemporary Ceramic Metaphors; from Yoruba proverbs to Florida Bumper Stickers (none so good as the conference's own, METAPHORS BE WITH YOU). There are linguists with a research programme, like Claire Lerman on Masking Metaphor in the Nixon Conversations, Allen Read on the Criteria for a Class of Jocular Words (absquatulatize, explunctify, spizzerinctum, catamawpous); others with a single valuable observation, like Briggite Ludgate of the Defense Language Institute, who has noticed that 'German terminology sounding like English taboo words are learned faster by US soldiers than any other feature of the German language'. There are sociologists and psychologists trying hard to be funny, and philosophers trying hard to remain straight-faced. And there are large numbers of English postgraduates doing their thing, many of whom would doubtless be happy to read a paper at a symposium on Contemporary Plumbing. There is Sexual Irony in Philip Larkin, there are levels of Incongruity in Tom Sharpe, there is Wit in Whitman and Duality in Twain and the Hanged God metaphor in Steinbeck's *Sweet Thursday*; and Bellow and Derrida and Faulkner and Gaddis and C. B. Greenfield and George Horace Lorimer. Margaret Drabble is given a bad time: 'the author is chary of allowing her characters – or readers – philosophical insights. Compare her with Camus, Sartre, James, Conrad, Murdoch, Bowen or Lessing, let alone Hardy, Bennett or Charlotte Brontë'. And J. J. Lambertson writes mystifyingly about the humour of *Ivanhoe*: 'It is undoubtedly significant that Sir Walter Scott's literary career coincided almost exactly in time with the reign of George III of England. It is a period seldom distinguished by historians as a singularly glorious one in British military prowess . . .'

Other unconsciously humorous pieces include (I think) the record of a jokey conversation between Mel Brooks and a friend of his called Mel Tolkin; 'note the inclusion of at least fourteen funny words: *psychoanalyst, Freud, number One, nickel, little, couch, smut, dirty, puke, Oedipus complex, mother, Jewish* and *Greek*'. (Jewish, I guess, counts as two. A small prize will be awarded to the *TLS* reader to use all these words in the least funny sentence.) In the script, Brook's interlocutor is called Tolkien, which adds a fine surrealist top-dressing.

More solemn are Lana Rings – 'Four factors determine humor in a given situation. They consist of the humorist (or "speaker"), the audience (or "listener"), the situation and the text' – and keynote speaker Warren Shibles with his seventy types of fly-in-the-soup joke: AMBIGUITY HUMOR *Waiter*: Just a minute, I'll unzip it. PARADOX HUMOR *Waiter:* The fly is and is not in your soup. And there is a notably sombre piece by A. Blake of New Mexico U. Sociology Department, on Defusing the Tension Barrier in the classroom through Creative Humour: 'I love to throw a class off balance. I may stop and talk to the students in the back row, then drift through class spouting *limericks*, and eventually arrive "up front" with some "off the wall" story about a day spent at sea with Irish fishermen. I use puns constantly: "the Buddhist priests were singing en-*chant*-ingly" or "the Eskimo were 'dog-tired' after being *polar*-ised all day long".'

It is worth quoting in full, for its succinct grimness, the report by Ronald Hoppe and Joseph Kess on Ambiguity Arousal Reduction and Humor:

> Multiple meanings of the word 'shot' were used to play a joke on subjects participating in a psychology experiment. Subjects either alone or in groups anticipated receiving an injection ('shot'), and their physiological and psychological levels of arousal were increased by this anticipation. When the time came for the administration of the 'shot', it turned out to be a 'shot' of liquor and not an injection. The subjects' arousal level as indicated by several tests showed a general reduction. A direct relationship between the amount of arousal reduction in the subjects and their appreciation of the joke was found, and those who showed the least reduction saw the joke as least funny. Theoretical implications of these results and related empirical research are discussed.

☆ *10-16.3.89*

The *TLS*, for reasons best kept hidden, does not have a bridge column; in consequence their impoverished founts do not include the (heart) sememe, making it harder for me to give you a truly relevant update on the progress of world-wide tee-shirt and bumper-sticker literacy. Consequently I am forced to Desperate Shifts: and as it happens Desperate Shifts Inc of Redondo Beach were the first to release the Adult (or at least Parental Guidance) shirt on to a market all too ready for it. Let us adopt the humble ampersand; wherever you see this sign, imagine instead a full-bottomed, blushing, pounding cardioid.

Thus I & NY (the aboriginal utterance in the business), I & LUCY, I & A LASSIE, or even I & NY IN JUNE HOW ABOUT YOU.

It is necessary now to distinguish between the pictographic (& = heart) and the ideographic (& = love) functions of the symbol. There is a single rare example of the sign being used phonetically (&=&) – I LOVE C&CAMPING has been recorded near C&lly. A few examples will make the distinction clear: On the one hand H. P. &CRAFT RULES; I'M IN C&R; PROUD TO BE A S&N, or indeed PROUD TO BE S&NE, together with the translated YA & &NA (YA LJUBLJU LJUBLJANA). On the other hand BRET & LIVES and I ADMIRE & CRANE; YO & AQUINO has been spotted in Manila.

Perhaps I had better sign off. Signing myself of course, Disgusted of &fordshire (or his French equivalent, *é&é de C&res*).

☆ *31.7.81*

I've been feeling a trifle idistic recently. If you have too, you could join the British Idistic Society, if it still survives. This is far less fun than it sounds, being formed to promote Ido, and its associated ideals of World Peace through Vegetarianism and Dhammapadha. Ido was an artificial language designed to supplant Esperanto (Esp. '-ido' equals 'son of . . .'). 'Idistic' is unrecorded by OED (can I have a contributor's tie, please?) but is attested to by a printed sticker of around 1911, one of the items in an album of idistic postcards and ephemera, once the property of a Cambridge hotelier, which I have just semi-accidentally acquired.

It appears that the moment the hotelier publicized his adherence to the movement the postcards came flooding in, offering congratulations, requesting the exchange of cards and stamps, and reproaching him for his prose style (which was full of 'Esperantala vorti'). From France, Germany and outlying portions of Austria-Hungary they came, portraits of Comenius, 'our great Bohemian', views of Mala Strana in Prague and Krakow townhall, Jenny Hasselquist the Swedish bombshell. There is a note of encouragement from Louis Couturat, the mathematical philosopher and architect of Ido ('refutar la Esp-isti' – the Esp-isti still regard him as Judas), propaganda postcards showing the Ido star or the Ido dove shedding respectively light and olive leaves over a battered globe – one card, curiously, bears the stamp of the Stassfurt Volapükaklub Zenodik, which suggests that some chapters jumped straight from Volapük to Ido without calling at Esperanto on the way. (Volapük was the first of the international languages to become a movement: the trouble with it was that it was extremely ugly, and much harder to learn than any natural language. 'O fat obas kel binol in süls' is the start of the Lord's Prayer in Volapük and that is enough about that.)

Through peace and war, peace and war, the Idists ploughed on, earnest for peace but with the most minimal influence on history; there are conferences here and there, a photograph of sepia congressists gathered round a waterfall, the sticker of the 'Internacia Uniono de Vejeteriani Idisti', 'Venez ad Sopron dum 1930', sheets and sheets of very pretty labels advertising Tobler Suisiana Lakto Chokolado, evidence of some great schism ('mi sustenas la Programa dil Demokrata Opozanta'). The Crusade against Babel petered out at last, alas. The correspondence thins and the last postcard, from the vice-president of the English group, is poignant: '... me ofte pensas pri mea old amiki ... quale sempre, Idisti trovas kordial bon-acepto in Lewisham.'

One of the most curious items in the collection is a round-robin postcard, evidently a minor pastime before the First World War. It left Cambridge on the morning of January 12, 1912 with a penny stamp and a minuscule address in Brussels. The Belgian recipient added (on January 14) ten centimes, 'kordyala saluti', and the address of a friend in Italy, leaving plenty of space for more addresses. From Italy it went to Germany, from Germany to Luxembourg and from Luxembourg, on January 24, it headed back to Cambridge, where we may safely assume the sender received it within two weeks of despatch. Dare one contemplate how much this would cost and how long it would take today, if it was not instantly confiscated as infringing a score of regulations? Of course thanks to the miracles of instantaneous data transfer, geosynchronous satellites and telephone answering machines, you can now ring yourself up and get an answer within minutes.

☆ *24.12.87*

Like most people, I go to the United States mainly in order to watch Public Broadcasting, and see all those wonderful British television programmes, undiluted by advertising, or by not-so-wonderful British television programmes.

Some folk are called to a higher service, and their duty demands a higher level of sacrifice. I think continually of Nancy Johnson, who emits a daily soapwatch column for the *Boston Globe*, and for all I know for a spread of papers from the *Biloxi Beagle* to the *Juneau What*, from the *Portland* (Maine) *Cement* to the *Portland* (Oregon) *Vase*. The column is unequivocally called a review, so I must assume she actually downloads these narratives from screen to brain to print, heroically risking massive damage to the delicate nervous tissue, rather than merely receiving summaries and summarizing them.

Reviewing soap operas is a high-definition activity, in Ken Tynan's phrase, with a format as precise as haiku. Three sentences, three separate linear propositions, six or seven subjects, with a single link between the synthesis and the leitmotif. Consider this one:

> Bobbi is still looking for Melissa.
> Felicia learned that Autumn once appeared in an X-rated movie.
> Quentin thinks Autumn is trying to kill Herbert.
> *(General Hospital)*

This is close to the classical form, in which the first two themes are without apparent connection, and the third statement, or apodosis, closes the loop. There are purists who would argue that the reference should always be to the first subject, thus:

> * Quentin thinks Herbert is trying to kill Bobbi

while other prefer a complete closure, thus:

> * Quentin thinks Autumn (or Felicia) is trying to kill Bobbi (or of course Melissa)

Modern critical opinion, in general, regards this as too severe. There is a welcome for the introduction of third subjects into the protasis, and similar rococo flourishes, as in the much-admired *As the World Turns*:

> Holden is haunted by thoughts of Lily making love with Daisy.
> Corinne admitted that she wanted to shoot James.
> Kim doesn't know about Andy's drinking.

Here there is no closure of any kind: 'the exquisite ornamentation of the first two figures may deceive us; but the intellectual core is severe, almost ascetic; only the delicate assonance of haunted/admitted saves the fragile structure from dissolving into a staccato disorder', comments a leading critic.

The reduced form called *savon maigre*, of two lines only, is popular in certain regions:

> Brooke fantasized about a romance between her and Ridge.
> Ridge was upset to learn that Caroline had accepted Thorne's marriage proposal.

This is also heterodox in that one of the characters has a name which indicates gender. Traditionalists would prefer, in place of Caroline, a name like Cranny or Clumber or Crop or Conglomerate or Carboniferous. Multiplexing of pronouns is much admired too:

> Maeve overheard Fletcher say that Meredith had killed her own Mother.
> Roxie realized that Rick still cares for her.

I think I'm getting the hang of it. How about:

> Bracken meets Viaduct at Sledge's pachinko parlour.
> Oslo realizes that Algol is afraid that Trad has found out that she is really his uncle.
> Viv accuses Bracken of simony.

Although there are some resemblances to Hemingway's ministories ('Nobody has ever explained what the leopard was doing at that altitude'), the closest genre is the narrative of the language manual:

> Cass saved Nicole, who was about to get flattened[1] by a truck[2]
> Billie tried[3] to seduce Wade.
> Gina came on strong[4] with Scott.

[1] Future perfect passive semelfactive. [2] Lit. 'with a truck'; *vagonom*, or more formally *wagon-litom*. [3] Use the imperfect or iterative. [4] Trans 'she was especially kind to'.

I have been saving the finest specimen for last.

> Adrienne and Justin were married in Greece.
> Victor saw Diana and Roman kissing.
> Diana learned that Serena is her mother.
> Roman shot Serena.

Genius can always transcend stylistic rules.

☆   24.12.82

T-shirt of the Month Club's special Spring Award goes to this one, spotted, sorry, sighted at a *vernissage* in Hackney:
        H. H. MONRO IS A WRY SWINE
No, really, the answer isn't upside down at the foot of the column. Just say it over a few times.

And as a change from tea-shirts (ORANGE PEKOE FREAKO, OOLONG U.,) here's a coffee-shirt:
STRONG DRINK IS A MOCKER
MOCHA IS A STRONG DRINK.

☆   23.12.88

Other people who write in these columns go around the world under a proper aegis, with all the right introductions. After my lecture, they say, just as if it was nothing, after my lecture I sat in a comfortable *pivoczna* with members of the semi-clandestine Illyrian Writers' Circle. I was taken to the nondescript suburban home of the celebrated Jaime O'Higgins, I drank a bowl of steaming *drepung* with a man from the Ministry of Public Guidance. Me, I make my own way, and get it wrong. Continuing my policy of familiarizing myself with a list of the world's vital strategic and economically powerful nations (starting at the bottom and working up), I visited Belize, once British Honduras, once the Logwood Coast, once the land of the Chol. Its major distinction, according to my old unreliable standby *The Book of International Lists* (Macmillan), is that it is the country with the fewest professors in the New World: twenty-three is all it can muster, fewer than anywhere in the world except New Caledonia and the Seychelles. In terms of professors per million, it doesn't rate so poorly, well above South Yemen with 8 per million, if nowhere near the Vatican City, which is said to have 1,192,000 professors per million population. (I suppose some of them are visiting professors or maybe some have more than one chair, the lay and the papal as it might be.) Belize is not a chart-topping sort of place: though it is cheated of one of its great merits by the *Book of Lists'* bizarre editorial policies: it could be the country with the smallest number of daily newspapers (1) but this crown is given to the Vatican on the extraordinary grounds of its being last in the alphabet. (Countries with no newspapers at all get left out of the list altogether, which detracts from its meaningfulness, I feel.) On the ground, Belize turns out to have several daily newspapers, although none of them manages to come out every day. Belize City's one newspaper seller was still offering Friday's *Amandala* on Tuesday morning on the grounds that he'd been round to the press a few times to collect Tuesday's paper and they kept telling him to come back in a few hours and he wasn't going to bother.

This and similar happenings have led many people to argue that Belize is too small or has too few (about 160,000) people. It cannot support an adequate daily press, or a television station (it gets a few minutes of its own programming on the satellite) or an FM radio, or a sufficient number of university professors, or a subway system, or a secret police force. (There is the SIS, but as the paper, yes the government paper, now you mention it, points out, 'only persons engaged in wicked crimes against Belize and Belizeans need fear it'.)

For this and for other reasons, I am inclined to argue that 160,000 is an ideal population size, and the sooner megastates like Guatemala or Denmark are split into a score of independent statelets, the better off we shall all be.

It is true that Belize makes but a small impact on the world scene. The delegation from the tourist industry that attended a regional jamboree in Acapulco reported back to *Belize Today* that there was a strong demand for 'basic geographic information', ie 'where are you and is there such a place?' ('¿Somos* en Nicaragua?' asked a worried man in Which Spy sun glasses as we pulled into Philip S. Goldson International Airport, which interested me, as I had always wondered what an inverted question mark sounded like.) To provide just such information I had to eke out a terrible existence on armadillo, lobster (actually crayfish) and the dreaded gibnut, a large stewable rodent.

Belize is an exciting place, where nothing much happens. I went into all the bookshops (which didn't take long), equipped myself with at least two-thirds of the country's available literature, leaving only the surfing books behind. I read two textbooks on Belizean history and one on politics, the history of the local Maya and Carib, some Creole proverbs ('Man weh caca 'pan di beach forget; de man weh waak eena it rememba' - 'the deed is remembered by the victim long after it has been forgotten by the perpetrator'), a recipe book, and what seemed to be the only local novel in print, a rather melodramatic piece called *The Sinners' Bossa Nova*. I made a

---

* It has been suggested to me that what he must have said was 'Estamos . . .' Quite so, if he was an idiomatic Hispanic; not necessarily if he was a CIA insert. Memory holds to 'Somos'.

brief architectural survey (the Governor's House was built in 1814 by Christopher Wren, or so my guidebook says). Instant expertise! Short talks will be delivered at no charge, lengthier presentations for a reasonable remuneration. Stand by for this column to become a major Central American bore.

Here, amid the pieties of a drink-and-dry-Christmas campaign, I enjoy looking back on the Belizean anti-drug campaign, which was visible but not deeply felt. 'Americans spray we good grass, so we haves to deal that bad coke' said Man in Street; and a local filling station, maritime admittedly, gives away a bottle of beer with every six gallons of gasoline.

☆ *22.1.88*

A word-processor, they tell you in the literature, is every kind of faithful servant: a hyper-intelligent secretary, infallible social hostess, inenarrable amanuensis, tireless muse, more-than-admirable Crichton, universal Egeria, organizational genius, incorruptible valet, supershimmering Jeeves, indefatigable aide-de-camp, a veritable Johannes Factotum. All of that, no doubt: but it also incorporates in its cast list the lineal descendant of those slatterns that made accidental holocausts of literature. Morning Mr Carlyle, grand day for a good blaze. What, those old bits of scribbled-on-paper, Mr Rossetti? Let me just draw back the curtains here, so you can see what you are doing, Mr Fox Talbot.

Nowadays it calls itself 'disc manager', rather as an intelligence department seeks to prevent intelligence and a man charged with eradicating the countryside might be called (for the sake of argument), 'Minister for the Environment'.

'Morning Mr User, Sir, need some more space for our alphanumeric ruminations do we? I'll just tidy away these bits and bobs here, shall I?'

Whoops.

And half a megabyte of exquisitely crafted prose goes to join the cloudcapped towers and gorgeous palaces, goes wherever the Red King's dream has gone. Did you hear the twang of a golden cord, a lost chord over Tufnell Park last Monday, a scent of burnt roses fleeing towards Highgate, the ghost of a flea airborne over Alexandra Palace? Gone where all past years are, to that left-luggage office in the sky ('parcel for you, Colonel Lawrence'). 'Couldn't you have asked and asked again?', one chides: 'didn't you think . . . ?'

NOT PAID TO THINK, it smirks greenly.

☆   *10.3.89*

I'd been back to Belize again to check out a few things I hadn't got down right last time. Is there really a newspaper called *The Coconut Wireless*? There is. And do they want a columnist? They don't. Also I needed an update on the economic news ('The public is hereby informed that Nico Marine has gone into voluntary winding-up leading to disillusion', *Belize Lookout*, 19.2.89).

World news filters through to Belize as through a pillow of softest grass, and I didn't know what to make of the report that the Ayatollah had launched a jihad against penguins. I assumed that he had discovered a *hadith* which demonstrated that creatures were created to swim or to fly, but not both, and legions of devotees, veterans of the Gulf War, were off to exterminate the wretched ratites and liberate South Georgia from the uncircumcised wing of its usurpers. I might even have referred to the uncircumcised yoke but representations from the Royal Society for Protection of Birds ('a yolk in poor taste') made me desist.

☆   *25.12.87*

I worry about you, I do really. The general book reading, generally book reading public I mean, reading regardless with no sense of ills to come, no cares beyond today. While all the while, on a certain hillside, in a distant plantation under a tropical sun, they are growing the silicon which will yield the chip which will make the apparatus which will destroy you all. The world will not be a safer or saner place when publishing is no longer the perquisite of a moral and intellectual élite but available to all. Samizdat will soon be joined by tomizdat, dickizdat and harizdat. The desktop publication gives way to the coffeetabletop publication, to laptop publication and eventually to kneecaptop and bustop, busstop, busttop. By the early 1990s the airlines will suspend inflight movies in favour of inflight word processing: at flight's end, as the 797 descends majestically like a stoned pigeon, fulfilled passengers will prepare to disenjumbo, clutching 200 novels, sixty cookbooks, forty sales manuals, and uncountable memoirs and uplifting thoughts, spiralbound in economy class, serviceable buckram in business, full levant elegant extra in a choice of eighteen toolings for passengers in what will by then no doubt be called hostage class. (Every first-class passenger insured to the value of a shipload of near-contemporary weaponry, dispatched without questions asked to any Gulf Port; mesocrat class guarantees two assassins released;

economy class passengers subject to NEVSCID – Not Entirely Voluntary Sudden Change In Destination – will get prayers in the church or temple or holy place of their choice.) Those few born authors deterred by the costs of vanity publication will leap into print. The space between pen and paper, where fell the shadow, will be abolished in the cause of instant gratification. I trembled for that day. Like monkeys on typewriters, they will produce round every half successful writing a dense penumbra of near or more and more distant misses extending to infinity. For every Hamlet, a score of Gamlets, Homlets, Hamjets, Hamlyts, Hamlegs. No more mute inglorious Miltons, but a host of noisily inglorious ones: for every Paradise Lost a Paradise Last and Paradise Lust and Paradise Liszt and Paradise List. (Of Man's first Disobedience, and Man's second Disobedience, and Man's third Disobedience, and . . .)

☆ *29.10.82*

Nobody carries bumper stickers any more, except the kind of people who don't know that nobody carries bumper stickers any more, and they tend to display sordid mottoes like GLASS-BLOWERS DO IT UNTIL THEIR CHEEKS CRACK or ANTIQUARIAN BOOKSELLERS DO IT IN A RING. One use (the only use) of CB might be to address, in a tone of reason and restraint ('While there is a certain specious logic in what you say, I can indicate the fallacy if you will spare me a few moments') drivers exhibiting opinions like GUNS CAUSE CRIME LIKE FLIES CAUSE GARBAGE. (An alternative option might be to pull out your Magnum or Kalashnikov and blow them away.) The wickedest sign says MORE PEOPLE HAVE DIED IN TEDDY KENNEDY'S CAR THAN IN NUCLEAR ACCIDENTS IN THE USA. The best triple-take came from a sign reading MY BOSS IS A JEWISH CARPENTER, which I thought was just a piece of pawky religious humour (I've always wanted to use that word, I wonder if I have it right) until I saw that the van carrying it belonged to Levine Lumber Corp.

☆ *31.5.85*

It isn't true about those six monkeys with the typewriters, and that's official. A recent *New Scientist* (I spend a lot of time in waiting rooms) reports the calculations of one David Osselton, a Gradgrindian sort of chap it appears, who proves that given all the time in the world and then some, they not only could not type the Works of William Shakespeare, they couldn't even type 'The Works of William Shakespeare'. It is true that 10^{12} monkeys, that's a trillion (US) or at least 4×10^9 waggonloads, could eventually type 'William Shakespeare' (or any other spelling you prefer), but it would take them 10^{12} years, a wilderness of years. This is only working the monkeys eight hours a day, with time off for Lincoln's Birthday and Up Helly Aa, and typing quite languidly: take away their holidays and sleep, replace them by superfast computers, you still need more time, space, print-out paper and energy than the universe has available. Which means that chance does less, or explains less, than we may have thought: which means a serious rethink for anyone who thought chance had anything to do with *The Complete Works*.

☆   2.9.83

I was sent some questions once by a man who wanted to start in the book business. They began:
1. Where can I find antiquarian books?
2. How do I find out what to pay for them?
3. Who can I sell them to?
4. What should I charge?

And at a dismal venue, Denbigh or Doncaster, I was asked: 'Is there a small book I could get that will tell me what everything is worth?' 'Yes,' I snarled, 'I have it right here but I'm not allowed to show it to you.'

This was churlish, and I'm now able to offer the Caxton Universal Bibliopolic Implement. This elegant little device incorporates an eraser at one end, a lead pencil at the other, and around the barrel a simple but accurate ready reckoner. Seize your book. Erase the previous price (after first making a note of it). Use the ready reckoner to multiply this figure by Antiquarian Booksellers' Secret Profit Coefficient (sent under separate cover). Inscribe new price legibly in book. And now you are a bookseller. The writing end of the implement may also be used to place the letters 'w.a.f.' on the flyleaf of your purchase, thereby absolving you of any responsibility for its completeness or condition. As you gain experience you can enlarge your vocabulary with phrases like 'scarce' (= not many in stock) 'curiously scarce', (= not many in stock considering that the remainder turned up recently) and even 'elusive' (= only one in stock *and* I've been asked for it).

☆   13.3.87

It has been a funny old time, lately, what with the alleged reappearance both of Marilyn Monroe's dad, clutching his marriage lines, even in death, like some drowned Victorian heroine, and thereby spoiling all those legends about the star's bastardy, and, simultaneously, with his claim not to have been kidnapped after all, of the Lindbergh baby. Next, no doubt, we will be having Ambrose Bierce, sunburnt but healthy, Irvine and Mallory ('we got into conversation with this splendid monk chappie, Sherpa Untensing I think his name was, and he made us see that the whole idea of striving to be first up a mountain was just maya, so we wandered into his monastery and the time passed without us noticing it') and Captain (now Lieutenant-Colonel) Oates ('I have decided to come in out of the cold').

Unlike history, fiction is immutable. No chance of further research revealing that Maggie Tulliver could swim, that Regina v Durbeyfield was overturned on appeal, or that Silas did it after all. 'If that train driver hadn't had his wits about him, you'ld have been a gonna, Anna.' 'No, she survived the fire; we got an annulment.' 'Gotcha, you big white bugger.' (I was thinking of *Moby Dick* but I suppose it covers *King Solomon's Mines* and *Seven Pillars of Wisdom*.) The theatre, of course, does run the risk of unplanned revisions, notably all those Shakespearean short circuits: 'I seem to have dropped my handkerchief.' 'Try the lead one.' 'Cross-garters? Not on your nelly.' 'Stuff the senate, I'm going to the circus.'

☆   19.6.87

If you go down to the woods today it will be no surprise to you to find antiquarian booksellers popping out of every dry tree and damp bit of woodwork: for every dealer that ever there WOZ is in Bloomsbury or Mayfair for certain BECOZ this week's the week the ABA the ILAB the PBFA and the BBFA and other marauding gangs with no acronyms have their No-picnic-I-can-tell-you (see ads for details).

In case you are a novice at the book-fair caper, here are a few tips to help make your visit more enjoyable and to assure you of the attention of the stall-holders.

There is no real guide to the value of a rarity but the bookseller's instinct of how scarce and how desirable it is. He is thus eager to get feedback from you the public, 'the most important person in his business' as he will smilingly hasten to assure you. So feedback –

along the lines of 'We've got shelves and shelves just like that at home' or 'You wouldn't catch me laying out good money for a grotty old thing/brand-new book' is invaluable. It is a courtesy to introduce remarks with some modest phrase like 'Of course I'm not a collector' or 'I'm one of those peculiar people who buy books to read them'.

Similarly, the original published price of a book is often a useful hint to its second-hand value: many booksellers, especially modern literature dealers, are busy people who don't have time for all the research they would like to undertake, so they will be particularly glad if you point out the discrepancy between the published price (say three shillings and sixpence) printed on the dust-wrapper and the often considerably greater price (say £350) pencilled on the fly. (The third volume of my autobiography, *Pencillings on the Fly*, will be available shortly from all good remainder shops.)

Naturally, most people visiting bookshops or book-fairs are not interested in adding to their collections ('it's not the money, it's the space'), but are often eager to find out more about the books they already own. The sort of information they are looking for is something along the lines of 'What's it worth?' or 'What's it worth to you?' or 'Can you direct me to a bookshop that will give me more?' So here are: TEN STEPS TO BOOKSELLING FOR THE NONPROFESSIONAL

or
TURN OLD PAPER INTO NEW £££££

1) *Reconnaissance*. Wander about the stand, refusing all offers of assistance. This will also serve to unsettle the dealer. Murmur 'Just browsing' in a firm but assertive manner. Alternatively, either approach ceremoniously and ask if you are permitted to look at the stock, specifying that they are not your class of book, that you are afraid of being tempted, that you are just a simple academic, humble collector, parsimonious millionaire, unsparing perfectionist (whichever role appeals).

2) *Foreplay*. Establish your own standing as nongreenhorn and unwillingness to be fooled. Make it clear that you are an insider. This is best done by examining a few books at random, looking at the prices and returning the volumes hastily to the shelves, while fixing the dealer with a conspiratorial nod. A whistle of astonishment would be merely vulgar, but a low appreciative chuckle of complicity will not be out of place.

3) *The Feint*. Approach the subject by indirection. If you are hoping to place a copy of the *Illustrated London News* Souvenir of the Coronation of George VI, express an interest in constitutional law. If you wish to sell Mrs Trimmer's *Prints illustrative of Sacred*

History (Volume I only), ask to see the work of English engravers of the late eighteenth century. The price the bookseller demands for what he shows you (a copy of *Songs of Innocence*, for example, likewise a children's book with amateurish hand colouring) will give you an indication of what to ask for yours.

4) *The Engagement*. Find out if the bookseller buys books, by asking him directly ('Do you buy books as well?') or indirectly ('I suppose things like this are pretty hard to get hold of . . .'). It is important to do this, since only a minority of booksellers obtain their stock by purchase. Do not be deterred by a waggish answer ('No I printed all these myself, they fell off the back of a lorry, I only buy at jumble sales' etc): many booksellers fancy themselves as drolls.

5) *The Ambuscade*. Get an estimate of the value of your book before you show it to him. This is paramount. As soon as the book is in his hands he will start turning pages, now fast, now slow, now racing through the book as if counting, now stopping to attend to some invisible feature: there will be cluckings and gobblings and clicks as in the language of the !Kung and well-simulated cries of surprise and regret. Your expression must make it clear that none of this takes you in for a moment. Your position will be immeasurably strengthened if you have coaxed him into uttering a price – any price – without the distraction of a hostage in his hands. Thus:

Aspirant: What is Shelley worth?
Bookseller: Which Shelley?
Would-be seller: Percival Bysshe Shelley, 1799-1822, is the one I had in mind. He also used several pseudonyms, but they are my little secret. [Caution here: there is no record of the approach I-am-interested-in-the-local-history-of-south-west-Buckinghamshire-have-you-anything-by-the-Hermit-of-Marlow? meeting with success.]
Bookperson: I meant what works of Shelley and in particular what editions. Many are in print at popular prices.
Aspirant: (who owns a limp leather *Gems of* with yapp edges and a green bow, *circa* 1895, slyly): No, I was more interested in nineteenth century editions.
Bookfellow (with the patience for which etc): Well of course some of them are extremely rare. The first English *Cenci* is relatively common, but *Queen Mab* might set you back ten grand.

However he may wriggle later, this constitutes an offer.

6) *The Proffer*. Some preparation is required. Do not be too delicate to draw attention to rubrics like 'This is a very rare old book' in an antique hand or 'My grandfather, who was lord lieutenant of St Vincent, said it was the only copy he had ever seen', or best

of all 'Keep this carefully my son, as I am sure it will be worth pounds and pounds some day'. Unscrupulous book dealers may seek to erase these telltale indications, so it is best to go over them in indelible pencil. Little sums like

1927
1724
———
203 years old!

add considerably to the charm of an old tome and you would be doing nothing improper by embellishing the book with a few.

This is probably as much as you can absorb at once. Stages 7–10– *The Incredulity Courteous*, *The Expostulation Direct* (discretionary), *The Discreet Mention of Sotheby's* (essential), *The Unashamed Appeal to Philanthropy*, *The Acceptance Grudging* – will be unveiled in time for the 1988 shindig.

You can get a hint about scarcity from the number of requests for a book in the columns of those magazines which consist of nothing but columns of requests for books. (These, even their editors would admit, are profitable to read but not truly loveable.) The idea is that hungry seekers after truth or profit drop in on their main man and give him a shopping list, he sends the lists to the magazine, and thousands of book scouts throughout the country write in with competitively priced offers. The dealer then uses his expert knowledge to select some of the offerings and recommend them to his customer. (What happens in my case – the computer hasn't been built that could make my business run more efficiently – is that the scouts write in and I lose the name and address of the customer; so if you are looking for the nineteenth impression of the Penguin *Ulysses*, get in touch: it could be your lucky day.)*

Charting this is terrifically misleading, of course, for it only tells you about the demand for a book, and nothing about the supply. I have a theory which flies in the face of all economists, not a bad thing to do to them, that the price of fashionably rare books, unlike the price of rational commodities, depends exclusively on the demand: once everyone decides their library is a contemptible sham without Kathy Acker's first book (a pseudonymous volume of sermons) and that the price is $1,750, they will go on paying out their $1,750s (or $14.95 without the dustwrapper) long after it should have become apparent that someone in Brooklyn has a truckload.

It is also misleading in that some books are asked for week after

---

* He did. It was.

week without success because they are of supreme rarity ('works of the Hermit of Marlow avidly sought for keen collector of S. W. Buckinghamshire local material. Several copies needed. Best prices paid. Without dustwrapper may do'); others because no one will risk the price of a stamp quoting them, and yet others because the advertiser has got fourteen copies and is trying to create a demand, still others because the advertiser has got the name wrong and is trying to summon up a ghost.

☆   3–9.2.89

'But why on earth pick Buckingham?', asks Mr Sanders-of-Oxford plaintively in his latest catalogue. A question many have asked, and the reply 'Because they couldn't spell Milton Keynes' is one of the few prose answers that leap unbidden to the reader's mind. What Mr S of O has in his hand is a piece of French eighteenth-century controversialism: *Lettres à Emile sur la Mythologie* by DeMoustier, 'plainly printed in France' (booksellers can tell these things) but with the imprint 'Buckingham'.

Buckingham sounds pleasingly classy to the French. It and similar places turn up in scrofulous French novels:

> 'Oh Sir Burmingham', gapsed Lady Lovepleasure, 'Do not spare me with your monstruous tool!', while the noble rogerer's valet James industrously souhgt to satisfy her fair cousin, the Marquise of Finsbury.

☆   5.8.83

How numberless are the boons that have been showered upon all orders of Society by what we might call the Book Fair Movement – making it sound akin to those nineteenth-century reformers like the Rational Dress League, the Sunday Society (they favoured Sabbath opening of museums and the drabber sort of art galleries), the Total Abolition (of Scotland) Crusade! Like latterday Chatauquas, we have spread the secular gospel of literacy, bibliographic awareness and a modest annual return on investment through every Drill-Hall, Assembly Rooms, Jubilee Hotel and Armoury throughout this land and our sister states across the seas.

If there has perhaps been any minute compensating disadvantage, it is that expertise and consequent expense have been spread a touch too far and wide. Whereas the provinces previously existed for the metropolitan bookseller to visit and plunder, returning with his shooting-brake laden with unrecorded provincial imprints and unrecognized pseudonymous rarities for which the grateful hayseed or hick has taken pennies ('Thank ee Muster Metropolitan Bookzeller, zurr; Ya'll come back real soon, hear?') we are now all of us reduced to the status of assistants in the global village bookshop, with distressingly rapid access to specialist knowledge and prices. I have warned you again and again about the dangers of adopting, in a trade whose heart is obsolescence, such modern devices as the electrical computing machine, the steam-press, the biro (TM); but my Cassandrologies (TM) have been ignored. See the consequences: there are nearly no non-specialist booksellers any more, and no non-specialist books.

Client comes into premises with half-a-dozen *Victor Sylvester's Modern Method for the Tango and Foxtrot* for sale and you send him on his way with a sneer; next day he comes back and says he thought you would like to know (see my *800 things not to say to booksellers*) that he'd offered them to Quickslow Quartoes of Covent Garden and they had snapped them up with cries of gratitude and a tenner apiece, just the thing for the Semiotics of Body Movement Collection at Stoke Newington U. Meanwhile the fiction department of the Royal Institute of Nursing would like to study hospital romances, and some book-sutler is buying 100,000 titles for them, and a private collector in Esher needs to complete his collection of variant printings of Old Moore's, Foulsham's and Ferguson's Almanacs. From time to time one is visited by a superscout, a sort of high-grade marriage broker, a sort of high-grade pimp actually, who knows who is short of what and how badly they need it. 'Anything on mink-farming since 1940 or penicillin before 1940? Any of Alfred Austin's prose works, *Round the Farm with Romany Again* but only in blue cloth? Incunables from Toledo, Toulouse or Trier? Anything on diverticulosis, Ethel M. Dell in parts, anything on seaweed as fertilizer on any of the Channel Islands save Herm, no, not *Vraic, Vraic, Vraic: Songs of a Sark Maiden*, he's already got that . . . ?'. When they leave, usually empty-handed, you look at your books with fresh contempt and feel as though you have been checked out and passed over by the entire Seventh Fleet.

Other people's shelves offer no relief. What looks like the final reject pile, containing, say, *An Outline of the History of the Blennerhasset Family, Our Curling Tour Through Alberta* and *Crowned Echoes: the Story of the BBC in Coronation Year*, turns out to be awaiting collection, urgently required by *Relatively Speaking, Rink-a-dink Books*, and *Volume Control*, bookeramas that cater respectively for the genealogy, hockey-and-allied-skills, and radio-history markets.

It is quite rare to find the sort of cool dusty basement with a million books, where every volume is thirty pence, uncollated, and without fly-leaf references – 'Zamenhof 486', 'Froom-Jenkin's "A" binding', 'Not in Terwilliger', references which only tell you that someone out there has already amassed everything on tea-tasting or Arminianism. ('Terwilliger' turns out to be a collection of the hundred best books published in February, so 'not in T' is a poorish distinction, particularly as you know that Terwilliger only got to ninety-six before they carted him off to Hotel Hebephrenia).

When you do find such places you rapidly wish you hadn't, places with books that mock the theory that every book has a customer if you wait long enough, books stillborn a century ago and decomposing since, books so dull I dare not even name them, books that you keep on returning to, like a desert wanderer circling a mirage, each time discovering anew that it is the wrong George Herbert or lacks the frontispiece and chapter nine, places where you emerge haggard and hopeless after several hours with a copy of a school magazine where you vaguely remember that Louis Mac-Neice was a supply-teacher in the 1940s and might have written the First XI reports, books with stimulating titles like *Early Days in the Gambia* or *Fierce Fights in Tahiti* which turn out to be missionary narratives of the kind that don't even tell you what she died of but what hymn she requested as she departed, lives of eminent preachers – there's one called *Lax of Poplar* who sounds like a newspaper letterwriter, Lax of Poplar, Disgruntled of Broadstairs, Tired of Reading (God yes!) . . .

☆   *10.10.86*

I have this problem that I think of as creative dyslexia. The world is full of joy and woe, and sometimes my retina does the work that my philosophy cannot. For instance, I always read Piazzas as Pizzas.

I just happen to have in front of me some promotional material for a historical novel based on the exploits of the Albanian hero George Castriot surnamed Scanderberg, and the author remarks, 'The story of Scanderbeg is, unfortunately, better known in Europe than it is in America. [He writes as an American, you understand.] Both in Rome and Tirana, large statues of Scanderbeg grace piazzas in memory of the man's exploits.'

And I, whimsical dog that I am, suddenly see all those fast food outlets (the Victorians called them tachyphagotopias, but it didn't catch on) doing a daily-special deep-dish old-fashioned finger-lickin' four seasons (send your friends a Vivaldigram) topped with peperoni *and* cheese *and* bell peppers *and* olives *and* capers *and* a tiny but exquisitely carven, no moulded, statuette in marzipan with lifelike and entirely non-toxic natural food colourings (ecco she is veritable una artista con E4628, no?) representing the Hero of Croya with his foot on the neck of Sultan Amuret II.

Likewise when an architect announces his plan to revivify the environment of London by knocking down a railway station on the North bank of the Thames and providing a new monorail link to one on the South Bank, what gives the scheme its charm and human appeal is the promise of the provision of space for pedestrianism and other aspects of gracious living. On the site of Charing Cross Station, which will be demolished, we are to have a huge pizza.

'Londoners deserve to have the kind of pedestrian pizzas which Venice enjoys.'

I'm just glad that it is going to be pedestrian. A motorized Pizza Veneziana would be more than one could bear.

☆   17.6.88

There has been a lot of creativity around in the antiquarian game of late, much of it, admittedly, criminal, but demonstrating none the less the vivacity and enterprise of those rare and special folk. Hot on the heels of Hoffman, forger, assassin, bombmaker, onlie begetter of The Freeman's Oath and of assorted Mormon historical documents (with generous impartiality he produced evidence which underpinned or undermined the early witnesses, confident that the elders of the Mormon Church, for one reason or another, would eagerly purchase both: for the full story get the current and last quarter's *Book Collector* or wait for my opera) comes news that a modest but significant proportion (roughly everything bought or sold there for the past twenty years) of the documentary history of Texas is undergoing painful reappraisal. Some treasured relics cannot be reappraised, it is said, as they became unfortunately incinerated by fire in a well-insured building. The Governor of Texas, who recently bought a copy of the *Declaration of* (Texan) *Indepen-*

dence for $30,000, is said to be displeased with his purchase: which means that it's bullet-proof vest time in Austin.*

But patriots may be wondering what has happened to British ingenuity and know-how in the cut-throat business of fraud and forgery. They need not be ashamed of their fellow countrymen: the land of Chatterton and Ireland and Wise and Psalmanazar and Payne Collier has not lost its competitive edge. The uninspired used to forge famous books until the Blessed Thomas J. showed them that the way to slow down enquiries was to forge books which no one could compare with the original because there were no originals. The latest conceptual triumph is to dispense with books altogether and tempt the incautious greedy without any production costs at all, apart from a few bob to duplicate empty promises.

And a few privileged book collectors and dealers in North America recently were dangerously excited by a catalogue emanating from Macclesfield, a name guaranteed to lull suspicions, even if the seller's name, Ian Fox, was unfamiliar and might have perhaps sounded a warning. Did they think, any of them, of La Fontaine's remark that foxes always want to be wolves, never sheep? Of the fox and the cheese, or the fox and the grapes? For these grapes certainly were sour and their children's teeth were set on edge: the cheese was hard indeed.

Imagine: you sit at your breakfast in Austin or Boston or Los Angeles or Baltimore, at your orange juice or hominy grits or home fries or alfalfa sprouts, idly reading a catalogue, a curiously terse catalogue, short on charm and detail and waggish commentary and scholarly footnotage and descriptive detail. 'Orwell *Wigan Pier* £25; *Animal Farm* only v.g. £60. John Osborne Look back in Ho Hum; Mervyn Peake *Titus Groan* groan; *The Bell Jar* Ezra Pound *How to Read*, Ezra Pound *Quinzaine for this Y* . . .'

Forgotten the hominy grits, untasted the alfalfa sprouts. *A Quinzaine for this Yule* turns up once a decade, commands telephone numbers. At a modest £425, a month in Mustique looms. Has this naive dealer in laughable Macclesfield stumbled on a treasure trove, bought from the illiterate children of some unrecorded Bloomsburyite? There's *At Swim-two-Birds* for a friendly £67, a fine *Echo's Bones and Other Precipitates* cheap at £175. The Greenes are healthily marked up though, and the early Waugh positively pricey, at £175 for *Rossetti*. Wasn't there something in

* HRIW. An ex-president of the ABAA, ornament of the Texan trade, has just been found fatally shot (May 1989).

the notes about dj's, though? Indeed. 'COMPLETE WITH DUSTWRAPPER WHEN PUBLISHED WITH SUCH, unless stated otherwise'. Suddenly, in Austin and Boston and Houston, it's Christmas. Visions of sugarplums dance in their heads from Santa Barbara to Seventy Ninth Street. Those Doyles in dj! Golding's *Poems*, 1934, Hemingway *Three Stories and Ten Poems*, all that early Agatha Christie, normally tattered? Nor are Modern First dealers the only beneficiaries. A complete run of *Rupert* Annuals. A *Frankenstein* at £1,200 will do very nicely, and so will the *Boz* and the *Desperate Remedies* and heavens, the Jane Austen! Would it be greedy to order *Pride and Prejudice* at £1,000 and *Sense and Sensibility* at £500 AND *Emma*? A feverish eye scans the conditions. Mr Fox of Macclesfield has no telephone number, to ensure no doubt that everyone has an equal chance. He is plainly a conscientious fellow. 'I only purchase and offer for sale books whose condition is likely to satisfy discriminating collectors'; 'If any customer is dissatisfied . . . a full cash refund will be given. I extend this guarantee unreservedly but am pleased to point out that no customer has yet needed to take advantage of it.' (A proud boast and, in the event, perfectly justified.) Oh and one thing more: 'PREPAYMENT is required from new customers, both private and trade.' Seems reasonable enough, or does it? From Yale to Yuma a rat, a veritable ratking was smelt.

Caution triumphed over greed. English dealers were disturbed at their respective teacakes or cocoa by dealers from East Coast or West, not all of them even customers, and ordered or begged to send their fleetest assistant to Macclesfield to grab the books by their spines, if they existed, or alternatively to string up by the fambles the villain who had raised false hopes. British booksellers, a cynical breed, phoned a long-established bookman in the region; he was indignant that any Southerner or Westerner could imagine that books like that could be around on his patch and someone else have the plucking of them. Within hours, mostly spent trying to persuade sceptical constables that a book could be priced at £1,000 and still be too cheap to be true, the fox was earthstopped. Unsmiling men, non-collectors in blue uniforms, sought to enquire whether the goodies were available for inspection, found only an accommodation address with a lot of envelopes with foreign stamps lying on the mat. The Cheshire Fox-hunt gets under weigh. A person has been charged. End of affair. Except for alleged Fox (case comes up in September) and a few red faces: the most embarrassing thing was to have been caught having believed, but not having believed enough to order everything in sight. 'We regret we cannot fulfil your order', purred a Well-Known London Bookshop to a be lucky client; 'but thank you for leaving us the Genuine Suppressed First of *Alice*; we really needed that.'

☆ 3.6.83

Enough has been said, by me at any rate, about forgery, fraud, cozenage, imposture, superchérie (the title, of course, of a newly-discovered Colette MS), illaqueation, bamboozlery and pflamdoodle. Away then, at least for a spell, with Payne Collier, Thomas Wise, R. H. Hearne, Cora Pearl, Paul Kammerer, Cyril Burt, Francis Pym, Arthur Gordon Pym (at least one of the names in this list is not a fraud) Geoffrey Howe, Cat Geoffrey, Mousecuddler, the Cat for Disarmament, Geoffrey Crayon, Washington Irving, Clifford Irving, Henry Irving (who was really John Henry Brodribb), Edward Irving and all the Irvingites, Ossian, Ireland, Tommy Chatterton and all the Marvellous Boys.

Let us turn to something clean, straightforward and manly, of which you could not ask for anything more so than Finn Havnevik's *English for Fishermen*, published by Fabritius and Sønners (Oslo, 1951), in their ever-admired 'Fagbøker for Fiskere' series. (Other fagbøoks include Hodson's invaluable *Trål og Trålfiske* and Jo Norling's *Pogo på Snurpefiske*: 'Pogo', a folk-hero among trålermen, I believe, is obviously related to the English 'poggy', a variety of menhaden, or cod, if not to 'pogy', a small Arctic whale; while the at-first-glance obscure 'snurpefiske' is evidently a compound of 'fisc', the Scottish legal term for the right of the Crown to the escheat of vacant estates, and the onomatopoeic 'snurp', an expression of uncontrollable disgust at the machinations of Scottish lawyers.)

English for Fishermen, which despite its title is largely in Norse, at least at the outset, comes bound in sturdy and reliable boards with a stout canvas backstrip, in a reassuring shade of North Sea green, portraying a stalwart fisker hollo-ing something in a clean-limbed and trustworthy manner. (I have always wanted to run a littoral tavern called 'The Mariner's Hollow' – 'Every Day, for Food or Play', Coleridge.) What the Norwegian is shouting is possibly 'Have you any steam on the windlass?', which turns up as early as page 21 to illustrate the verb 'to have': 'John's father has a fishing boat. The boat has four oars. Has your father a fishing boat, Jim?' With Jim's arrival, however, the dialogue turns sinister: 'May I ask you to do me a service? Can you swim? Must you go now?' – which is doubtless where Jim gets the push and goes to feed the menhaden, and serve him right for trying to mix with the men when it's notorious that his father doesn't have a fishing-boat, being resident ballet critic of the *Grimsby Pilot*.

Every quirk of English grammar is illuminated by the same relentless cold fishy light: a *few* mackerel, *many* halibuts, *much* herring; the fisherman *hauled* in the rope/the rope *was hauled in* by the fishermen. There is also plenty on the English way of life ('This is a kettle. In the kettle there is coffee. Some people like condensed milk in their coffee') and wholesome advice on how to conduct oneself in Fleetwood or Lossiemouth: 'you have some leisure hours when your boat is in port and should use your time in a practical way. There is much to be seen, monuments, beautiful churches, houses of unusual architecture.'

There's obviously an infinitely expansible market for specialist language books, Gulf Arabic for oil riggers, Spanish for bull-fighters, Japanese for robots, Turkish for deconstructionists, Etruscan for brain surgeons, Wendish for surveyors. Have you a theodolite? Yes, I have several theodolites. Jim's theodolite is green, but Lydia's (the-of-Lydia) is purple (Skprz. pürr-pyll). No doubt one could go on.

☆   18.5.84

How to enrage your bookseller: no. 258 of an occasional series.
'But it says six shilling on the spine.'
'Of course I wouldn't dream of selling it, but I was just curious. . .'.
'But it says thirty-one and sixpence on the spine.'
'I had that when I was a little girl.'
'I can see I'd better look through my chuckouts a bit more carefully.'
'Where do you get all your books?'
'It must be very old, it belonged to my grandfather.'
(No more than three of these should be attempted on any one bookseller.)

And no. 259:
leave on his answering machine a slurred request for *Her-Bak 'Chick-Pea'* by Isla Schweller de Lubicz. (If you are wondering, it's an Egyptological fantasy, full of *tekh, Neters,* Ptah, and Ptah's *Ka*.)

REMAINDERS

☆   *25.12.87*

A long time back I had a schoolfriend who collected bus tickets. Most of us were simply stockpiling tickets whose digits added up to twenty-one, since it was well-known that a wealthy eccentric would come around one day and pay us ten pounds each for them, but my friend (it wasn't me, I swear it) only wanted tickets with numbers like U238 or Cl 355 or Zr 9122 – tickets, I need hardly explain, where the letters were the symbols for chemical elements and the numbers were an approximation to the atomic weight. It was an arduous business, and whenever he got within sight of success, the Nuclear Physics Laboratories at Brookhaven or Oak Ridge would come up with some new artificial element with a tricky combination of letters, Lawrencium or Mendelevium; or would announce that on closer inspection, Masurium and Illinium had been declared non-existent.

None of this, plainly childishly obsessional behaviour, has anything to do with the desire and pursuit of car licence plates whose letters reflect some aspect of your personality, your initials or age or character (CAD, ACE, YUP). These are called 'élite registrations' to show the importance of their owners, and those who deal in them belong, or the best of them do, to the Cherished Numbers Dealers Association, which has a Code Of Conduct. (What behaviours can this code exclude? Killing the owners of desirable plates? Trading in trigrammata which are obscene or blasphemous in remote languages, which insult foreign heads of state or invite the attentions of traffickers in drugs or deviance?)

I've a price list in front of me with more than a thousand Cherished Numbers, ranging from HN 1 at £16,900, surely close to the twin acmes of desirability, which I take to be ER11 or I AM 1, down to YKT 38J at £30, which seems to be hardly desirable at all, unless you are Yolanda Kallipygia Thighworthy, or live at Number 38 J Street, Yakutsk, in which case it is your lucky day. Certain rules emerge: two letters is better than three letters, any low number is better than any high number, no matter how elegant (thus TPR 9 sells for £1,500, but you can get SAD or PUB or LUX or RED or TEX for only a couple of hundred); letters before numbers is better than numbers before letters (6 PT is a few hundred less than PT 16); an extra letter at the end reduces value sharply (with the exception of TON 1Y, a cool £11,500). There must be other hidden variables, such as whether you get a car along with the plate; or else why is TMF 640 selling for £747 when WOK 383, the very thing for a man who owns a chain of chinese take-aways (takes-away?) is a mere £469?

There are bargains to be found. OVA 1, which would suit a rich and egotistical obstetrician, if such a person exists, likewise a chicken farmer or a dyslexic umpire, is plainly worth every penny of £7,800; by comparison KH 983 seems exorbitant at £2,697. There's no great demand for subtlety. Dull 88 LG is £2,255, while LCK 1T is given away at £520, and a mere £240 will purchase you XUF 1Y, a must for any boustrophedontist.

☆ *10.10.86*

Attentive readers will have observed that on rare occasions a tiny cirrus of criticism beclouds the effulgence of my admiration for auctioneers. To the carping few, it sometimes seems as though the great auction houses do not wish to share equally with their customers that risk of disappointment which all of the runners who in life's race must run, must run. Few, however, protect themselves as thoroughly as the folks in Bunbury whose conditions of sale are in front of me as I speak. They disclaim responsibility for authenticity, age and condition. They disclaim responsibility for default by the buyer. Or by the vendor. Or both (if the seller turns out not to own the lot and the buyer doesn't pay, Bunbury still want their commission). They will execute bids, on the understanding that they will not necessarily bid the right amount on the right lot, or at all. 'No one in the auctioneer's employ has authority to make any representation of fact.'

'You said it was a Rembrandt'; 'You said it wouldn't rain'; 'You said it would bear my weight'; 'You said the very important antique cannon was not loaded.' To all such plaints a smiling officer of the company will indicate with a gesture that the buck has passed on.

OK, they won't tell you what the picture is or whether the guy has the right to sell it or whether they will accept your bid or not. Just sit tight and hold your tongue and you will be all right.

Well, maybe. Everyone there is deemed to be there at their own risk. We are not responsible for any injury or accident that may occur.

Well, look, I mean we are all grown up around here, right? Man goes to an auction, auctioneer's gavel flies off the handle, auctioneer's clerk gets sauced and does likewise, can't expect chap on the rostrum to do anything about it. One of our clerks dropped the grand piano (Taiwan Bechstein Baby Grand) on you and it deconstructed a couple of ribs? Hard cheddar, old chap. Threw a follower-of-Bernini bronze at you and knocked a tooth out?

Really, where did it go? Not the tooth. Through the window? Mister, that's our window that's your bronze at fall of hammer. Like it says here, you are responsible for any damage you or your purchases may do to the other lots, the staff or the premises. Not likely though Sir, is it? Substantial place we have here. For instance, feel these magnificent Corinthian pillars. Steady as rock. Put your whole weight against it. That's right Sir, like that. Oh, Oh lor'. What have you gone and done now?

☆ 7.10.83

I am very happy to welcome the return of Joseph, or 'Joseph' as he signs himself, punctilious about the inverted commas. He was one of the busiest wall prophets of the sixties, taking a firm line against abortion, sex, drugs and all those pastimes of the period. He appeared on every hoarding, overpass, canal bank and railway cutting, and I wondered if it was the *nom de pentel* of a whole team. Then he stopped, like Job, and took up with his own affairs for several years. Now he is back in business. In Clerkenwell I saw 'FOR YEARS WE ACCUSED THE SIN OF OTHERS: NOW WE CONDEMN OUR OWN' and near the Hayward Gallery a bit of Job-like self-flagellation about being guilty of the greatest sin, the sin of silence. And last week I saw the man himself, an unassuming person by no means as colourful as the MEAT FISH AND EGGS=SEX man, sandwichboarding the Psychics' and Mystics' Fair in Earl's Court. Inside, the Aetherius Society had a special on Holy Rocks from Charged Mountains ('between July 23rd 1958 and August 23rd 1961, nineteen Mountains throughout the world were Charged by The Cosmic Masters.' £30.70 Postpaid and Insured Inland. Vat Included) and there were recordings by another man called Larkin, this one in favour of The Planetary Initiative for the World We Choose, and harmony on Earth via music and the arts. Outside was Joseph in the chill evening. In front his message was: 'The Bible says Christ came from Heaven. The Psychics say he came from outer space.' At the back it said: 'The bible says Jesus returned to the right hand of his father. The Psychics say he left in a flying saucer.' Welcome back Joseph, the Cities of the Plain need you.

I bet Amos got invited to lots of cocktail parties ('Do your woe-to-the-bloody-city shtick again. Cyn hasn't heard it.') and Cassandra was a wow on Trojan Breakfast TV. She may even have made it to the main current affairs show, *Priam Time*.

Forget I said that about the holy rocks will you? I see the pamphlet may not be reproduced, even in part, without the written permission of His Eminence Doctor Sir George King, OSP, Professor of Human Relations, Western Master of Yoga, PhD, DLitt.

☆ 16.3.84

It hasn't been a bad month, all things considered (things like *The Desert a City* by Derwas K. Chitty; *La Vie Sexuelle* par Auguste Forel; *Marriage in the Melting Pot* by George Ryley Scott), but the recent sale by Sotheby's of divers lots of blank paper – granted, ornately blank paper, glittering green and gold, used for binding eighteenth-century children's books (I mean used in the eighteenth century for binding children's books, of course, nothing else) has once again prodded me into semi-furious rumination about the motives of collectors of books and auxiliary materials.

Love of literature has nothing to do with it: people who collected cellos because they liked listening to cello concertos would be rightly judged to have seized hold of the wrong end of the stick, bow or baton; while if I said that I was partial to a bit of Brahms played by an Oistrakh or two, but what I really specialized in was lumps of raw vulcanite, that I was so passionately fond of having my ear ravished that I had collected eleven hundred varieties of blank tape, you would conclude that I was out of, or off, my prahm, or Brahm. (*Pram*, also *prahm, praum, prame*: a flat-bottomed boat or lighter used especially in the Baltic or Netherlands for shipping cargo: 1548 '*for the prame hyir havand thair gudis to the schip*'.)

Given that the collecting urge (an urge is less biological than an instinct, but more respectable than a mania) is always based upon some false premiss about the association between matter and spirit, ie, a magical delusion, there are still categories, ranks and orders of collectors. One may collect truth, another beauty, and these are very different things. Others may collect for rarity, for importance, or for literary value; and here logical problems arise. For a book may be visibly beautiful or demonstrably rare: but a book cannot be of literary importance or merit, for the merit and value do not inhere in the single book, which is essentially a replicate.

We all adopt various stratagems to cope with this epistemological scandal at the heart of our trade. A sophisticated bibliograph from a very senior booksellers reckons that one sells not a historical datum but a historical object, and therefore that a book that has been in any way sophisticated or is less than perfect (*they* never sell books that are less than perfect or in any way sophisticated) is not a second best but an absurdity: a book lacking a half-title is as relevant as a tripod lacking a leg. The trouble is that historical validity is a very imponderable sort of commodity to be dealing in: what you are collecting is the good faith and good sense of the bookseller and of each preceding owner and handler.

One solution is to collect only important copies: author's own copies with corrections, critics' copies, dedication copies. Adam Smith's copy of *Decline and Fall*,* Leavis's *Seven Types of Ambiguity* have recently been offered for sale – so briefly, was Emerson's copy of *Walden*, or was it Thoreau's copy of *Representative Men*, but it disappeared in a flurry of recriminations and lawsuits when the real owners discovered it had gone. You can go and inspect Darwin's copy of *Das Kapital*, and observe that it is unopened and thus unread; from the near-sublime to the near-ridiculous, I drove my family mad the other night, as they watched *Riddle of the Sands*, by reminding them that my copy of the book was a presentation from Erskine Childers to one E. Heaton Ellis, a yachtsman and later Assistant Director of Intelligence, Admiralty, *and did they realize what that meant?*

☆ 2.11.84

Charles Darwin is at his most approachable when he is giving way to enthusiasms: exploring with grave delight the 'exhaustless fertility of Nature in the production of diverse yet constant forms' of barnacles, living or fossil, recounting with astonished precision the craftsmanship of orchids or of earthworms, or, best of all, describing, as naturalist rather than biologist or theoretician, the curious behaviour patterns of the Darwin domestic animals or the Darwin infants.

Those books of Darwin's that gave the least theological offence have been the least popular. The works on barnacles, though they remain essential references for any balanologist (or do I mean cirropodist?), were out of print from the 1850s to the 1960s; *The Formation of Vegetable Mould through the Action of Earthworms* ran through thirty impressions in its first thirty years, but none at all during the next thirty; his orchid book (*On the various contrivances by which British and foreign orchids are fertilized by insects, and on the good effects of intercrossing*) was last printed in 1904, except for a facsimile edition, no longer available, of the sixth

---

* Gibbon, not Waugh.

American impression of the second edition; and the *Biographical Sketch of an Infant*, where, in the course of a dozen delightful pages, the doting but clear-sighted parent managed to adumbrate the chief lines of the next century of research in developmental psychology, was for nearly three-quarters of that century obtainable only in Armenian or Russian, although, to be honest, I doubt if the Armenian edition (Yerevan 1914) was at all widely available for very long.

The Expression of the Emotions in Man and Animals has not been so neglected, having been sporadically reissued, but the critical and bibliographical esteem it commands have both oscillated. Sobersided Darwinists have been a trifle sheepish about it, perhaps because it shamelessly exudes wonder and enjoyment, and because it is based not upon any serious (painstaking, pain-giving) experiments, but upon hearsay, anecdote and informal observation (it is a great source of comfort and stimulus to dog-owners) and also upon the responses to the wonderfully absurd questionnaire ('Does shame excite a blush when the colour of the skin allows it to be visible: and especially how low down the body does the blush extend?'*) which Darwin had printed and circulated among missionaries, anthropologists, tropical surgeons and others into whose purview a dusky flush might properly fall. The originals of these questionnaires are hugely rare, Questing Beasts whose capture brings to collector or bookscout hundreds of brownie points (readily convertible into currency): but they have been reprinted (Freeman and Gautry, *Bull Brit Mus Nat Hist* [hist series] 4, 1972) as well as in the *Expressions* itself, where anyone can enjoy Darwin's idiosyncratic common sense: '15) Can guilty or sly or jealous expressions be recognized? though I know not how these can be defined. 16) Is the head nodded vertically in affirmation and shaken laterally in negation?'

The queries were propounded because Darwin thought it important, for the purposes of evolutionary theory, to ascertain 'whether the same expressions and gestures prevail, as has often been asserted without much evidence, with all the races of mankind, especially those who have associated but little with Europeans'. Of necessity, Darwin took evidence at second hand, but not uncritically: 'General remarks on expression are of comparatively little value, and memory is so deceptive that I earnestly beg it may not be trusted.' The same scruple led him to insist that the illustrations of

---

* 'Sir J. Paget, who necessarily has frequent opportunities for observation, has kindly attended to this point during two or three years. With English women blushing does not extend below the neck.'

the diverse expressions should be those now-celebrated heliotypes of photographs by Otto Rejlander and others, the howling infants displaying what Lavater called Simple Bodily Pain, the young lady disdainfully 'supposed to be tearing up the photograph of a despised lover', the whiskered gentleman (perhaps Rejlander himself?) simulating disgust ('A smear of soup on a man's beard', muses Darwin, 'looks disgusting, though there is of course nothing disgusting in the soup itself'), and the horrible electrical rictus in the faces of M Duchenne de Boulogne's faradized madmen.

Expression of Emotions is crammed with curious anecdote (monkeys close their eyes when given snuff), with happy observations from Shakespeare, Lady Mary Wortley Montagu, Rajah Brooke, and Sutton, the observant keeper at Regent's Park and with striking imagery: 'I remember seeing a man utterly prostrated by prolonged and severe exertion during a very hot day, and a bystander compared his eyes to those of a boiled codfish'; but it is the photographs which excite bookpersons. At 7,000 copies it is much the commonest Darwin first edition; but demand, and consequently price, rose abruptly when it came to be thought of as a sort of photographic incunabula (which it never was).

Things grew more interesting when Darwin's bibiliographer detected two distinct issues of the first edition, differing in minor but unmistakable points concerning the arrangement of preliminary and final leaves, differences of setting, punctuation and capitalization. (Does Agony have a capital A on the list of illustrations? Is there a comma or a full-stop after the word 'portrait' in the advertisements? Has an inverted comma fallen on page 61?) Priority was easily established, all the differences pointing towards increased clarity and consistency with the Murray house style. There were already two states of the plates, presumably because the masters wore out and had to be replaced. The more obsessively one compared the two variants, the more differences emerged: but they stayed remorselessly trivial, so I was always rather ashamed about the whole business when it emerged, as it frequently did, in the course of salestalk: 'Of course, it is quite vital that a discerning collector like Sir should have the first issue as it first sprang from the press. Now, while the alterations between what we professionals call Freeman 1141 and Freeman 1142 are not momentous, quite erm the reverse actually, erm, you don't really want an example, well for instance on page 59 there is a drawing of a 'Cat in an affectionate frame of mind, by Mr Wood' and in what we take to be the second issue it says 'Cat in an affectionate frame of mind. By Mr Wood', I'll write it down shall I? So you know that it's the drawing, not the cat that is by Mr Wood. And on page ten "expounder" gets a hyphen, and on page 208 of the second issue there is a brand new misprint "htat" for "that" . . .'.

The more one goes on in this strain, the more one is convinced that this is not a fitting activity for a full-grown lad or one in possession of a moiety of one's marbles. Sometimes I would ramble defiantly on, about collecting as an exercise in pure style or stylish purism, about the properly pious collector and his proper platonic love of the Platonic first issue or prototype, even if there were no visible mark to distinguish it from a later issue; only a crude logical positivist would settle for less. It is what the eye doesn't see that the heart grieves after. Trivial typos were only the outward and visible sign (or *signes*) of an inward and spiritual difference (or *différance*), even though it may be a zero différance. The words take on an entirely new significance in a new historical context, as Borges understood.

If there are two impressions, the tone of the passage alters, even if the words remain the same: what the author first merely *proposed* he is now *reasserting*, with all that that implies.

And at length I would offer the corrupt lure of some possible meaningful Textual Variation, on some as yet unscanned page. For the true devotee this is of course just a rationalization, like saying that you eat fish on Fridays because the body needs additional protamine phosphate at the weekend.

But rationalization or no, there *are* two significant textual alterations I have just spotted, a small victory in the unending battle against common sense.

On page 104 of the first issue Darwin observes, apropos of inflating the body to excite fear in the foe, and the Fable of the Ox and the Frog, that 'according to Mr Hensleigh Wedgwood, the word *toad* expresses, in all the languages of Europe, the habit of swelling'. In the second and all subsequent issues this reads 'in several of the languages of Europe', someone in the meanwhile having told Darwin, or maybe Wedgwood, that the generalization didn't hold for Basque or Finnish.

And on page 307 of the second issue two toes of a footnote are amputated, and several lines of text reset, to remove a reference to Hensleigh Wedgwood's assertion that the sounds of horrified expiration, like *ugh* and *uh* and *gugh*, gave rise to many words like 'ugly' and 'huge'. Hensleigh Wedgwood, author of the *Dictionary of English Etymology* (2nd edition 1872) was simultaneously Darwin's first cousin and his brother-in-law. *DNB* speaks of him as 'displaying an extraordinary command of linguistic material and great natural sagacity, marred by an imperfect acquaintance with the discoveries of philological science', which is pretty comprehensively damning for a philologist. In August 1872 Darwin was correcting proofs at Leigh Hill Place, the home of another of his Wedgwood cousins, Hensleigh's brother Josiah. Hensleigh might well have been in a privileged position to make last-minute corrections. But it was just a vacillation, for in *Contested Etymologies* (1882), a critique of his superseder Skeat, he has returned to the *ug–ugly–huge* hypothesis. He scorns Skeat's derivation of *huge* from Old High German *arhohjan* as 'far fetched'; on the other hand 'the pedigree from the interjection of shuddering – *ugh* – and the connection with Scandinavian forms like Icel. *ugga* and the corresponding E. *ug, ugge* to feel a repugnance to, an abhorrence of (Halliwell), remains unimpugned'. Personally, I can't take sides, except to doubt the sensitivity of anyone who can use *ugga, repugnance* and *unimpugned* in the same sentence. There's a lot more about Swedish dialect *hugg-da* and Wedgwood signs off with an Anglo-Norman lager commercial:

> Out une biere merveillose
> E laide e ahoge e hisdose.

These seem to have been the only published changes in *Expression of the Emotions* in Darwin's lifetime. The first edition (both issues together) of 7,000 copies was published in November: 5,267 of these were taken up at Mr Murray's autumn sale. A further 2,000 were printed at the end of the year, dated 1873 and described as 'tenth thousand' on the title: they resemble the second issue, except for a further rearrangement of plates. This reimpression had unfortunate consequences: it sold so slowly that there was no call for a new edition until after Darwin's death, and his revision did not appear until 1890, edited by his son Francis.

This is dull enough as far as it goes, but it may not be the whole story by any means. I've looked at painfully few copies, and must examine more. I've prepared a little questionnaire of my own for any reader who owns either 1872 issue.*

Another curious bit of microdarwiniana, perhaps less trivial. In *The Descent of Man* Darwin gives the wrong date for *Hereditary Genius*, the *magnum opus* of his other kinsman, Francis Galton. He gives it once, correctly, as 1869 and then four times in succession as 1870 (there was no 1870 edition). This mistake occurs in the first edition of *The Descent* (1871) and has never been corrected. Might Darwin have had some unconscious reason for confusing these dates? He might indeed.

Hereditary Genius was published in late 1869, and immediately

---

* I received many replies. They add nothing to the story.

on its appearance Darwin wrote to congratulate Galton in the most enthusiastic terms. (Francis Darwin dates the letter December 1870, but this is certainly wrong. Galton's equally enthusiastic reply does bear a date.) Galton was emboldened to undertake a series of rather clumsy experiments on transfusing blood among rabbits to test Darwin's pangenesis theory. He kept Darwin informed of the results, and must have thought that his methodology had Darwin's support. He published a paper, suggesting that his results seemed to argue against the theory in March 1871, just after the appearance of *Descent*. To his chagrin Darwin published a refutation in *Nature* the following month that suggested that Galton had misunderstood his theory and his experiments were not a crucial test (and therefore, by implication, a waste of time). Darwin seems, for once, to have been less than straightforward, though Galton was magnanimous in response. Did Darwin, correcting proofs in January 1871, by chance have a bad conscience about Galton's activities in 1870? Bizarrely, in the second edition of *Variation of Animals and Plants* (1875) he attributes his own *Nature* paper to Galton, confusing its date with that of Galton's reply to it.

Well, even Freud made mistakes. Ralph Colp is a wise and scholarly psychiatrist and Darwinian (he may practise Darwinian analysis, which would be alarming) who has written on the unconscious determinants of Darwin's ill-health (*To Be an Invalid*). He has also had a major part in unravelling the origins of a curious bit of modern folklore, the myth of the Darwin–Marx letter, in which, allegedly Charles thanks Karl for his kind thoughts, but no, he'd rather not have *Das Kapital* dedicated to him. (In brief, there is such a letter, but it is to Edward Aveling about Aveling's book on Darwinism; there is also a letter from C. D. to K. M. thanking him for sending a copy of *Das Kapital*; comes a busy day in 1931 when the director of the Marx-Engels Institute in Moscow is being purged and some Upwardly-Mobile Young Apparatchiks put two and two together and get eleven . . .) I have read Dr Colp with pleasure and profit: but when I found in one crucial context the date of a letter from Darwin to Marx given as October, 1973, my chief emotion was, to coin a phrase, *Freudenschade*.

It's all stuff about *toads*, anyway. The *OED* says *toad* comes from Anglo-Saxon *tadige* (give or take the odd extinct letter) and that has no known cognates in any other language. But the real mystery, to my mind, is what the Aztecs were doing associating toads and toad stools. They associated them in stone artefacts of toads sitting under toadstools (or according to another construe, toads with toadstools growing out of their heads) which can be found in various colours and sizes scattered all over the meso-American cultural horizon. Only three explanations come to my mind, *viz*: 1) The Aztecs spoke Anglo-Saxon. 2) In addition to the well-known hallucinogenic mushroom-eating cult, they had a clandestine hallucinogenic toad-eating cult, having anticipated Western pharmacology's discovery of Bufotenin (the toadskin-factor) by several millennia. 3) Toads actually do have toadstools growing out of their heads, or did in Tewkesbury and Teotihuacan, possibly as they piloted tiny flying saucers between Pyramid and Henge.

☆   6.5.88

Selling books to flighty New Yorkers is always a tiptoe business: it only takes the smallest tremor – a melt-down, an outrage, an unkindly word from a foreign creditor – and it's pursed lips and zipped purses all round. This year there were altogether too many happenings. Hostages and primaries; the Gaza Strip as violent as the South Bronx: everybody's team was doing badly. Midnight of opening night was the deadline for paying taxes: in an extraordinary national sacrificial rite every American by the same hour of the same day must take out his-her pen and write 'Pay the IRS the sum of . . .' (fill in bucks or megabucks). No wonder the cheque-writing musculature went into *rigor*, no matter how willing the spirit. Then the Dow dropped a hundred notches, like a droughty river, leaving the rich alluvium perished for want of a drop of the hard stuff. Useless telling these people that the Dow that can be communicated is not the eternal Dow: they know the smell of cooking goose. Next day was announced a foreign trade deficit in Martian numbers: eighteen billion simoleons in February clear – imagine what it might have been in a month with thirty or thirty-one days! Any spending was risky, spending with aliens downright unpatriotic.

But I think it was the closure of the Williamsburg Bridge, discovered between one rush hour and the next to be a mere collective delusion, constructed of rust, corruption and flaking paint, that threw indigenous dealers and collectors most off their stride. One moment ten thousand vehicles, rumbling or jammed: the next emptiness and the overhanging shadows of tall cranes – whooping, Stephen, Hart: 'Out of some subway scuttle, cell or loft, a bedlamite speeds to thy parapets.' Firm foundations give way; certainties buckle in the rain like limp linguini; a ferry runs once again from Manhattan to Brooklyn, Whitmanesque revival ('the ferry-boats, the black sea-steamers well-modeled, / the down-town streets . . .') Thirty-seven other bridges in New York City are said to be in dangerous condition. A spectre is haunting Manhattan: the spectre of literal, littoral Isolation. Technology is on the run: what might be next? Your collector-in-the-street, the average joe-first-issues-of-L.-Frank-Baum-in-a-dust-jacket, looks over his shoulder and hunches against the wind, chilled through for all his dust-jackets. Will typography be disinvented, and all its artefacts blow away? Who collects gas-mantles?

Then there was the Tamara factor. *Tamara* is 'a walk-through drama, a living movie, a scented soap, an Italian "Dallas", a voyeur's dream come true, more fun than Disneyland, Magic Mountain and Marineland rolled into one, great high-trash fun'. (Advt). A number of scenes from a day in the life of Polish painter Tamara de Lempicka, calling on Gabriele D'Annunzio in his country residence, she with portraiture in mind, he with lust, and various incidents of 'daily life in Il Commandante's preposterous villa cum brothel cum mausoleum' (Advt) are simultaneously enacted in numerous rooms of whatever suitably contorted locale the troupe can lay its hands on. The audience wander from room to room or follow a favourite character about: 'every choice is valid. Every whim or dedication will be rewarded in its own way'; afterwards, or during, they compare notes to find out what exactly they have missed. Or – the company hopes – they will go and see it again and again and again. (After the fifth visit the price drops to $50.) To make the whole experience still more enticing, the acts, if that is the word, are irrigated and girt around with hightone food and drink: little floating isles of drama in an ocean of Perrier Jouet, Tamara Cocktails and 'Le Cirque's legendary Crême Brulee' (Advt).

Tamara has visited various cities. In New York she shared premises with a bookfair. My bookfair. At irregular intervals entrances were closed, toilets were sealed off, and from behind screens came the sounds of nosh, drama and voyeurism. This was unsettling enough; but I had no way of being sure that the action was all the other side of the partitions. Was there perhaps a hastily-scripted addition, 'Scene 23: Gabriele and Tamara visit a bookfair, where he tries unsuccessfully to buy her a marble-bound bejewelled copy of his own *Opere scelte* but is frustrated by a rascally bookdealer from Muswell Hill?' I don't recall anyone actually asking me for D'Annunzio, in fact I can't recall anyone ever asking for D'Annunzio (though I do have a lush edition that, come to think of it, is more like a prop than a real book), but the behaviour of some of my clients is explainable on no other hypothesis. They were standing about – I see it all now – trying to be inconspicuous, waiting for a dramatic confrontation which never came off.

☆ *17.7.87*

Not all the book-fairs and all the auctions in the world can bring me a volume that conveys more rapture than my small octavo *Canadian Pacific Railway List of Designating Numbers of Stations* (1st September 1913. Destroy all previous lists. They did, that is why it is so rare).

What we have here, or rather what I happily have here, and what you are not going to get your sacrilegious hands on, is a magical epic of found poetry 9,950 stations long, every station a melody, together a rosary of names, the litany of the stations of the cross-Canada expresses and the chugging locals from Halifax by way of Beaver Bank, Fenerty's Siding, Hibbitts, Duffys, Tuckers and Stillwater (he leadeth me beside the Still water to Sissiboo, Sigogne and Hectanooga) by way of Basque, Saptsum and Toketic, by Spuzzum, Saddle Rock, Yale, Choate and Hope; clear to Port Moody, Crabbs, and Vancouver. (Not Port Moody Crabs, which would be more than the human frame could bear.)

The blending of Romance and Cree, of Saxon and Salish, of Latin and Na-Dene, is inexpressibly poignant. Mazeppa and Melgund and Medora; Matsqui, Malakwa and Medunkieunk. The voices of desolation – Fort Steele, Wasa, Skookumschuck – blend with the cries of commerce – North Star Ballast Pit, Cranbrook Sash and Door Co, Alice Broughton Mining Co. What a story could be gleaned from sequences like Payne Spur, Monitor Spur, Three Forks and Alamo Concentrator; what an astonishing new verse form is adumbrated by nos 3,604 to 3,609: Hawkins, Bellamy, Canadian Cooperage Co Siding, Jelly, Bell, Yule.

In the Kenora Subdivision they commemorate Telford and Rennie, Darwin and Whitemouth Shelley, a lovely epithet: near Chalk River they speak mockingly (Mallocks) of the Dominion Explosive Coy. And explosive and coy the Dominion may be by turns, Forget Stoughton Holdfast Liberty (Sask); Ridout Kinograma Tophet Nemegos (Ont); Gautier, Pettapiece, Floors. Forget Payne's Spur, the Pettapiece that creeps from day to day: listen again to the sound of the last end:

Bellamy
Jelly
Bell
Yule.

But the way forward is the way back and the midnight of winter brings renewal: Yule, Bell, Jelly, Bellamy – a merry sequence indeed. It would be a bold traveller who bought a day return.

☆   8.4.83

Arthur Koestler had the quality of ominpresence. When I was growing up, whatever tempting intellectual systems threatened or enlivened the time, he had already been there, from kibbutz to condemned cell, like a precise and uncensorious physician (though the censoriousness came later), describing the pleasures and the consequences of indulgence. The world was peopled with his vivid and exemplary heroes.

I never met him, and as that hugely energetic and diverse career of his went on, agreed with him less often; but it was never possible to read him with indifference, without enthusiasm. As malignant or indifferent fate would have it, I never managed to write about my gratitude to him; on the contrary, frequently found myself reviewing books by his associates with whom I was not in sympathy. I tried to say my thanks in connection with Iain Hamilton's originally authorized, later anathematized biography: I doubt if that helped.

We honour none but the horizontal: why not write a fan letter today to the literary idol of your choice? Don't be shy: I do not believe that the eminent object to receiving letters from total strangers provided they are couched in sufficiently flattering terms.

Not everyone honours the horizontal. The *New Statesman* (in which he frequently wrote when both stood on the humanist democratic left) signalled the death of this various and independent-minded man with a squalid piece by David Murray which ignored much of his most enduring work: the novels, the autobiography, the campaign against capital punishment. Instead, taking Koestler on his own valuation of himself as a systematic metaphysician rather than a wonderfully stimulating speculative writer, it sees him as the would-be creator of a malignant obscurantist ideology, to push 'the false claim that society is harmonious and organic' and so on, a closed system to replace the closed system of Marxist mechanism to which he once adhered. (His adherence was at best tactical: he was having 'oceanic feelings' of a deplorably idealist nature way back in the 1930s.)

'Just the sort of system the bourgeoisie needs as it pursues a policy of retreating from the terrain of rationality', concludes Murray, in a tone faintly reminiscent of Rubashov's interrogators in *Darkness at Noon*, who see no 'objective' difference between disagreeing with Party policy and plotting to poison Stalin. His last phrase has a particularly unforgettable, ingrowing-toenail, quality: 'There will be many more Koestlers.' Well, no there won't, and this is not only because people are not interchangeable. I'm unique, you're unique, David Murray is unique: and some people are slightly uniquer than others.

Koestler makes (he hinted) a wonderful subject for the bookcollector: variant titles, significant translations, collected and corrected editions, elusive pamphlets and a fine batch of rarities. His first book (*Von Weissen Nachten und Roten Tagen* Kharkov, 1933) may not survive, if it ever existed. His next, *L'Espagne Ensanglantée*, is merely very difficult. *Darkness at Noon* is about as hard to find as a normally published book put out by an ordinary commercial publisher can well be: I have to make do with a cleanish first edition in a fourth impression dust-wrapper – it took, incidentally, from November 1940 to April 1943 to reach that fourth impression. And then of course there is Professor Arthur Costler and his sex manuals, found usually in post-war editions which had been largely rewritten.

Publishers' errors add to the fun. Do you want the reissue of *The Gladiators* dated 1949, which appears to be a first edition, or a copy with a pasted-in slip which says 'First published elsewhere, 1939/ Reissued by Macmillan 1950'? (Neither or both, depending on the degree of collecting zeal or mania.) The French translation of *Arrival and Departure*, called *Croisade sans Croix* (Editions Penguin, 1947) gives the copyright as 1939, which would make the book, set in Lisbon in 1940, prescient as well as perspicacious. Most embarrassingly, the Left Book Club was obliged to paste over the title page of *Scum of the Earth* a slip deleting the words 'translated by Daphne Hardy' and explaining that the work hadn't needed a translator because it was written in English. And of course no collection would be complete without the scurrilous pamphlet *The Philosophy of Betrayal* (Russia Today, 1945) which takes the line that Koestler was, even if only objectively, a hireling of the fascists who repeatedly jailed him and came close to killing him. Anyone who had reservations about the Soviet legal system was giving the camp of reaction and warmongery just the support it needed. There would, the authors imply, be many more Koestlers.

☆ *11-17.3.88*

Here is an enthusiastic leaflet for the Historiorama at Tombstone, Ariz.

> See:
> *Licking Flames engulf the town
> *Surging waters flood the mines
> *Law men and lawless shoot it out
> Hear:
> *The dread Apache warcry pierce the ear
> *The sharp snap of the muleskinner's whip
> *The terrifying clang of fire bells!

Which begs to be versified:

> When surging waters flood the mines,
> And licking flames engulf the town,
> I think of something rather good
> Observed by Dr Thomas Browne:
> 'There is no road nor ready path to virtue';
> Apache cries may pierce but cannot hurt you.

☆ *19.12.80*

I had just stopped for tea and biscuits at Madeline's Caff (it used to be called 'Chez Swann and Guevara') and was waiting my turn at the newest videogames (Rapist, Holocaust, Brain Tumour), when I surmised wildly that inside every literary person there is a head waiter, waiting with napkin on arm to tell you what is on the menu and why you should enjoy it.

I have certain ambitions in the entrepreneurial direction myself, the most overweening being my plan for a gigantic globular restaurant in Hyde or Central Park, its surface a gigantic relief map of the world crisscrossed by cat-walks and chair-lifts for the obese, while under its surface thousands of booths serve food appropriate to the region. The problem is that you will end up with a great surplus of Siberian and Pacific Island cuisine, unless you can create a vogue for long pig luaus ('the ribs were fine but all that pineapple turns me up') and whatever Siberyaks eat (baked kamchatka with a soupçon of salt and a certain *Yeneseiquoi*). Less grandiosely, I plan a cheap-nourishment emporium selling casseroles, daubes, scouse, and Mongolian and Lancashire hot pot, a sort of brothery or broth-house, to be called 'The Stews'; a few academic kaffeekellers ('The Cat's Paideuma', 'The Urbane Gorilla', 'The Gratias Agogo', 'The Salad of the Bad Café'); and a chain of pancake houses – 'The Load of Crêpes', 'The Crêpe Hangar', 'Crêpe Soul' (with chitlins and collard greens) and a Chinese takeaway called – of course – 'Crêpes de Chine' . . . come to think of it, that last one could have a whole range of those celestial snacks called 'Dim Sum': *Dim Sum, ergo mon cogito*.

Meanwhile, since listmaking is fashionable, here is a genuine one, more in the nature of a found poem:

Beans Cabbage Cauliflower Broccoli Artichokes
Macaroni or Kindred Italian Pastas
Soup (except Beef Tea)
Omelette
Scrambled Eggs
Jam (except in small quantities)
Scotch Kale.

It is a list (from *Soyer's Paper Bag Cookery*, 1911) of things that cannot be cooked inside paper bags. Everything else, including Irish Kale with small quantities of jam, fried, poached and shirred eggs, and Albanian tagliatelli, can.

☆   31.10.80

Those of my readers who were not even short-listed for the Booker should not despair: they have not exhausted all possible sources of subsidy. Here I have two timetables of the world-wide gravy train, *Literary and Library Prizes* (tenth edition) and *Foreign Literary Prizes (Romance and Germanic Languages)*. They come from R. R. Bowker and Co at £16.50 each, a snip when you consider that each page could repay your investment many fold – unless of course you were unlucky enough to land the Premio Piquer of the Real Academia Española, which was worth 1600 pesetas at the last count and would hardly keep you in calamares, let alone clover. But here they all are, the P. C. Hooftprijs and the Count Dracula Society Awards, Doblougska Priset and Nit de Santa Llúcia, the R. T. French Tastemaker award for influential cookbooks and the Wheatley Medal for an outstanding index.

The two indispensable guides list aims, conditions, composition of juries, recent winners, and – above all – addresses. There is some pharisaic stuff in the preface about how one might use the information herein to trace, for example, the career of John Steinbeck from California State Literature Award in 1936 to *Bestsellers* Paperback Award 1964, by way of Pulitzer and Stockholm; very useful, no doubt; but what your average reader wants is to be pointed in the direction of the crisp green folding stuff, the rhino, moola, fric, deng or spondulicks. Which makes it the more regrettable that the editors have decided to omit 'prizes that are little known or only of local importance'; no doubt they are keeping to themselves, as who would not, hot tips about obscure funds with lots of money and little competition, semi-private soup tureens like those wonderfully manipulable Oxbridge scholarships that used to be offered in the first instance to the younger sons of red-haired congregationalists from the Soke of Peterborough and, failing that, to the first person to apply when I say *go* – and fancy that, another of my nephews seems to have won it.

I looked in vain for an award of five million escudos for an unpublished, indeed unwritten, literary project, restricted to elderly Kentish Town booksellers; there were instead lots of ambitious awards for the writer who – more or less – had done most to bring about the millennium. There is the Cortina *Ulisse* ('culture ought to be a common instrument of civilization and not the privilege of the few') which goes to upbeat titles like *Weil Alle Besser Leben Wollen* and *We Too Can Prosper*, the Viareggio (culture, fraternity and peace) or the Lecomte de Noüy (special concern both for the spiritual life of the age and the defence of human dignity, *now discontinued*).

The Christopher Book Awards seem to want it all ways: they are judged 'on the bases of their affirmation of the highest values of the human spirit, artistic and technical proficiency, and a significant degree of public acceptance'. They have gone in the past to such publicly accepted affirmers as Fulton Oursler and Malcolm Muggeridge (twice each), Herbert Hoover and Marion Sheehan, author of *The Spiritual Woman, Trustee of the Future*.

There are no awards, officially at least, for the writer who has done least to advance human dignity and understanding, or the author who has shown the most sustained contempt for his readers; though the French do have the Prix des Enfants Terribles which went in 1972 to Alain-Chedanne's *Shit, Man* (I wonder what they called the English translation), and we are also given a list of the recipients of the city of Hamburg's awards (1933–43) in commemoration of the death (by alcoholic poisoning, according to William

Shirer) of Dietrich Eckart, the Nazi poetaster. Less odious, but none the less unattractive, sounds the Unesco International Book Award, which in 1975 went to the USSR National Committee for International Book Year for its initiative in having 1972 proclaimed as International Book Year.

Much more sympathetic are the various consolation prizes, like the $2,500 given to an English or American poet by the Friends of Russell Loines (his very name a poem), 'not as a prize but as a recognition of value, preferably of value not widely recognized'. I suppose no one feels – or is – recognized sufficiently, but I would not have thought of Robert Graves as obscure in 1958, nor Larkin in 1974. Similarly, the Richard and Hilda Rosenthal Foundation rewards novels that have not achieved commercial success, though some of their medallists have surely succeeded since, like *The Poorhouse Fair* or *The Crying of Lot 49* or *The Assistant* (which also won Malamud a gold medallion encased in Lucite from the National Council of Christians and Jews).

Less invidious altogether are those prizes with really precise rubrics, like the David D. Lloyd Prize for the best book on the life of Harry Truman, or the Howard W. Blakeslee Awards for popular books about heart disease, won by *The Living River* in 1960 and *The River of Life* in 1962, and – my personal favourite – JoAnn Stichman and Jean Schoenberg's *How to Survive Your Husband's Heart Attack*, a book which might be very short indeed. (Entries of four words or less, on a postcard please, to the Academy of Sciences of the Chuvash ASSR.)

There are, of course, innumerable regional awards, for writers from Freiburg and Oxford, South Carolina or North California. (There used to be one for Southern California too, but something strange seems to have happened to it. It was founded in 1972, awarded for the first time in 1975-6 to John Gilmore for *Blowout*, and then immediately discontinued.) Texas does pretty well, with a variety of goodies like the Jesse H. Jones Award and the Friends of the Dallas Public Library Award, which you must not think of as the Jesse James and the Friends of the Dallas Book Repository. There are all those ethnic awards: the Alex Haley Foundation African Roots Award, Jewish American, Greek American, the Godfather Award for the study of the Sicilian contribution to American culture. There are awards for the known and awards for the unknown (Bread Loaf Writers' Conference Endowment Fund has eighteen separate funds), rewards for the young and awards for the old (Marjory Peabody Waite for continuing achievement and integrity), awards for the progressive and awards for the reactionary, like the Prix du Roman Populiste, founded as 'an expression of popular reaction against surrealism and the psychological and academic novel', and then given to *La Nausée* – not the first name that comes to mind when you think about populism.

In France, of course, there are enough awards for everybody to have a couple, from the 100,000 francs of the sporadic Prix de la Nouvelle Vague to the fifty francs of the Goncourt and the two *louis d'or* of the Prix Voltaire (the Prix Littéraire de 500,000 Francs is actually cashless). In addition to these there are the Prix Roger Nimier ('to maintain the permanence of a state of mind and a style'), the Quai des Orfèvres prize to encourage respect for the workings of the French police, and a best foreign book prize (not a translation prize), won rather belatedly in 1949 by James Hogg, the Ettrick Shepherd, since when it has honoured more contemporary titles like *Le Seigneur des Anneaux* and *Enterre mon Coeur (à Wounded Knee)*. Tolkien, by the by, also won the Gandalf medal, which seems supererogatory, and shared the Benson Medal of the Royal Society of Literature with Rebecca West. *Prima facie*, they wouldn't seem to have a lot in common, but no doubt were able to come to some amicable arrangement about wearing it alternate weeks; more logically, Mary Shelley shared a Hugo with Mel Brooks and Gene Wilder for *Young Frankenstein*.

A few tips for the ambitious: the most bemedalled literati, judging from the index of the British-American volume are, equal first, Robert Lowell, Richard Wilbur and Marianne Moore, so there may be some winning formula to be deduced; but poets win few pence, and it is perhaps better to go for the big one, which is the Premio Planeta, worth 8,000,000 pesetas unless this is a misprint. Be warned also that if you win the Gran Premio de Honor de la SADE all you get is a gold medallion of José Hernandez (and perhaps I should just mention that SADE is the Sociedad Argentina de Escritores).

Literary prizes are wholly pernicious, encouraging competition and setting man against man, nowhere more clearly than in Germany where the Bundesrepublik offers 10,000 west-marks as the Thomas Mann prize, and the DDR 18,000-east-marks for the Heinrich Mann (making an exchange rate of 1.8 Henries to the Thomas, but a Mann's a Mann for a' that). The one I would really like is a small replica of Charles Russell's 'The Horse Wrangler' from the National Cowboy Hall of Fame in Oklahoma City, but I'll settle for the D. H. Lawrence Fellowship, to spend eight weeks on the Lawrence Ranch near Taos, New Mexico. Please consider this as an application; I'll bring my own pyjamas for the heat.

Apropos of nothing at all, a snake came to my water trough the other day. I was sitting at my typewriter staring at the roses in a deep dream of peace, when a small Indian child knocked at my door and asked if I knew I had a reptile in the garden. I explained condescendingly that he was not in the tropics now and should adjust his imagination accordingly, but he insisted I look and, sure enough, wrapped around Mrs Miniver, or it might have been Madame Chiang Kai-Shek, was an enormous green mottled ophidian. We exchanged apprehensive looks, while sundry loafers on the wall shouted useful advice along the lines of 'look out mister he gonna bite you Babylon white ass'. While I was hesitating about whether to phone the Zoo and admit that I could not identify it, or call the police and say yes it was me that called them last month when an unfamiliar neighbour who had lost his key took a short cut through the back garden but I was only doing my duty as a concerned citizen and would they come and look at a giant tropical snake, the serpent lurched into the undergrowth and disappeared. He left me with an obscure sense that there was valuable literary material here if I could only put my finger on it: meanwhile, if anyone has mislaid a python, or a baby . . .

☆ *16.10.87*

Hell yes, Virginia, it is a moral issue! At least I don't know of any bookseller who can read the catalogue of a colleague or rival, one who has found a way of asking pounds where others ask pennies, who has substituted coconuts for peanuts, without adopting a moral stance. Or more often two moral stances, one aloud ('The public should be protected') and one under his breath ('Where did I go wrong?'). Now this is remarkable; your run-of-the-mill baker or candlestick maker, coal merchant or coke dealer, doesn't feel guilty at undercutting the competition, at failing to realize the full market potential of the product: it shows what deeply ethical creatures we bookfolk be.

This rumination is triggered by the arrival of a booklist from deepest Ulster that sets new benchmarks on the upward path (although I think the point about benchmarks is that you use old ones, but I'm not sure of my surveying terminology – if you have the light of nature you don't need theodolite, I always say). In the places where they gather, one bookperson is going to another and asking 'Shouldn't someone tell them that Ian Fleming's *Live and Let Die*, as published by the Reprint Society only two years after the first edition, cannot be sold for twenty-five pounds?', to which the other may reply 'What makes you think they don't know?' Booksellers will point to further evidence of unsophistication, like the £75 tag on *The Scallop* (a handsome work of romantic conchology, but produced by the Shell Company in quantities roughly sufficient to satisfy the needs of all users of petroleum-based products) or the failure to grasp that for Indian Railway Library editions of Rudyard Kipling to be truly desirable (at prices ranging from £70 to £350) it is not sufficient for them to carry the words 'Wheeler, Allahabad': they must also *not* say 'and Samson Low, London'. This gives us, but only briefly, a comfortable sense of superiority: if they knew, they would go about things differently. A knowledgeable specialist dealer may, indeed has, offered the rare printed catalogue of the twopenny lending library in Haworth for 1820 (when the two elder Brontë girls were aged four and five) on the unquestionable ground that although their father is not listed as a subscriber, it is inconceivable that they should not have browsed its shelves during their critically formative years a decade later, if the library was still in existence then, a matter concerning which there is no evidence. When he offers to sell this book for £550, both he and the prospective purchaser know what is going on: we are being invited to applaud a daring speculation, to put our money where our imagination is. When an unknown asks £65 for an undated edition of the poetical works of James Russell Lowell, or £201 (can this be a misprint?) for the Cabinet Edition of Tennyson's *Queen Mary* we feel that he has offended socially. The Brontë contract, if it occurs, is between consenting adults: £65 for Tennyson is just not done.

Unless it is done. For this is indeed the terror that flies by night; what if someone does pay it?

☆   11.7.84

Borges and me
The trick, of course, is not to try and sound like him: there is an imitable Borges, and it would not be hard to manage his deep notes without his depths, like a monkey playing the doublebass.

I had been reading Borges for some years, even from the days when it was still chic to enjoy him. I didn't know much about the man, like how he pronounced his name or – perhaps – what he was getting at. I'd heard he had some kind of eye trouble and that was a pity. Nevertheless, I was ready to do reverence.

I had a reverence too for Philip Henry Gosse, father to Edmund and brother to Plymouth, was intrigued, as is every chop-logic, by *Omphalos*, that late triumph of scholasticism, a work of unexpected warmth and fairmindedness in which an honest creationist confronts the lessons of geology. There could be no doubt, for Gosse, that the geological and the fossil evidence pointed to the great antiquity and slow processes of the world; equally, or perhaps unequally, there could be no doubt that the world had been made in seven twenty-four-hour days, for the Bible said so, and the Bible bore God's own affidavit. But the world had been created perfect, and perfection demanded a past; fossils were not the 'gigantic and superfluous lie in the rocks' that Gosse's appalled friend Kingsley thought he had described, but necessary and lovely traces of the intrusion of time into Eternity. God, it seemed, had started the film of History in the middle: but in pre-entropic Victorian physics history was a causal chain extending forwards and backwards to infinity; wherever you started watching would seem like the middle. (All the more so if the history film was a filmloop. Gosse's own metaphor was a wind-up toy set going by a street-showman on its circular path.)

I was new to the book-trade then, and I thought that *Omphalos* (the name refers to Adam's navel, another sort of fossil) was a common book, for I had found two copies on two successive days. Later I found it was relatively rare; later still I found it was no rarer than such misleading coincidences. But the book had sold badly and had been bound up from the sheets as needed in job lots of fifty or so at a time, bound in a variety of colours and patterns of cloth; one of my copies was a true first issue, and that genuinely was rare. The other was bound in a prize calf; pretty but of no merit to the punctilious collector. Two copies of an obscure book seemed excessive. 'Send one to Borges', suggested a friend and showed me the essay on *Omphalos* written in 1941 and published in *Otras Inquisiciones*; Borges, naturally, had been fascinated by this perfect and doomed thesis, but knew the book only from the accounts of Edmund Gosse and H. G. Wells, for he could find it in no library in Argentina. I was too shy or too mean to do so, but later that year Borges came and gave a series of readings in London, in Westminster I think, ringmastered by Norman Thomas di Giovanni, to attentive spell-bound audiences. I attended, I was spell-bound. (Actually I thought he was a little slow, a little simple; but I assured myself that such simplicity lay beyond cleverness.)

To the last of the lectures I brought a copy of *Omphalos*, carefully wrapped. After some thought I had decided that I could not afford to give away the better copy; after rather more thought I slipped my business card, as if by inadvertence, into the book, but did not inscribe it. A note of acknowledgement would be something I could treasure. It would also be a commodity.

After the lecture I jostled and coaxed my way to the speaker; Norman Thomas di Giovanni granted me an audience. I explained my errand, unwrapped my gift as I was asked, put it in Borges's fumbling hands, realized two things: he was more profoundly blind than I had obtusely gathered; and I had accidentally brought him my precious first issue, though Borges, holding it graciously but upside-down, would presumably never know this. He seemed moved; I was blinded.

But still I was mildly disappointed, over the next few months, not to get some acknowledgement from the punctilious Borges. Only at this moment do I realize why. I had, of course, put my card in the other copy (now in the History of Science Library of a Midwestern State University); a small, merciful miracle, unobserved, had switched the books around and removed from my act of homage the intrusive evidence of self-seeking, like a dinosaur bone in the wrong bed.

☆ 29.8.85

Treasures of the British Heritage,
or How We Acquired our Unique Charm
(No XLIV is a slightly condescending series for tourists.)

Before 11 o'clock see that your waitress has plenty of cakes to serve with coffee and that these are arranged in dishes in a closed cupboard, where they will not get dry.

Coffee should be made overnight and strained off before 10 o'clock in the morning. Everything in the front of the shop should be ready to receive shoppers and coffee-drinkers by 10 am.

Chapter 8 – 'The Day's Routine' – from *Running a Successful Teashop* by Griselda Lamb (London, Jordan & Sons, 1947, 96pp, 5/-).

In the same series are R. G. Nettell's *Your Career in Poultry Breeding*, Phyllis Lovell's *Domestic Science: 50 Well Paid Careers*, and *I Want to Go to Sea* by Norman Lee, which goes into my private case alongside *The Middle Way* by Lao Tse and *The Weary Blues* by Langston Hughes and (when they become available) *The Crystalline Salad* by J. G. Ballard and *Whatever Her name Is* by one or other Amis.

☆   *26.8.88*

You can keep tumid Gatwick and humid Domestos, jewel of the Ionian: this column took its hols in pluvious Aberystwyth, lured by word of a new, fresh-minted recording of *Under Milk Wood*, the centrepiece of a residential course of advanced D. Thomism run by the University College of Wales. I was enthusiastic about the jaunt, thinking no doubt that droll Celts would make easy targets for low-level waggery: the Welsh, though courteous, were cautious. What kind of a journalist was I? Understanding journalists – there had been some very understanding journalism in the *Western Mail* – were of course welcome. But irresponsible journalists were a different matter. An irresponsible journalist had visited a previous conference and had used the phrase 'culture vultures'. What kind of approach did I think that I would take? Whimsical? They didn't think they needed whimsical, thank you. At length I was given my *laissez passer*, without actually having to give an undertaking about 'culture vultures'.

We warmed up by visiting Laugharne, where we drank at Dylan's table (offers have been made) under a photograph of Dylan and a poster that said 'All books about Dylan are out of date after this one'. We drank with the book's co-author, genial but saturnine owner of the local bookshop: 'Seventeen Japanese tourists bought postcards but they didn't buy no *Collected Poems* so what's the use? If this goes on I shall be in the workhouse.' I had offered my great idea for opening a winebar called 'DT's'. The others looked at me sourly. 'DT's' was up and running, thank you, and they didn't need great ideas from abroad.

But the welcome in Aberystwyth was more than cordial. Professor Walford Davies of Extra-Mural Studies had lured some sixty people to the Old College, Coleg Hên as we say, from places with better climates (there was no one from the Falklands, which might have a worse one) to spend two weeks being lectured to (John Wain, Ralph Maud, John Ackerman), read to (John Rhys Thomas, Aeronwy Thomas, R. S. Thomas), sung to (Lyn Davies) and acted at (Swansea Little Theatre Company); being fed and wined and bussed about Wales, to Laugharne, to Fern Hill, to Rhossili, walking in the white giant's thigh and soaking up, soaking in or just soaking. In the intervals they had seminar groups, whereinto I was very properly not permitted to pry. They came from campuses across America, many from Italy, from divers other parts of Europe. I saw no Japanese; the one Indian face belonged to one of the local enthusiasts, who were given listening privileges. Mostly they were academics ('some of them have been teaching Dylan

Thomas without ever seeing the scenes that surrounded his genius'); all were highly motivated, committing two weeks and a fair sum of money; I saw no blue rinses or birds of prey.

George Martin, producer of *Under Milk Wood II*, arrived to be greeted by the Dylanists and a few surviving Beatle-crushers who demanded autographs. It transpired that we were not to get the première, for the work was still in progress: 'the ingredients are all assembled but not yet cooked'; thanks to modern technology what took Dylan an afternoon and Richard Burton three days would take George Martin months of mixing. But there were lots of facts and a tape full of samples.

The cast is prodigious. No false Cymric had lingered shamefully in his or her home when George Martin was on the march to Llareggub (though Shirley Bassey had pondered and havered and finally decided she wasn't Welsh enough). But there were Anthony Hopkins (first voice, the Burton part) and Harry Secombe and Geraint Evans and Bonny Tyler and Angharad Rees and Siân Phillips and Victor Spinetti and Jonathan Pryce. Tom Jones, Freddy Jones, Aled Jones. And Alan Bennett. Alan Bennett? He gets to be the voice of the toffee-nosed Saxon guidebook.

It would be unfair to pass judgment on fragments of raw sound, unremixed. The music is pleasing, largely George Martin's (Mark Knoeffler of Dire Straits is briefly heard); there seems to be rather a lot of it. Anthony Hopkins's voice is remarkably like Richard Burton's burrtone, less remarkably when you learn that they were born a hundred yards apart and went to the same school. (But this is a Welsh Factoid; the truth, I'm told, is that Anthony Hopkins was born a hundred yards from the school that Richard Burton went to.) He seemed – but this must be my imagination – to grow more confident as he went on, diverging more from Burton's readings and timbres. But how can one distance oneself from that authoritatively over-every-possible-top performance except by self-restraint? There is less honeyed rubato, more sibilance and nasality. Less cucumber and hooves, but a more ominous tone, perhaps a more thoughtful reading. In a word, less schmalz (smwyllch).

On the other hand Captain Cat's musings on his drowned comrades are enriched by a moving orchestration; perhaps they were already moving enough without plangent chords and echo-chamber effects.

The text has been established by Douglas Cleverdon, incorporating many afterthoughts known from letters or manuscript corrections of presentation copies. There are two new names in the list of boats. Polly Garter has a petticoat and combs (to rhyme with rhombs), an obvious improvement on her petticoat and combs (to rhyme with Holmes). Mr Waldo gets his song back, too shocking for the BBC, which clucked disapprovingly like the chorus of old Welsh wives at his 'using language'. (There's a *Festschrift* title for somebody: *Using Language: The Deconstruction of Dylan*. I asked Professor Davies if there had been any ideological dissension in the seminars, but he, scenting irresponsible journalism, refused to be drawn.) We wondered if there was some plot to produce a new text and alter the copyright position, provoking the ire of some Welsh Kidd. But Martin didn't think so, couldn't say anything about cover designs, theatrical projects or video rights. A modest man, he thought that the new recording would take a modest place beside the old favourite: but certainly the time has come for a cover version before the standard becomes a strait-jacket.

That is really all I can say. I'm forbidden by the terms of my agreement to make any further references to warm Welsh rain, warm Welsh beer, or goodnights, gentle or otherwise.

Oh yes. Bonnie Tyler, a name of power in some circles, sings Elton John's Country-and-Western-style version of Polly Garter's Song in a little choked-up smoky-mountain voice, Willy Wee's Kentucky blue-grass widow. The single will probably sell millions and make Dylan Thomas as famous as that fellow who wrote *Cats*.

☆   *7.10.83*

I've just bought a half interest in four tea-chests of Curiosa, ex-property of a noble Lord; well, I was only half interested, anyway. 'Curiosa and Curiosa', as you can well imagine Alice being made to say in some scatological lampoon of Dodgson. *Down the Rabbit Hole and What She Found There*, or some such title. The thing would practically write itself: (The Caterpillar! The Croquet Mallets! The Cheshire Cat! The Marmalade!)

I think I got the tackier two chests (trade enquiries will not be countenanced), the kind of stuff where they not only call the gardener in, but the gardener's mate, the gardener's mate's mates, the garden hose and seventeen pounds of asparagus. The sort of stuff that circulates furtively (like a hangdog blood corpuscle) round the seedy purlieus of Purley, the bawdy beaux lieus of Bewdley, or whatever.

My interest is bibliographically pure, purely bibliographical. I love the false imprints: Paphos, Jerusalem, À l'enseigne du crinoline, Maison Mystère, Foutropolis, Priapeville, Sadopolis,

Birchington-on-Sea. The dates are either evidently spurious, like 1786 on a scrofulous French novel of a century later, or obscurely spurious, as though by a reflex mendacity, 1900 for 1910 or 1910 for 1900, 'An III du XXe siècle foutatif' for 1899 or 1907 or anything but 1903. They all claim to be printed on papier de chine or japon or pur fil lafuma or esparto or crease-resistant crimplene; all are strictly limited editions of seventy copies for amateurs of which this one is unaccountably unnumbered. Some have the bookplate of the Marquess of Milton Keynes, whose device, entertainingly enough in view of his special interests, is 'In Honour Bound'; one has the arboreal ex-libris of Henry Spencer Ashbee, 'Pisanus Fraxi' himself, the great erotographer. (Most of Ashbee's collection is in the British Library, as is most of the Noble Lord's, the deal allegedly was that they had to take his not-so-fine erotica to get his fine stamp collection: my volumes do not seem to be BL duplicates or escapes, but the remains of some less distinguished stratum.)

Among the low-lights are *Age-rejuvenescence in the power of Concupiscence: or the Return of the Old Man to the Strength of Youthtide in the Power of Copulation* (Carrington 1897), the charmingly titled *Mémoires d'un Vieillard de vingt-cinq Ans* (Auguste Brancart, 1886) and two volumes of *The Romance of Lust* ('London 1873' or perhaps not), which has sentences as syntactically controlled as the activities they describe. Let me quote one supra-Jamesian *tour de force*, replacing the improprieties with some emollient and inoffensive expression, thus:

> It was now my own loved Mrs Benson's turn to experience the inexpressible delights of the double junction. From her love to my splendid Booker Prize, of which she had taken the first sweets, and initiated in her deliciously adulterous Booker Prize into the divine mysteries of love, and the still more sacred joys of the second altar dedicated to the worship of Priapean unutterably sensual raptures; from this circumstance and the constant use of the rear receptacle practised by her husband, whose Booker Prize was a very fine one, the initiation into the double jouissance was less nervously effected than with the less used Booker Prize of the more delicate Egerton, not but that at the same time two such Booker Prizes operating at once made her wince a little before we were fairly engulphed to the very Booker Prizes, the banging together of which in their close proximity added greatly to the stimulating of our own London Library.

And then there is *Raped on the Railway*, ineffectually amended on the spine, with a second, ill-fitting lettering-piece, to *On the Railway*, but within subtitled *The Story of a Girl who was first Ravished and then Chastised on the Northern Express.* This work is of course much sought after for the light it sheds on LNER train-handling practices at the turn of the century: the title page is dated 1894, which would carry more conviction if the text did not contain a reference to *Untrodden Fields of Anthropology*, 1898, though this date may also be factitious, and if the hero did not participate in the Boer War, leading the sketchy narrative to the splendid climactic, I mean not climactic but dénouemental line: 'By Jove! The Woman I raped on this Very Train!' Just the thing for steam memorabilia maniacs, branch line buffs, or possibly Paul Theroux. Or it might provide a script for Memorable Train Journeys of the World no 55.

There will, I conceive, be those who think that this is a distasteful subject, and who will not be mollified by the author's manly stand, I mean his firm position, I mean his succinctly expressed opinion: 'I have always, as a doctor and man of the world, had a horror of rape upon infants and children. Nothing can be more shocking than to take a helpless child and endeavour to satisfy one's lust upon its innocent body. Cases of rape on vigorous adult women come under quite a different category.' There will be those who maintain that rape is not a subject to write satirically about, and that to make jokes about a topic is to countenance it. It must be hard to read Swift if you think that.

For myself, I try the transposition test, to make sure I don't class my sensitivity as fine feeling and yours as squeamishness: 1) 'Nothing can be more shocking than to take a helpless child and mutilate it. Cases of castration on vigorous adult booksellers come under quite another category.' Strong, but serviceable. 2) 'Nothing can be more shocking than to take a helpless pamphlet and endeavour to satisfy one's greed on it. Cases of breaking the plates out of a sturdy antiquarian volume come under quite a different category.' Yecch. Ugh. Is nothing sacred?

☆ *16.3.84*

I hope your appetite for transcendently bad verse is as voracious as mine, for it keeps on coming. An amiable Californian has sent me some Idella Clarence Hoobler, of Worcester, Mass, including the poem 'People of Today':

> Many people of today
> Think they're cunning and funny
> And plan to enjoy others' money

> By calling them their lasses and honey,
> And never appearing grumbly.
>
> Many people of today
> Are soothsayers, surveyors,
> Bricklayers, weighers, players,
> Adulators, complainers
> And contemptible constrainers.
>
> Many people of today
> Are conveyed o'er the world in various ways
> By steam vehicle and bicycle speed.
> The latter is enjoyed indeed,
> And will supersede.

A remarkable and talented poetess . . .

Ms Ge Polter: Why do you choose to employ a condescending word that specifies the poet's gender when you would not dream of specifying the poet's race, haircolour or socksize?

Not my word, but Ms Hoobler's; listen again: 'The Poetess':

> A poetess I should like to be
> With intellect to link as fast as think
> And from it never, never shrink
> And continual work complete,
> And never be left in the cold and bleak.
> Nor of unaccomplished work to think
> And impatiently grow weak.

My sentiments exactly.

☆   2.7.82

'James Joyce, is it? Dat gobshite dey trew out of the country for his dirty writings?' asked the taxi-driver, giving me the perfect opening (but you don't believe me) for an account of Bloomsday celebrations in Dublin in Joyce's centenary year.

Others spoke more generously. 'It is time to repay some of the honour and fame he has brought to Dublin', said the President of the Republic, unveiling a bust by Marjorie Fitzgibbon on Stephen's Green. 'He's got a fine head on him', said a bystander appreciatively as the covers came off, for all the world as if he were a glass of Guinness ('James's Choice', say the adverts). But the bust's grandson noted sourly that the monument was paid for by American Express, and stayed in Paris. Other absent invitees (or invited absentees) were Norman Mailer, Marguerite Duras and Samuel

Beckett, but Sir William Empson and Dennis Potter and Tom Stoppard and Burgess and Borges were there, and Simon and Garfunkel, though perhaps on a different errand, and Hugh Kenner and Salman Rushdie and 'I think I have been talking to Lech Walesa', mumbled a name-numbed citizen at the State reception.

'Here Comes Everybody', they called the Symposium, all too truly, and here too came I, in a trainload of Scandinavian Scouts and Scoutesses (integrated of course) filling the corridors with canoe paddles and reading something called *Dublinbör*. I'd chosen my travelling edition of The Words with a dandy's care ('not the vellum, I suggest, Sir, it might seem a trifle *parvenu*'): a stout two-volume paperback of *Ulysses*, Hamburg 1933, Stuart Gilbert's authorized revision, in the sought-after second impression, with the first literals repaired and no time for entropy to do its ugly work, the correctest edition, supposedly, until a perfect text issues from Munich next year[*]; and I carried a neat tranny, so that Radio Telefis Eireann's thirty-one hour reading, every word from Stately to Yes uninterrupted by sleep or weather forecasts, could go whithersoever I went.

So I came Bloomsberrying into what seemed an indifferent city, until I observed that all the magazine covers featured Joyce's features, and *The Inside Guide to Dublin* had filled its odd corners with encouraging titbits: 'Did you know that James Joyce invariably overtipped?','Did you know that James Joyce's favourite wine was white?' And the bookshop windows were Joyceful with Finnegan Calendars and Biographies of Bloom, with *The Wake* annotated at IR£25.48, with maps and vade mecums and pilgrims' guides to the Stations of the Odyssey, with postcards and every text imaginable, and (fairly unimaginable) a book by a Jesuit, *James Joyce's Schooldays*. (He has a sensational find: the punishment book from Clongowes, with no mention of four on the hand with the pandybat for breaking his glasses and being a lazy idle schemer: but instead J. Joyce four for vulgar language, a mild dose compared with Lynch's eighteen for not knowing Virgil and Nasty Roche's ten for 'constant lateness at duties'.)

Literature began breaking in: at Newman House they were collecting signatures in the entrance hall for the Tsar's petition against War, though some cack-handed scholar had just put his elbow through the photograph ('he has the face of a besotted Christ') frame; and David Norris, Chairman of the Centenary

---

[*] Up to a point, Lord Copper. A text issued from Munich, but unanimous agreement on its perfection has not been forthcoming. Blood on the floor, more like.

Committee, was complaining gloatingly that in the morning, when Hugh Kenner had gone to put a plaque on 52 Upper Clanbrassil Street, where Leopold Bloom would have been born if he had been, know-better neighbours had gathered round to tell him he'd got it all wrong, the Blooms hadn't lived there at all, you must be thinking of Lower Clanbrassil Street, we knew them well, decent folk. There was a marvellous exhibition on Joyce's student days, giving flesh and feature and family to those epiphanic glimpses of his fellows in *Stephen Hero*; and all kinds of good things like the Minute Book of the Literary and Historical society and J.J.'s copies of Ibsen, and the reviews from *The Irish Booklover* ('no cleanminded person could possibly allow it to remain within reach of his wife') and one of the most memorable throwaways in all literary reminiscence, from William Bulfin's *Rambles in Eirinn* (M. H. Gill, 1907):

> We intended riding to Glendalough and back, but were obliged to modify this programme before we reached Dalkey, owing to a certain pleasant circumstance which might be termed a morning call. As we were leaving the suburb my comrade said casually that there were two men living in a tower somewhere to the left who were creating a sensation . . .

And there was a copy of Lamb's *Adventures of Ulysses*, used as a class book in the College. I was nudged. 'It's published, do you see, by Brown and Nolan, BRUNO NOLAN', said a stranger, temporarily deranged by paronomasia.

I went and listened to the Home Team, as it were, having a little quiet fun at the expense of cosmopolitan critics so full of symbols and structuralism they don't know who actually won the Gold Cup in 1904. Chuckles were had at references to the dangers of foot and mouth disease causing sterility in bullocks, and how this represented all kinds of sterility, references made by unworldly academics who don't know that bullocks are generally infertile. The critic who says that the crucial symbol is Stephen's refusal of the coffee, representing Communion, was collated with the critic who says that the crucial symbol is Stephen's acceptance of the cocoa, representing Communion, to their mutual disadvantage. The moral seemed to be that you must understand Ireland to understand *Ulysses*, and while you are all welcome and we need your advice ('I think of Matthew Arnold; I think of William Wordsworth; I think of all those great critics, none of them, alas, Irish . . . ;) you needn't think a week in Dublin will give you the insight that is our birthright.

It became clear that there was a certain diversity of approach. On the one hand the international academic community, serious persons by and large who simply wish to spend every waking moment discussing the works, a laudable ambition. The International Joyce Symposium, of which this is number eight, has a commodius vicus of recirculation between Zurich, Trieste, Paris and Dublin, and its more single-minded participants are fairly indifferent to locale, though some of the younger students did become a little ecstatic, as though the Tolkien Society was actually meeting in Hobbiton this year. These professionals organized the fifty-odd workshop sessions at which Joyce's name was linked with almost everyone else's, in which every line of *Finnegans Wake* was teased of meaning; around them an irrational penumbra which became overstimulated by anagrams ('all Joyce's works begin with a dairy and end with a diary') or numbers (especially 22 and 39), or the Romanian component in the *Wake* ('but this is also a phrase meaning peasants' cotton drawers, exactly of the kind worn by Brancusi'.)

On the other hand, but considerably overlapping in personnel, there was the largely Dublin-based Centenary Committee, Joycean triumphalists, to whom Joyce's acceptance, indeed apotheosis, in his home town, is a personal vindication, people with the equally laudable aim of establishing Study Centres and statuary, memorials living and stony, and ensuring that everyone has a good time; and properly not averse to accepting subsidies, even from those to whom Joyce week, however admirable, is just an event to squeeze in between the Ballsbridge Horse Trials and Gay Pride Week. 'James Joyce, Patron Saint of the Tourist Bored', wrote a spiteful pavement artist under his physiog: you couldn't take a step without treading on a Portrait of the Artist. And thence it is a step to Thomas Gear's Official James Joyce Medallion in gold or silver or platinum, in a strictly limited edition that won't be exhausted till Thomas Gear has turned over five million dollars, and to the exhibition at the Guinness Visitor Centre, and Bloom's Hotel with Avocado Plurabelle in the Anna Livia Room and Sole Bloom and the Martello Tower in sugar lumps in the Blazes Boylan Coffee Lounge and Patricia Levinton doing Molly Bloom's soliloquy every evening in the Earwicker Bar. She was one of a posy of Blooms, a coddle of mollies: you could take your choice of Fionnula Flanagan and Siobhan McKenna and Pegg Monahan on the radio. But I went to another one-person show: Eamon Morrissey's *Joycemen* at the Peacock, though it meant missing the evening lecture at the Mansion House, where the hideous acoustics, together with a sound system apparently designed by Vincent and Ludwig, audio engineers, had just utterly defeated Sir William Empson. In the event, the sound system was hastily ripped out and rewired, and Anthony Burgess's bravura performance, 'To Say Nothing of Another Membrane', was one of the week's triumphs. But there was excellent fun with Morrissey, a spirited if not a profound performer; for him the central episode of *Ulysses* is 'Cyclops', Bloom's encounter with the enraged Citizen who hurls the biscuit tin, the sequence that ends, memorably, with 'ben Bloom Elijah . . . at an angle of forty-five degrees over Donohoe's in Little Green Street like a shot off a shovel.'

Bloomsday itself began with a various and chilly crowd of devotees at Sandycove, some swimming at Forty Foot ('If I had a scrotum it would surely have tightened', remarked an Irish author of the female persuasion), others shaving on the gunrest, absurdly with electric razors, or toasting the day in Buck's Fizz in honour of plump Buck Mulligan – well you couldn't eat Mulligan Stew at that hour.

But even before that the radio began the reading, a vivid and respectful performance with an immense and accurate variety of Dublin voices (though Bloom was too unIrish for some) and innumerable obscurities illuminated (Roland McHugh, called in as textual adviser on the curious grounds of his familiarity with *Finnegans Wake*, complained of the problems of assigning narrative to the optimum number of narrators without creating false boundaries, a little like colouring a map with three inks). I carried it everywhere, feeling absurd at first, but no one objected except a pernickety Faculty wife from Ohio, and so many people were doing the same that gradually the air of Dublin began to fill up with Joyce's words. The time of the narrative moved sometimes ahead of, sometimes behind the sun: miraculously, it marched precisely with it at 2.55 when a hundred-odd costumed characters from the Mayor of Dublin (playing the Viceroy) to various unofficial improvisers, took to the streets to recreate the 'Wandering Rocks' sequence. It was moving, absurd and delightful. Spectators rushed hither and yon along the crowded quays, or struggled with an oversized map to decide whether to catch Dilly Daedalus upbraiding her improvident father along Bachelor's Walk and watch Bloom and Blazes Boylan pass, or dash to the Dublin Bread Company in Dame Street where Buck Mulligan sees Parnell's brother-in-law. There was rather a surplus of ladies in Edwardian underwear for strict textual accuracy, though this is not a complaint, and while some of the minor characters showed extraordinary conscientiousness (old Ben Dollard, flies agape, explained his domestic problems over and over again to Father Cowley for all to overhear) some of the principals reacted to the anachronistic excitement of cameras. Leopold waved his copy of *Sweets of Sin*, enthusiastically; the blind stripling kept getting helped across a road he wasn't meant to cross; 'Would that be Mrs Daedalus?' shouted a bemused camerawoman, and in the benign confusion many innocent passers-by were interviewed.

The Ormond Hotel, where most of the cast find themselves at the end of the hour's peripeteia (except of course Father Conmee SJ, away in Mountjoy Square, and Molly and Blazes at it in what remains of no 7, Eccles Street) added to the confusion by letting slip that their share of the celebrations would be to sell beer at 1904 prices, although a secondary rumour, that they were only accepting pre-decimal currency, had earlier started a run on the piggy banks; a thirsty crowd, not all literary scholars, blocked the approaches and caused a traffic jam that may still be reverberating.

There was more street theatre later, when David Norris took the keys of 35 St George's Street, a crumbling mansion once Signor Maginni's Dancing Academy, as the future home of a museum and poetry centre. 'Why spend money on the dead when there is none for living artists?' shouted a passing figure, presumably that of a living artist, and did not stay for the swift riposte: 'We always have begrudgers and Brendan Behan had the word for them.'

Brendan Behan's word, I'm informed, was 'Fuck the begrudgers', but it was a more elegant toast that Borges offered at the Bloomsday Banquet later; once again the sound system, and an ironic samba from the next ballroom, victimized the speaker, but a wonderful Borgesian phrase snatched my ear: 'if these books last long enough – and I think they may last for ever . . .'. Dublin had done its best to ensure this. The costumes and the critics, the devotion and the exploitation, together had scraped a little hole in the surface of reality, through which the myth could shine.

And it is early on this second Bloomsday morning, and they are grilling kidneys in Bloom's Hotel, and in Jury's Hotel and the Clonakilty Hilton, the fine tang of faintly scented urine (page 56 line 5) faintly falling on the Royal Tara China Bust (£287+ p and p), on Davy Burns,* and farther westward, on the Chapelizod Bridge, renamed the Anna Livia, and faintly falling, like the descent of their last end, upon all the living and the Dead.

---

* See below, 30.7.82.

☆   20.3.87

I had a dream about a deadly new ailment that was transmitted by money. The first people to go down with it were usurers and croupiers and everyone said 'serves them right', PAY PLAGUE: GOD'S PUNISHMENT FOR AVARICE said the headlines; SERVE THE DIRTY BANKERS RIGHT said the graffiti. But they changed their tune, didn't they, when they found that any exchange of goods and services, even casual labour, might permit the spread of the dreaded Surplus Labour Value or SLV. Didn't the Government then lend its backing to a campaign against excessive monetarism, pointing out that while Safe Earning was some help (they encouraged the use of letters of credit, the so-called 'plastic johnnies'), real protection lay in abandoning the modern heresy of financial permissiveness and free growth, and a return to the mediaeval virtue of poverty? Closed down the Stock Exchange ('a cesspit of their own making'), denounced capitalist propaganda in the media and the loonies who taught business studies to the young, leafletted everybody saying that the real culprit was the profit motive, didn't they.

In my dream that is.

☆   30.7.82

It's been a busy week, looking (in vain, in vanity) to see if the new *OED* has accepted any of my neologisms (how are you going to manage, I wonder, without 'pseudoquantification'?) and apologizing to Dubliners for misspelling Davy Byrne's moral pub.

'I was in the bar the other week', recounted a local raconteur, 'and the sign there said DISH OF THE DAY BEEF BURGUIGNONNE. 'What'll it be?' asked the curate. 'The spelling's wrong', I said. 'No, it's just the way he writes his bs. What'll you have?' 'A pint of stout and a word with the manager', I answered. 'Have you considered', I asked the manager "that shortly the town will fill with visiting professors and persons from the media and perhaps a team of reporters from *Time* magazine looking to write a droll piece on how Dublin landlords can't spell?" "You are absolutely right", he said "and do you have any ideas for a Bloomsweek special?" I thought for a moment. "Bloom's lunch, special, burgundy and gorgonzola, £2, it's all in the book." "Marvellous," he said, "we'll do it." And there's the sign: BLOOMSDAY SPECIAL: GORGONZOLA AND BOURGANDY.'

☆ *25.1.85*

There isn't a tremendously strong tradition of oral poetry among the fiercely independent hill-folk of NW6, where I grew up; but it just so happens that I learned to recite (quite imprecisely, as I found out later) large portions of 'The Battle of Lepanto' before I could read. So I count myself a Chestertonian, and ought to be pleased that suddenly lots of people are invoking (not to say recruiting) his chubby spirit. But it isn't the far, fierce G.K.C. that I used to read. It is the jolly patron saint of Englishness, fairmindedness, good ale and good fellowship ('the world was old and ended: but you and I were gay') that is being trundled out and trained on the Enemy like an unwieldy cannon. Even his religious ferocity is somehow filtered out, as though Roman Catholicism were just an eccentric expression of the English Dissenting spirit. It isn't, mostly, the Left that quotes him (so much the worse for the Left), despite his fierce anti-capitalism and anti-imperialism ('Lancashire merchants whenever they like / Can water the beer of a man in Klondike / Or poison the meat of a man in Bombay; / And that is the meaning of Empire Day').

Just the other day in *The Times*, Bernard Levin, taking time out from reprimanding Labour politicians for not standing up when Mrs Thatcher enters the Chamber, enlisted Chesterton in a new crusade against Single Issue Fanatics – animal liberationists, seatbelt enthusiasts, miners' pickets: that whole class of person. Well, yes, he'd have enjoyed a Crusade right enough; and raised the banner of Fanatics against Fanaticism. Chesterton could be quite funny at the expense of other people's intense convictions ('Chuck it, Smith'), but when his own were threatened it was Swords about the Cross. He relished confrontation and his heroes were Single Issue Fanatics to a man, ready to die or kill for the Free State of Notting Hill. His own enthusiasms were not always so charming; his class-hatred, his xenophobia, spiced with more than a dash of antisemitism ('The happy jewelled alien men / Worked then but as a little leaven'), the unreasonable ferocity of his way of putting things:

> And they that rule in England,
> In stately conclave met.
> Alas, alas for England
> They have no graves as yet.

Does he have anything to say to 1985? I doubt it, but here's a little relevance, just five pages away, in my edition, from 'The Horrible History of Jones' that Mr Levin quoted, called 'Sonnet with the compliments of the season to a popular leader much to be congratulated on the avoidance of a strike at Christmas':

> I know you. You will hail the huge release.
> Saying the sheathing of a thousand swords,
> In silence and injustice, well accords
> With Christmas bells. And you will gild with grease,
> The papers, the employers, the police,
> And vomit up the void your windy words
> To your New Christ; who bears no whip of cords
> For them that traffic in the doves of peace.
>
> The feast of friends, the candle-fruited tree,
> I have not failed to honour. And I say
> It would be better for such men as we,
> And we be nearer Bethlehem, if we lay
> Shot dead on scarlet snows for liberty,
> Dead in the daylight upon Christmas Day.

☆ *25.12.87*

If, by some chance, there isn't enough chaos in your life, the effect of a hurricane on a television aerial is to turn teletext into a symbol and a meter of hyperbolically increasing disorder. In seconds, it can do to a text what several generations of oral tradition could not.

As in the speech of the drunk, hidden truths emerge: TEN TORIES REpEl it exclaims; FAIRER VEAL URGED – DEEPER CUT SAYS GRKmK; NO CxcmDENCE VOTE ON MP. Other messages become progressively more opaque; SOVIET LEADER ARRIVES IN USA became SO IET LEADEER ARRI ES IN U A, then SO£££££ ADER ARRI*** in U++, and then the frankly obscure Wa COZ TROCI. Colours shift and change, symbols and diacriticals flicker like butterflies, the very time pulsates like an anemone, sense collapses into the language of night. By a miracle of unplanned Burrovian in-folding, a story about Gulf mayhem is interlarded with homely details about the menu at an Anglo-Russian microsummit. EXPLOSION AND FIRE FOLLOWED BY RASPBERRY VACHERIN. VICTIMS INCLUDE THATCHER AND GORBACHEV.

☆   *9.7.88*

'I don't see what on airth keeps him so late, unless maybe, he can't sell his head', says the landlord of the Spouter Inn to one Ishmael. 'I told him he couldn't sell it here, the market's overstocked.'

Herman Melville treats the matter of Queequeg's merchandise lightly: but when a London sale-room catalogued for auction a nicely tattooed Polynesian pate recently, the response was less flippant. (They were forced to withdraw it from sale, and, making a virtue of necessity, restored the object, with appropriate ceremony, to a representative Maori body.) And none less flippant than Bernard Levin, who reckoned that it is the auctioneers who are the cannibals.

Heavyweight harpooner B.L. reaches transports of indignation: anyone who would sell a head would sell a human lampshade, would sell his mother for ghee and his daughter for snuff movies, his son for abominations and his body for spare parts. There was a sense, as he perorated, of someone working themselves into unspontaneous rage, which made me want to quote Levin's favourite poetic source: I found myself muttering 'Chuck it, Smith', which was Chesterton having a go at some poor Welshman getting worked up about something dear to *him*. G.K.C., always ready for heroics in his own causes, could be unpleasantly patronizing when another man's wither was being wrung. (It wrings for thee.)

Never trust a man who quotes Chesterton, as my old Rabbi, Mordecai Braun, used to say, as he helped the Whitechapel police solve many a knotty case.

But the things that move Levin are not the things that move me, or at least not in the same direction, and the fact that he may be the best welterweight prose stylist in England since Hazlitt (not in Scotland, and certainly not in America) shouldn't cloud one's judgment. Levin was recently sighted quoting the fat racist (and the fact that G.K.C. was the best overweight prose stylist in English since Belloc should also not cloud one's judgment), quoting with approval from *The Napoleon of Notting Hill*, the Chelsea Bootboys' Bible, a sacred text to every microchauvinist, village hooligan or Himmler, in reference to the fact that Caucasians, chaps from the Caucasus, are still ready to shed blood, preferably one another's, for Armenia Irredenta or Greater Azerbaijan. Levin is unsurprised and delighted that after seventy years of Stalinist and post-Stalinist supranationalism, the Azeris still love their natal sod – ie, are ready to start massacring Armenians at the drop of a veil. You don't have to be a Utopian socialist to find this depressing, I should have thought: but Levin looks forward to the liquidation and fragmenting of the evil empire, not believing that the evil will live on with the fragments. He offers to attend the independence celebrations for Lithuania and Byelorussia, boasting that his ancestors came from those places, and overlooking, it seems, their reason for leaving. Do you believe that when the Grand Metropolitan of Kishinev crowns King Petru the People's Capitalist, or when the Grand Mufti of Alma Ata gives his blessing to the Sultanate of Pan-Turanistan (and a jihad against the Georgians) there will be a warm welcome to homebound expatriates of a Levinitical persuasion? I do not.

☆   26.8.88

Two correspondents of notable courtesy (they didn't call me 'remote and ineffectual') have rushed to the defence of G. K. Chesterton, whom I inaccurately attacked last month for jeering ('Chuck it, Smith') at the deeply felt convictions of 'some hapless Welshman', as it might be Smith the Smith of Bettws-y-coed, or Aneurin Smith the Anthracite, when the jeeree was actually, they forcefully point out, the anything-but-hapless, anything-but-Welsh F. E. Smith of Birkenhead, sticking his oar into convictions not his own for the sake of political advantage. Well, all right: but – without getting into heavy textuality – it still sounds to me as though G. K. C. thought the convictions funny and not just their defenders. It was Smith's reference to the conscience of Christian Europe being aroused ('Are they clinging to their crosses, are they Smith?') that got up the Chesterton hooter, as though the very idea that any foreigner could care about Welsh disestablishment was risible. It is, of course: but Chesterton was very ready to invoke the Spirit of Christian Europe, Last Knights and all, when his own universal apostolic creed seemed under threat. Generous Chesterton, defender of the quirky and private, too easily became Immenso Champernoon, the school bully's fat sidekick.

☆   14.8.87

If we are at the dawn of a bright new era of bookbanning, bookblockading and – who knows – bookburning,* the noon will bring an ill wind of good to those who supply the precious com-

* HRIW.

modity. The less free people are to speak, the more time they spend in bookshops and libraries. It is hard to ban so many books that there is nothing left for the dealer to deal in, but they had a brave try in what was then Rhodesia. I have here the list of banned books, periodicals and records as of year's end 1970, and it doesn't leave a whole lot to chance, starting with Abrahams's *Tell Freedom*, Aldiss's *Hand-Reared Boy* and the Beatles Lyrics illustrated by Alan Aldridge. Sex, race, and rock 'n' roll: the triple motif is clearly stated in the opening bars. James Baldwin, Lenny Bruce and Jack Kerouac; *Hotel Orgy*, *The Liberation of Guiné*, *Been Down So Long It Looks Like Up To Me*. Anything by Burroughs, anything with the words Black or Sexual or Freedom or any combination of the same, anything (it appears) in Swedish. *Eros in Capricorn* never stood a chance, any more than *Not Now, Sweet Desdemona, If this be Sexual Heresy*, or *The Literature and Thought of Modern Africa*. A bar on the Tropics of Cancer and Capricorn, on Plexus and Sexus but not on Nexus, on Whitestone Glamour Books numbers 83, 84, 85, 86 and 87, and a surprising lot of rugby songs and jokes, whose publishers probably thought they were on to a nice safe little earner in Salisbury. No room either for *The Origin of the Brunists* or *Absolute Beginners, Why are we in Vietnam*, and *Sock it to me. Alice*; or (fine demonstration of impartiality) W. B. Huie's *The Klansman*.

The list is strangely nostalgic today, with the dusty icons of abandoned revolutions: Simon Vinkenoog and Franz Fanon, Phyllis and Eberhard Kronhausen, Sheikh Nefzawi and Gaia Servadio. Susann J., Robbins H. and Collins J.: whatever happened to them? The Ginger Man and Jan Cremer, Candy and Myra Breckinridge, all gone under the hill. The curtains have fallen on O. as on *O! Calcutta*, and *Riot '71* no longer sounds like incitement.

You can hear the same music (those unheard are sweeter) in the list of banned records. *Hair* and Irish Rugby Songs, 'The Freedom Singers Sing of Freedom Now' and The Who, 'Je t'aime . . . moi non plus' (seven inches of grunting and panting) and 'Why I am Ready to Die' by Nelson Mandela. But then 1970 is a long time ago.

☆ *21.6.85*

I wouldn't dare to make fun of Sotheby's, but I was schadenfreudianly gratified to note that the cataloguer of Lot 141 in a forthcoming sale of Russian literature has not tumbled to the secret identity of the author of *Pionery* (Pioneers), transcribed by him as Uot

Uitman. Uot, whose name looks Finno-Ugrian (there is a language called Vottish spoken only by 128 people on the shores of Lake Onega, just across the waters from the 256 people who speak Vepsish) is none other than the sage of Boroklino, the good grey poet of *Leaves of Graz, Starting from Paumanovsk, Fancies at Novosinsk,* and the unforgettable *Oy Kapitan, Moy Kapitan.*

By a similar perverse ingenuity the same cataloguer translates *Voyna i Mir*, the title, in this instance, of a book of verse by Mayakovsky, as 'War and the Universe'. While it's true that *mir* means 'the world' as well as 'peace' (it also means 'parish council' for the matter of that), it is curious to ignore the Tolstoyan precedent, as though one were to translate Waugh's *Decline and Fall* as 'Decline and Autumn' or *A Farewell to Arms* so 'So long, elbows'.*

Of course it may be a tiny deliberate jest, like the charming throwaway in their latest brochure: here, the Folger Bifolium (two conjoined leaves of a Latin translation of Eusebius, probably written in Northumbria in the first half of the seventh century) is modestly described as 'perhaps the earliest English manuscript to come on the market since the Viking raids on Jarrow in 1022'. I hadn't thought of Viking sallies as essentially bibliophile forays, but no doubt the plunder did come on to the market: *Highly Important Contemporary Anglian MSS (slightly looted), the late property of an ecclesiastical establishment. To be sold by Søderby of Jarvik in the Great Mote Hall. 10% Danegeld charged on the Hammer Price.*

For anyone with money left after the June book fairs (someone say with access to *two* offshore oilfields or an offshore bank) there is an impressive sale of literary and historical manuscripts at the end of July. Tennyson's copy of *Maud*, Charles II's copy of the Declaration of Breda, Joyce's death-mask, a newly discovered Pound translation, a characteristically wimpish letter from Neville Chamberlain ('the German desire for peace must have its effect on Hitler and I hope too that the personal contact I have established will help'), a notebook of Yeats and the manuscript of Hazlitt's *Liber Amoris*. This unadorned account of his infatuation with the landlady's daughter, an indifferent and flighty person decades his junior and a class and a half below him, upset Hazlitt's friends ('This impotent sensualist', *The Times*; 'Disgusting', Crabb Robinson) but must now be the favourite reading of every melancholy middle-aged lecher. Sotheby's estimate of £15,000 for the entire MS seems trifling, when it is compared with the estimate on the same page for

---

* Wrong: before the Revolution, Mir and Mir were spelled differently.

an important letter from Piranesi with a drawing of the Warwick Vase: £20,000–£30,000. It shows how little books are valued,* as compared to things, and what a splendid idea it would be if you spent every available penny on them next week.

☆ *18.5.84*

It would be disingenuous to pretend the customers of Knockabout Comics and Airlift Books are in the main professional mycologists and students of botanical pharmacology. The titles they import, and which have been seized and held by the police for sixteen months pending prosecution (a delay equivalent to a savage fine, whatever the outcome of this week's Old Bailey trial), include *A Guide to British Psilocybins*, *Herbal Aphrodisiacs*, and *A Child's Garden of Grass*. By no means all the books held are cultish, recreational, or advocate illegality; they include *The Electric Kool-Aid Acid Test*, and *Fear and Loathing in Las Vegas* to say nothing of William Burroughs's *Junkie*, his first book, published pseudonymously as an Ace double-header paperback in 1953: it must have sold millions of copies since then. It is clearly only a matter of chance that they didn't seize *The Grass is Singing*, *Snow White* and *The Coke, Anthracite and Allied Industries' Yearbook*. In their leaflets, the defendants misspell *Junkie*, and claim darkly that De Quincey is only tolerated because he 'exists in many leather-bound editions on members of the establishment's bookshelves', a sentence that really gets up my nose, to coin a phrase: but they have come by their paranoia honestly, that is to say on the uncomfortable frontier where your right to read and mine to sell books is attacked and defended. They are being charged not under drugs legislation, which would seem legitimate, or at least possible (a conspiracy charge under the Misuse of Drugs Act 1971 has just been dropped) but under the Obscene Publications Acts of 1959 and 1964, some legal wit having decided that depravity and corruption are not limited to sexual matters (I'm with him there of course), and therefore that a 'tendency to deprave and corrupt' may be displayed by any book that someone disapproves of. Out goes *Oblomov* for painting an attractive picture of sloth, out goes every cookery book for counselling and facilitating gluttony, out goes Thomas Paine, out goes Thoreau, snip! out go *Casino Royale* and *The Queen of Spades* (offences against the Gaming Act – did you know that the Obscene Publications Squad had a squad tie that figured a scissor cutting a page? Some printdealers would proudly

---

* The Hazlitt made £20,000, Piranesi £32,000 (both – Quaritch).

wear it too), out go all left-wing books and most right-wing books and the *Rights of Man* and *Biothanatos* and *Little Black Sambo* and *Oliver Twist* and the Jorrocks books, shopped by the League Against Cruel Sports, out goes the Sermon on the Mount, grassed up by Mr Sholom Al-Jihad of the League of Extremist Copts, Hebrews, and Arabs Against 'Orrible Interfering Moderates (LECHAA'IM), and out goes you!

Knockabout Comics, whose case comes on first, is at 249 Kensal Road, London W10, and needs all kinds of support. It is a lovely warm spring day and the temperature is rising rapidly towards Fahrenheit 451.

☆ *21.12.84*

It's peaceful here in NW5, quite often. But at this moment in time there are rather too many pheromones in the air for tranquillity. Pheromones are those stirring chemical signals that, in handy aerosol form, are offered in the small ads of the vulgarer sort of journal, with gross sexist promises of mastery through pharmacology: 'just a dab in each nostril and you'll have to scrape the birds off with a trowel', they proclaim, unregenerately. But these pheromones emanate from the female dog that shares my house, one of three more-than-Baskervillian mighty hounds, one Russian and two Scots (Ivan, Ian and Iona as it might be) that we keep around in order to . . . I don't know why exactly, to keep the book population down perhaps. She is enjoying her first season, a particularly unruly, romping débutante, too young yet for matrimony. The reason dogs don't write poetry, are in fact the most mundane beings in the world, is that they are not creatures of the moon. A canine Camilla would have to wear marguerites, I mean a canine Marguerite Gautier would have to wear her red camellias 360-odd days of the year (though the parallel is not exact). With no cyclical moodiness to set their calendars, they try to cram an awful lot of living into a few days. For most of the year it's just bones and loyal packmembership; then for about a week it's roses all the way, the red rose and the white, the red camellia and the white, the days of whine and rrowses, all emotion and no remembrance in tranquillity.

It takes her two suitors differently: the Borzoi has gone all Slav, fallen off his Oblomovcouch in a Dostoevskian ecstasy of self-abasement. There is a Pushkin poem – one which regularly reduces Soviet expatriates and doubtless patriates too to sodden sobs –

about loving her so much that I just wish her another lover as tender and devoted as me (me, presumably being about to piss off to the Casino for an evening of morose cards and shampanskoye, and a bullet through the head at dawn), that catches his state of mind fairly accurately.

The other hound, coarsely vigorous peasant type, chopper-down of cherry orchards, seems to have realized that he is to be the eventual lucky one, the chosen legatee, and passes the time with boisterous but not deeply heartfelt complaints. Muscovite whimpers counterpoint a grumbling pibroch (is this possible?), and there is a lot of heading off, shepherding about, and closing this door before we open that one, as though the house were a multicultural spaceship with any number of airlocks between the life-forms that breathe bromine and the ones that dissolve in it. And now the humans are being affected. Last night the hounds were outside, breathing resignation and lust and yearning and general dogginess into the still night when something resembling Ragnarök broke out, crashes and curses and barks and breaking furniture.

I ventured to the window. An unfamiliar and belligerent voice challenged me to step into the garden. There, the voice's owner, who seemed in a state approaching melt-down, explained that while proceeding in a peaceable manner down the road he had been attacked, assaulted, nay molested by two ungovernable and rabid dogs, which had destroyed the very valuable property he was carrying, and in consequence he had, as anyone would, broken down my side door in order to make his way into the garden and strangle the dogs and possibly their proprietor, in lieu of compensation. I pointed out that the dogs could not have attacked him, as they were separated from the road by an eight-foot wall topped with wire. He accused me, picturesquely, of lack of imagination. The dogs had assaulted him *verbally*, causing him to drop his valuable groceries, and thereby provoking his need for vengeance.

I pointed out mildly, but with uncharacteristic firmness (splendid things these pheromones) that breaking my door down, to say nothing of threatening to asphyxiate my dogs and my family, might be considered an unfriendly and even an illegal act. His reply surprised and flattered me. It was, approximately: 'If you think that you are living in a clunking dream world. What do you do for a living, mate? You must be a clunking writer. Do you think you're Coldritch? Living in a clunking fantasy, like Samuel Taylor clunking Coldritch? You think you're in the clunking Company of Wolves, don't you?' And more of the same. As reinforcements for my side arrived, he evaporated. He went in fact like one that hath been stunned and is of sense forlorn, leaving behind him a curiously syllogistic non-threat ('I'm not afraid of any man, young or old, and you're neither') and the shards of his broken groceries, his Precious, a bottle of Porlock Pearmain Cider. We swept up the shards, surveyed the streets for him in vain, and dispersed the audience. 'It's good round here', said one of them, 'last time I was here they had a snake.' This was especially gratifying, as I was beginning to think that the snake was a false memory, something I had invented for a Remainders column a few years ago. But I invent nothing...

Enter Associate Professor Keelhauler of William Carlos College, Williams, Tennessee: Our writer is here wittily attempting to validate one of his fictions or factions (the snake) by reference to another of his narrative creations (this very *ad hoc* bystander). While this of course sheds no light on the ultimate veridicality of the experience outside the authorial frame of reference, he is surely making an ironic comment on the whole narrative and likewise on the whole historiographic process, and in having this irony pointed out by yet another literary construct (Assistant Professor Keelhauler) who am also a fictional figment or factual fagment, does he not thereby seek to invalidate the invalidation and thereby revalidate the validation?

(Dawn breaks. Freeze frame. The twanging of a string.)

☆   *20.3.87*

People write and ask me in various polite ways whether everything, anything, I say is true. We know you make things up, they say, but how can I join IMBROGLIO, the International Moral Brigade Resolutely Opposing Gays, Lesbians, Intersexuals & Onanists which you mentioned last week? And I have to apologize.

Or contrariwise, wasn't that stuff about the toxicology of tarantulas a bit OTT, they complain? And I have to point out it was lifted straight from the latest number of the *New England Journal of Medicine*, or not, as the case may be.

Yet it's always perfectly clear to me.

Well, no it isn't. From time to time the level of circumambient absurdity reduces me to a delighted stupor, until I realize I'm partly responsible for it. Observation is theory-loaded behaviour: paranoids do live in a threatening world, and I live in a daft one. But the rules seem to me clear. There is no point in a fictional Believe It Or Not, whose only interest is its improbability. It is remarkable if there is a Gisela Werberczek Piffl in the telephone book, quite unremarkable if there isn't. It is quite interesting, although by now drearily familiar, that two most respectable Canadian historians are Professor Careless and Professor Wrong: it wouldn't be at all interesting if they didn't exist. Fiction and autobiography do not depend on veridicality for their appeal; biographies and train timetables do.

Good. After that homily are you prepared to believe that the organization that supplies pure water to Northern Lower California (and perhaps other regions of Mexico) goes by the acronym CESSPT? That my holiday reading has included Victor Dunstan's *Did the Virgin Mary Live and Die in England?* (Megiddo Press. £7.50). It isn't so improbable, bearing in mind that she came of an old Cornish family, that when her Son's political activities had made Palestine too hot for her, she would think of retiring to the place where He had been Up (at one of the twenty-three Druidical Universities, highly regarded by Upwardly Mobile Palestinians).

I mean, what would be the *point* of my making up, if I dared, a book called *The Crows of Shakespeare* (1899) by the irreproachably factual Mrs Jane Blackburn, who also wrote *Birds of Moidart*. In the preface, she remarks that she has 'only endeavoured to sketch a few of the scenes which I hope may interest those who care for crows and induce young people to read Shakespeare'. This in itself tells us a lot, does it not, about the prioritization of intellectual pursuits among the English *haute bourgeoisie* – she doesn't speak of inducing those who love Shakespeare to study ornithology – and it would not tell us anything half so interesting if I had made it up.

☆   10.3.89

I didn't make up, or even misunderstand, the *Guardian* Law Report (McMonagle vs Westminster City Council in the Queen's Bench). McMonagle was the manager of a Peep Parlour or Sex Encounter Establishment, within which (it was common ground) were to be seen displays of those kinds of activities which family newspapers enjoy writing about. Westminster City Council grants licences under Schedule 3 of the Local Government (Miscellaneous Provisions) Act, 1982, to 'premises at which entertainments which are not unlawful are provided by one or more persons who are without clothes or expose' those areas which family newspapers are interested in. (That's why they are called family newspapers.) Accordingly, when the two hard-working police officers inspected the premises last February, they enquired of McMonagle whether he held a licence. 'Certainly not', replied McMonagle, or rather

McMonagle's brief; 'the licence is for "not unlawful" entertainment, whereas the activities in my drum [sic] were manifestly criminal". A court case ensued, in which, untypically, the prosecution tried to prove that the defendant's actions were lawful, while the defence tried to prove that they were criminal, obligingly citing four possible counts: of keeping a disorderly house, of keeping a bawdy-house, or keeping premises for the purpose of showing an indecent exhibition, and (flavour of the month) of outraging public decency. The magistrates decided that the show was lawful and therefore unlawful, McMonagle appealed, the Crown Court agreed.

McMonagle appealed again, and the Judges of Appeal, with that logicality that has marked the case throughout, ruled that though they thought that the Crown Court was wrong, and the proceedings amounted to an offence (that is the proceedings in the Peep Show Parlour, not the proceedings in the lower courts), they didn't think that the view was *so* perverse (that is the view of the lower court, not the view in the Parlour) that they ought to do anything about it.

And so they didn't.

I mean you can hardly blame the *Guardian*'s dance critic, on the very same page, for getting so worked up that she denounced a performer at the ICA for thinking that 'revealing one's public hair equals defiance and liberation'.

> Private faces in pubic places
> Are wiser and nicer
> Than pubic faces in private places.

That's what I always say.

☆   3.2.89

An English Bookman Foresees his Death

> I know that I shall meet my fate
> Upon some motel bathroom floor
>   Behind, a glass wall (toughened plate);
> A scalding cataract before.
>   There is a certain style of shower
> Where pipes and valves are so arranged,
>   ° , and   cu.ft/hour,
> (Like APEX tickets), can't be changed.
>   The taps are guarded by hot sprays

> And hands must stretch through waterfalls
>   The smallest splash of which would raise
> A blister on King Billy's balls.
>   A waste of energy, this stream
> Where temperature is uncontrolled.
>   What's death by superheated steam
> In balance with this hot, this cold?

☆   17.6.88

Gay Daughters of Pleasure, a flimsy wrappered twelvemo of unsightly appearance and disreputable content, bears the imprint 'Amsterdam 1926'. Pornographers are not constrained by a strict regard for truth, and if Amsterdam then why 'Prix 15 Fr' (and no bargain), but certain stylistic and typographic mannerisms suggest a Dutch origin: 'Dear boy she cried while she moved herself in a masterly manner. You have appealed to me very much I rather like you, and for that reason I too have enjoyed the pleasures we have indulged in as much as jou.' *Gay Daughters* is not admirable for its wholesome moral tone ('I beg her to embark in scenic art, it being my intention to make her not only a star in the theatrical world, but my lover, as her beauty and charm excited my admiration to the fullest possible extent') nor yet for the meticulousness of its proof reading ('my object was to plock and be sucked off, but I wented it done in an up-to-dafe mandee, and with this ojbect in view I . . .'). For some felicities the compositor must get the credit: 'she carressed it with all her unexcellent skill. It held me smellbound'. But it does have an impressive finish. Stopping the action in the midst of an ante-climax ('smorthing, carressing and robbing it from tim to time'), the authorial presence reminds us unambiguously of the arbitrary nature of text:

PART II
PART II IS MUCH BETTER
THAN PART I
DO NOT FORGET TO READ IT

☆   26.8.88

I spent a little time recently (courtesy Polytechnic of Central London Linguistics Department), learning how to make all the sounds that tongue can utter, tongue assisted by larynx, pharynx, syrinx and other apparatus on the inside of the face. Well, not all of them;

only those certified as authentic by the International Phonetics Association – such lobbying there was before they blackballed *khhhhg* on the grounds that you cannot articulate it without a mouthful of Listerine (TM) or rather a mouth full of Listerine (TM) (I did learn the difference between mouthful and mouth full, but less of that anon). And not all of *those*, because some I couldn't do because of an ill-fitting glottis, and I had to be in Hounslow the night they did retroflex clicks. (In PCL, not Hounslow: try a retroflex click there – or in West Drayton for that matter – and you are in dead schtuch or lumber as the case may be.) Anyhow, I toiled to acquire a nodding acquaintance with all these wheezes and grunts and delicate palatal glides ('Let me teach you the Delicate Palatal Glide', a Foxtrot *c* 1927), a vain accomplishment since only a few of them can be even hinted at by the exiguous character set employed by the *TLS*.

And now there's this new one:
*

It usually comes, remarkably, in threes (there aren't many triple consonants except in some of the less efficient Dravidian languages and triple vowels in Polynesian, I think) and normally follows the unvoiced labiodental fricative.

Suddenly the newspapers are full of it. From the contexts ('What the F*** goes on here, asks our outspoken reporter') it appears to be expletive (unvoiced bilabial expletive), but its occurrence is patchy, some regional or class-limited idiophon. It's common in what you might call the bonking press, likewise the *Standard* and the *Telegraph*: did I see it in the fearless *Guardian*? The rest of the posh papers still stick to fucking, but *Private Eye* goes 'f*** f***' with all the enthusiasm of a recent convert, *Private Eye* the bold, iconoclastic tabudefiant (probably the name of a small Berber village in the Anti-Atlas, the anti-Atlas I suppose being just the place for people who have the cares of the world on their shoulders).

I haven't charted this carefully enough. It may be that for some of the journals I've mentioned 'f***' is actually an advance on '(deleted)', 'a certain expression unsuitable for a family newspaper', 'the f word' (a genteelism that Reagan has made peculiarly his own) and other cringible euphemistics. But if *Private Eye*, that taught a generation to publish and damn the torpedoes, has gone tight-lipped and fizzing, how long before the more pusillanimous publishers and printers are racing to re-establish the Victorian Values of Vagueness, Velleity and Vulgarity.

O f***. F*******. It is the sound of lights going out all over Europe.

☆   3.2.89

Iblis House
Your ref SR/SV WHS
Our Ref 01/1989/1367

Your Diabolic majesty

I hasten to bring the report on *The Satanic Verses* affair up to date.
1) There is nothing material in the book in question to cause you any concern. The author, who was never more than a minor operative in the service of this department, had no access to privileged information. His book is a hodgepodge of rumour, speculation and the kind of unsubstantiated scuttlebutt that floats around any office. He is (according to the best available legal advice), under a contractual obligation of confidentiality, but opinions differ as to the best means of enforcing this. Legal precedents are discouraging: informal executive action may well be preferable.
2) The consequences of the affair can cause us the most profound satisfaction. The levels of prejudice, animosity, resentment and ill-feeling have been gratifyingly hellish. Delightful zealotry roams unchecked. Every person who takes offence at anything is sure that an offence has been committed, and looks for an eye to pluck out. Gloom, obscurantism and benightenment have advanced globally.
3) The situation in England is particularly pleasing. Everyone who eagerly shouted for the banning of *Gay News* and the banning or burning of its resident blasphemer is outraged to discover a mob of Pakis showing similar tenderness for *their* prophet. When a parcel of tinted zealots produced what might be called a Salman tandoori in the main streets of industrial towns, severe editorials had to be written to explain to them that they were guests in this country and should learn some English tolerance. Or else. Contrasts were drawn between Islamic bigotry and Christian forbearance by the very brushes that drew contrasts between proper respectful expressions of disagreement and intolerable slurs on the divine founder of the Church of England.
4) This can be used to boost our current recruiting drive, especially in view of our policy of positive discrimination in favour of those ethnic minorities that have been under-represented in the past.
5) I understand that Mr Rushdie has sought sanctuary in Bradford Freethinkers' Hall, chaining himself to the folio volume of Thomas Paine on the lectern. His deportation to Qum, where the Home Secretary apprehends that he is in no danger, is expected hourly. We are making preparations to receive him.
6) There seems no reason for you to interrupt your holiday. (Glad

to hear the skiing is going so well.) Our affairs seem to be well taken care of by the agents of the Enemy.

I have the honour to be,
>   Sir,
His disobedient servant
>   Baphomet.

☆   10.3.89

Some people are against the hunting of Rushdie – as Sydney Smith said about the anti-blood-sports movement of his day – less for the harm it might do to Salman than for the pleasure it would give to the Muslims. I thought there was nothing more to say except (loudly and by many): OVER MY DEAD BODY. But then a church dignitary announced that it showed the infinite superiority of his lot over your lot, and in a strange burst of polytheism, declared that the Christian Deity tolerated unspeakable blasphemies, and the Islamic Chap should do the same. Other bogus defenders have been squalling about European traditions of religious tolerance and freedom of speech. When did they start, for Voltaire's sake? Let us make it clear, while announcing that it is the ideological duty of any humanist to stick a red nose on the Ayatollah by March 10 ('a custard pie has been launched against the non-heretic'), that the windy fundamentalist trash of Islamic bigots is not an iota trashier than that of the Christian West's born-again book-burners, or the intolerant trash of Sikh, Hasidic, Lamaist zealots. We are a species that produces ideological trash as naturally as a nightingale produces song or a clam mother-of-pearl.

Stop Press.
The compromise agreed between the British Government and the Iranian Ecclesiastical Courts will gladden the hearts of all realists. Half the text of *Satanic Verses* is to be published in Teheran, and Salman Rushdie is to be half-killed. The blasphemy laws are to be extended to cover all religions, including Satanism, and Stonehenge is to be dismantled to forestall desecration.

☆   7.9.87

Consuming, or at least scanning, several hundred titles in an hour while never actually reading a book, creates an odd cognitive state. What stops one going spine-title-crazy or into the special kinds of alpha rhythm epilepsy that come from reading twenty-four lines a second is silly internal repartee with familiar titles: Hi there *Queer things about Japan*, good to see you, Lax of Poplar, how are Hoarse of Barking and Enormous of Wapping? Greetings to Watts on the Mind and Brain on Nervous Diseases and Payn on the kidneys and Miles on the horse's hoof and Head on Beer and *Rust Smut Mildew and Mould* (there's nothing like them for curing a cold) and my current favourite Böhm on the Flute. I heard the distant voice of Inspector Clouseau complain: 'But you can't go Böhm on a flöte; önly on a drøm.'

☆   9.4.89

I'm sorry, no I'm not, to come back to *The Satanic Verses* but noone else seems to have challenged the Islamic proselyte who explained in *The Times* that while execution without trial might *seem* severe, it was to everyone's advantage in the long run; more interestingly, he argued (he did not invent the argument) that the defence that the events complained of occurred in a dream was invalid, because dreams concerning the Prophet were always true, by the express ordinance of Allah, or rather God. (Muslims object, and rightly, to being called Mohammedans; they object less vigorously to having the name of God left untranslated, as though he were some particularist tribal idol. We do not say 'they worship an invisible spirit, supposedly the creator of the Universe, called Gott. The cult of Gott is widespread throughout their country, and many of the myths surrounding Gott are similarly to those related of Dieu, worshipped by the neighbouring tribes'.)

God permits the devil to imitate any creature, except the Prophet. Therefore if the Prophet appears in a dream, it is truly the Prophet, and what he says is true.

This view presents some difficulties. Certain dreams, it follows, for example a dream of the Prophet uttering heresy, *logically cannot occur*. If I thought I was restricted in this way, I should be afraid to go to sleep.

Or certainly afraid to recount my dreams. For you can be sure that if I, as let us say, a devout but somewhat unsound mullah in

Meshed, were to say over my toast and marmalade 'I say chaps, I had ever such an interesting dream last night' and then proceeded to recount a vision in which Mohammed had spoken injudiciously, my fellow Imams would not, munching their Rice Krispies, murmur 'How remarkable, our theology must be at fault.' They would more probably reply 'You cannot have had such a dream since the laws of the universe do not permit it. Therefore you are making up a blasphemous fantasy. How, as you say, interesting. I believe my nephew is well qualified to succeed you.'

No wonder they drink such a lot of coffee.

☆ *18-24.11.88*

I've got a new recipe for delay, have concocted a sort of hi-tech writer's block. (Writer's hi-tech bloch, hi-teck block: one can paddle, or puddle, happily for hours in the polymorph perversity of English spelling, like a child on a pleasure cruise of self-discovery.)

1) First catch, or rather case, your word-processor.

2) Find a cyber-naive, impressionable subject (perhaps a rarer hare). Demonstrate to your subject the near-miraculous flexibility of your favourite package, as it might be Wordintime (TM), Bookerpross (TM), or DOS / TextOperant / Joystick-Enabled / Word-Selection Keyboard input (Dostojewski) (TM).

3) Display the function FIND AND EXCHANGE, and your own charming lack of *gravitas* (TM), by instructing the machine to go through the latest file and substitute some absurd irrelevance for a common word. 'Commuter' for 'computer' makes a wondrous hash of sobersided instructions; 'aubergine' for 'the' has surreal results; various vulgar possibilities will doubtless occur to you. (Many years ago a literary journal suggested, for Christmas fun, reciting Tennyson's 'Oriana', substituting 'bottom upwards' for the name 'Oriana' wherever it occurred.)

3a) Repeat 3) *ad lib*

4) Leave the file to stew on its own machine-code for several days.

5) Forget the whole incident.

6) Return after several days, with a deadline or some other source of urgency. You will be astonished to find a rich cake of prose, entirely free of simple pronouns and conjunctions, but thickly encrusted and encrypted with the words 'sausage', 'pleonastic' and 'water-closet' or whatever ruderies you chose.

6 n1) Bear in mind you cannot now recall whether 'sausage'='the' and 'pleonastic'='and', or vice versa

6 n2) In my case it was 'tomato' and 'pizzle'.

7) This may be as much stupefaction as you can stand. But for those who don't have to watch their cholesterol, the cream on the salmagundi is to attempt to de-encrypt by using the same instruction to turn all the cauliflowers back into whiches, all the bums back into thes.

8) And get it wrong.

☆ *18.10.85*

What with the *TLS* being a newspaper of record an' all, I think it's the right place to get this set down in hard copy: Tuesday of this week (no tapes available, but there are independent witnesses) I heard a TV news announcer (what they like to call a newscaster, one who casts news about, on the analogy of broadcaster, one who casts broads about – likewise a man who tells Oedipal jokes is a Jocasta and a spreader of scatological jokes a Lucasta, but I digress) I heard a newscaster refer to the city of Hebron as 'the west-bound tank', thereby winning outright the Lunar Memorial Coral Spoon, the Spooner Memorial Laurel Crown, for 1859.

Moreover, there is a new lost Graham Greene novel come to light; the portrayal of the irascible Indian restaurateur from Hornsey makes *The Glower and the Puri* one of Mr Greene's most striking fictions. There's a moving scene where, though disbarred by the local MOH, he administers biryani to a desperate fugitive. Mr Greene's familiarity with English commercial practices has already been demonstrated in *The Mart of the Hatter*.

☆ *19.2.88*

HOW I SHOT J.R.

I should never have stopped off there for coffee. All I had in mind was a quick jolt of java, a moment of mocha, a poke of peaberry, with Jonathan Miller, old school chum and man of parts, both theatrical and anatomical. Miller, as every newspaper reader knows and knows wrongly, is a man who loves perverting olden goldies, wrenching the classics out of their God-given contexts. Who can forget his Welsh Macbeth, his Eskimo Carmen, the Mastersingers of Eilat?

Critical judgments may differ, but one thing is sure: he doesn't like to have the context-wrenching done for him. He had commissioned a new translation of *Andromaque* from a poet justly celebrated for his innovative skill and precision of language. Craig Raine (whom I revere) is not one to be cramped by a confining mandate, and had used Racine as a launching-pad for a flight of more than Martian distance from the original. His version was set in 1955, a parallel-universe 1955 where the Second World War is dragging out its Trojan length: situations, characters and sentiments were correspondingly modified. Picture Miller's chagrin: this was not what he meant at all. In desperation – his wife, children and cat had already turned him down – he turned to me. I inspected my qualifications: they seemed largely negative. I wasn't a poet and had no objectives of my own; I wasn't fettered by excessive reverence; my French was not sufficiently precise for me to be pedantic; I wasn't unduly alarmed by the prospect of critical abuse.

I was doomed.

A few strategic decisions were swiftly made. A prose Racine was unthinkable (I'm less sure now); you can't write alexandrines unless your name happens to be Alexander, at least I can't; other rhyming couplets produced a sea-sick jigjog. If the play was to be Englished, and refer, however faintly, to a poetic tradition, then more-or-less blank more-or-less verse seemed indicated. Approachability was the overriding objective: no archaisms, no poeticisms: Racine's narrow and intense vocabulary, those recurring *funestes courroux*, those *feux*, *fers*, and *voeux*, the *perfide*, *mépris*, *cruelle*, *ingrat*, would have to be avoided, varied and diluted. I wanted a diction nearly but not quite contemporary, not Sloane or EastEnder but faintly formal civil-service speech, reaching – in anger or fear or jealous passion – for rather dated colloquialisms and the clichés of sentiment, a language occasionally heightened but never attempting the sublime. The target was demystification: to let the extravagances of passion seem all the clearer for not being wrapped in extravagance of language, and to transmit as much of the original irony as might be.

My Amstrad (it has just corrupted a disc and has been sent to computer Coventry, but I must be fair) was ideal for scratching away at text, but I finished the last two acts in a self-induced rush, on trains, in station buffets and hotel rooms zigzagged about Kent and Hampshire in the wake of the hurricane. Everywhere statesmanlike oaks, queenly ashes and proud poplars lay felled or in undignified sprawls, like Racinian heroes toppled by blasts of emotion.

For all my intentions, I began to have ideas above my station. Characterizations began to impose themselves. On the basis of an astounding speech where Pyrrhus blames Hermione for the war-crimes he has committed, and then generously agrees to forgive her ('Madame, je sais trop à quels excès de rage / La vengeance d'Hélène emporta mon courage. / Je puis me plaindre à vous du sang que j'ai versé; / Mais enfin je consens d'oublier le passé') I began to see him as a Vietnam apologist, explaining how the Cambodians had bombed themselves. Likewise Hermione became the prototypical Crazy Lady of Yuppie-Nightmare movies: exchange a few words and you're on the road to psychosis. And Orestes, I regret to say, presented himself as Marvin the Paranoid Android from Douglas Adams's books. Their idioms began correspondingly to diverge: only Andromache's style should remain consistently elevated. Likewise I permitted the confidant[e]s to be fractionally more demotic in speech, nannyish or schoolmasterly or lady's-maid-like. Pylades, who is traditionally as princely as Orestes, I began to see as one in the long line of NCOs and other military gentlemen who come to clear the stage of the mess of corpses and emotions left by their betters, the municipal dustcart after the Lord Mayor's Show. This led me, delighted by my own daring, to one real extravagance: I translated the closing couplet ('Sauvons-le. Nos efforts deviendraient impuissants / S'il reprend ici sa rage avec ses sens') as

Lift him. Look sharp. There's fuck-all we can do
If he's still raving mad when he comes to.

I rubbed my hands, Saved To Disc, and smirked. I need not have bothered.

I could have handed over the text and gone my way, but a long-suppressed yearning for glitter and greasepaint led me to haunt the Old Vic. I watched entranced the embryological miracle of pages becoming performance, and was overcome by mawkish, Priestleyish Good Companionship at being allowed to feel part of a company. We worked at the text, changing a score or two of lines that grated or jarred when grating and jarring were not wanted: the cast professed enthusiasm. (Some critics, to whose insight I defer, tell me that this is not so, and that the cast were obviously unhappy with the text. If their enthusiasm was feigned then they are even better actors than I took them for.)

Buthrotum in Epirus, I discover, is modern Butrota, a small city on the Corfu Channel. Have we unjustly neglected the Albanian dimension? I make a number of ingenious suggestions, which are inexplicably ignored.

'Fuck-all' stood no chance. There is no tradition of proletarian backchat in Racine, and though the production may be designed to remove incrustations of veneration, it is not designed to subvert the author. Besides, everyone can predict what the press would make of a four-letter classic. I gracefully surrender and reserve my version for the to-be-published text, with a note which refers to Pylades as 'an NCO talking to squaddies, reverting thankfully to his idiolect when all the members of the officer class are busy elsewhere or dead or mad'. I am inordinately proud of it. The publisher has his doubts but passes the proofs.

I miss the first preview because I am moving house (three humans, seven quadrupeds and eleven thousand books). Jonathan Miller is a little perturbed at unexpected laughter at a few lines. We adapt and adjust: the following night there is unsought laughter in other places. We adjust further: what's left seems to be genuine discomfort, which is not unwelcome. Two lines which regularly get a murmur, for which the translation will come to be blamed: 'Who told you to?' – not a radical rendering of 'Qui te l'a dit?' – and Orestes' 'Thank you Heaven: my misery is more than I dared hope for', which is excoriated as a piece of ludicrously anachronistic post-Freudian paranoid posturing. The original is 'Grace aux dieux! Mon malheur passe mon espérance.'

The first night passes with the usual number of mishaps. Local ENT wards have been scoured for whoopers, hackers and gaspers: 'Come on Dad, wrap up warm and bring lots of hankies, the theatre air will do wonders for your poorly throat.' (We had a full *grand-mal* epilepsy in a preview: the cast responded with stoical professionalism, not unmixed with professional stoicism.)

Speaking of stoicism, my own pleases and relieves me. What does it feel like to be generally abused? Not much actually. The general critical opinion is that I have traduced a noble poet, besmirched a fine set, betrayed splendid actors. Racine, the argument in some places runs, is an old-fashioned poet and should be translated in old-fashioned words. I have turned a tragedy into a comedy or possibly a melodrama. A comedy, says the *Evening Standard*, which also says that Jonathan Miller wasn't there. More curiously, Milton Shulman in a not wholly hostile review, complains about various idioms, including one, 'shoot-out', that had been cut the previous day. Has he taken to reviewing previews, a frightful discourtesy to the actors? Or has he bought and read a script, an extraordinary compliment? I ask, but get an unsatisfactory answer. *The Times* complains that I am recklessly idiomatic, the *Mail* makes jokes about my name I had not thought to hear again. Hughschall B. Nameless of the *Daily Daily* says the gap between elevated sentiments and unelevated language can only be bridged by laughter, a curious view of the modern stage, screen, novel, and life.

The worst thing that happens is that I see copies of the text on sale and rush to buy one, only to find that the publisher has had last-minute cold feet about my ending: substituted 'nothing' for 'fuck-all' and deleted my note. I contemplate mayhem but am separated by the Atlantic. I reflect that it is, after all, the Old Vic text, and it is something to have one's words in print only fourteen weeks after the mere idea of the project was first adumbrated.

The best thing that happens that day is that I get a copy of John Robert Colombo's *New Canadian Quotations* and find three entries under my name. (Praisers of Toronto are welcome whoever they are.) Real fame!

Later reviews include a couple that are complimentary, others that are critical but at least assume that we sinned wittingly; understanding that an afternoon's editorial session could have removed the two dozen colloquialisms that so stuck in the critical craw, if director and cast had wanted them changed. One complains that the words were unsuitable for a production in seventeenth-century dress, as though the costumes were chosen first, and the translation an accessory like an ill-matched handbag.

But if I have committed myself to accessibility, I cannot argue with the audience. I cannot, in Brecht's phrase (nearly) dissolve the audience and elect another. How many false notes does it take to spoil a symphony? Not many: go Pa-Pa-Pa-*Oink* in Beethoven's Fifth, and you are dead, brother.

By the third performance, inappropriate laughter had vanished.

Critics I respect have liked it. (Didn't realize how much I respected them till now.) Watch out, Bérénice, I've got my eye on you.*

☆ *18.2.83*

And speaking of self, there was a poster in Bloomsbury offering a course in 'Gnostic Self-Freemasonry'. I didn't think that Freemasonry was something you could do to yourself, though you could stand in front of a mirror practising those rituals that sound so delightfully *risqué* when printed in Masonic manuals with a series of initials: 'Then the Candidate shall s. h. f. u. h. a. while the Lodge-Keeper d. y. b . . .'. But one man can no more constitute a Freemasonry than he can a conspiracy or a riot. What next? Self-Rotary? Self-Elks? Self-Independent-Oddfellowship? The same poster had the most engaging invitation I've seen for a long time:

> ENTER THE CIRCLE OF ETERNITY
> (Nearest Underground: Russell Square.)

THE END

The end is the end. After you and I and all shall have got to the end, no further can we go. But as the Preface of a Book is always the 'Bugler' of the subject matter of the Book, it is necessary, that the **end** should also tell us something of the sound of the 'Bugle' in front, who, in this A B C, is not commissioned to have the first and last say, as Mr. Turner – C, 305. The soldiers who go in front of a battle have forfeited their right to see behind; so are the soldiers behind, who, although they cannot see well in the front, yet, however brave the front soldiers may be, they can only lean their hope of victory on the power of the soldiers behind; for such I must say is the latter portion of the Reversible Book of 1862, you desire to be reprinted. I do not always believe in the first progress of a battle, but the last progress of victory. Nor is it my place to question my readers, how they have begun life; but how they will

---

* Bérénice remains unperverted. *Andromache* was produced at the Old Vic Theatre on 15 January 1988, directed by Jonathan Miller with a cast that included Janet Suzman, Penelope Wilton, Peter Eyre and Kevin McNally. It jogged for four weeks. The text was printed by Applause Books of New York, (£3.95) but as far as I am aware, never distributed. [I'm told it is now (autumn '89) available.]

end life! is the needful point of the question, which has given me the hope of satisfaction, in counting no troubles both by day and by night, in getting up the A B C Proverb, containing **2850** short sentences. I shall think myself fully compensated, yea! more than compensated, – if all who read this simple Book will answer NO, through faith in Christ the question in W – Big Man's A B C.

Again – your education begins from A B C, which have long since been set aside, handed to your children as finished on your part, without reference to any meaning than A B C, and this from generation to generation. You now find, that you have not finished the A B C, which are the hinges of our learning, the hopes of our hereafter Philosophers, and the riches of our country. For my part, I shall be fulfilling one portion of the promise in my last address to you – 10th May, 1862, to agree with the name '*Reversible*' you freely gave me, were I to be allowed to Reverse all big men and women in Africa and elsewhere, by saying ☛ **Go you back and learn the meaning of your A B C**. And be sure my friends, you will find sufficient reason from its meaning, to flog your hearts to Christ, as you would flog your little boys and girls to learn their A B C. May you therefore, through the assistance of God, be convinced by the good spirit of a childlike simplicity, after seriously contemplating and bringing to the home of your bosom, the question asked by no other letter in our A B C than W. Lastly: some of my friends call me 'Prince Alfred Johnson,' – these and all other names given to me, I have said more than enough already; **and as the end is always the end** in view with me, I must finish this by saying, – that the different names, although not so given to me by my godfather and godmother when I was born, nevertheless, by a close observation of my life (**nothing goes wrong yet**) they very nigh come to the interpretation of the name of my mother, from the fact of my going to England in 1860, with 'Prince Alfred' – the '**Crown**' – bearing the same interpretation of the name of my mother – 'TEJUMO-ADE,' – meaning '**Open your eyes upon Crown**' – T – 2557.

    Your most humble and obedient Servant,
GEORGE WILLIAM JOHNSON,
 Liverpool, 1st June, 1877.   NATIVE AFRICAN.
   GOOD BYE!!
  GOD BLESS YOU AT THE END. AMEN.